/

MW00390593

AN

EXPLORING THE
GOSPELS
MARK

EXPLORING THE
GOSPELS
MARK

JERRY VINES

LOIZEAUX BROTHERS
Neptune, New Jersey

EXPLORING THE GOSPELS: MARK
© 1990 by Jerry Vines. All rights reserved.

Published by Loizeaux Brothers, Inc., a nonprofit
organization devoted to the Lord's work and to
the spread of his truth.

Printed in the United States of America.

Library of Congress Cataloging-in-Publication Data
Vines, Jerry.
    Exploring the Gospels: Mark / Jerry Vines.
        p.   cm.
    ISBN 0-87213-895-X
    1. Bible.   N.T.   Mark—Commentaries.   I. Title.
BS2585.3.V56   1990   90-30942
226'.307—dc20   CIP

10 9 8 7 6 5 4 3 2 1

Contents

EXPLORING THE GOSPELS
GOSPELS
MARK

1

How It All Began

Mark 1:1-13

THE FIRST FOUR NEW TESTAMENT BOOKS ARE CALLED GOSPELS. These writings by Matthew, Mark, Luke, and John are not full biographies of the Lord Jesus. Rather, they are individual accounts of his life written from different perspectives. Each writer has his particular emphases and teaches certain lessons.

Matthew presents Jesus as the messiah of the Jewish people. Luke emphasizes Jesus' perfect humanity. John's gospel begins in eternity and pictures Jesus Christ as the eternal God, the one who came into time, wrapped himself in human flesh, and dwelt among us.

Mark's gospel, the shortest one, takes a different view. His purpose is to present the Lord Jesus as the suffering servant. The key verse is Mark 10:45. There we find in Jesus' words a summary statement of what Mark's gospel was intended to do: "For even the Son of man came not to be ministered unto, but to minister, and to give his life a ransom for many."

Our Lord came for two purposes: to serve, and to give himself on the cross as a sacrifice for sins. Mark's view of the Lord Jesus as the suffering servant accounts for the absence of many of Jesus' teachings in his gospel. It was not so much Jesus' words as his works that Mark emphasizes.

Mark's gospel is a gospel of action. We see Jesus on the move. He heals first in one city and then in another. He moves rapidly from place to place. In Mark, two words recur in the King James text: *immediately* and *straightway*—for example, in 1:10 we read, "And *straightway* coming up out of the water." In 1:12 we read, "And *immediately* the Spirit driveth him into the wilderness."

Those two words translate the same Greek word, which conveys the idea of action. Mark was so busy telling what Jesus did that he could hardly catch his breath until he moved to the next thing.

Who was this man, John Mark, who wrote a gospel that is so much on the move, so filled with action? From the book of Acts and other passages of scripture, we can piece together his story. We know that his mother was a Christian and that early believers met in her house for prayer. John Mark was brought up in a godly atmosphere. John Mark became a servant of Paul and Barnabas and went with them at the beginning of their first missionary journey. But a disappointing turn of events transpired as the party proposed to go up into Antioch in Asia Minor. John Mark left them and went back to Jerusalem.

Sometime later when Paul and Barnabas were getting ready for another missionary journey Barnabas wanted to take John Mark, but Paul said, "No, he left us on the first trip." So brother Paul and brother Barnabas disagreed. Barnabas held out for John Mark, but Paul said, "Not on your life." Paul went one way, and Barnabas went the other way with John Mark.

There was a happy ending, however. John Mark made good before the record ended. Though he started poorly he finished well. In Paul's last letter he said, "Bring John Mark with you; he is profitable to me for the ministry." John Mark was a man who understood what it means to have a second chance. This was the same man the Holy Spirit used to write the second gospel.

John Mark began his gospel a bit differently than the others did. Matthew and Luke began with the birth of the Lord Jesus. John began with the words, "In the beginning." Mark began his gospel with the ministry of John the Baptist. But before describing it he wrote, "The beginning of the gospel of Jesus Christ, the Son of God." The word *gospel* means good news, the good news about Jesus. The gospel is the message from heaven that God loves us. Though we are sinners we do not have to pay for our sins. Jesus paid for our sins on the cross. Certainly that is good news for all of us.

Notice the three names or titles that Mark used. *Jesus*—that tells us about his person. *Christ*—that tells us about his position, the messiah of the Jews. *The Son of God*—that tells us about his power. Together these titles make a strong statement about Jesus at the outset of the book. Is Jesus capable of living up to this? Is Jesus Christ really the Son of God? Is Jesus Christ able to do what Mark claims He is able to do? In these introductory verses John Mark was affirming the credentials of Jesus. He is trying to establish the credibility of Christ as the Son of God: Jesus Christ *is* more than able to be our savior.

We can notice three stages in Mark's articulation of Jesus as the strong Son of God, the suffering servant of the Lord.

I. HOW JESUS WAS ANNOUNCED (1:2-8)

John Mark reached back into the Old Testament and asserted that Jesus was announced by prophetic prediction. Next he pointed to history and said that in the ministry of John the Baptist Jesus was announced by proclamation.

A. Prophetic Prediction (1:2-3)

Mark 1:2 contains a quotation from Malachi 3:1: "Behold, I will send my messenger, and he shall prepare the way before me." "My messenger" is a reference to John the Baptist. Malachi predicted that before Jesus came there would be an introducer, a forerunner. God would send a messenger who would go ahead of the Lord and announce his coming. In those days, before an oriental king would come to a particular place, there would always be a herald who would go ahead and prepare the people for his arrival. He would announce to the people that the king was on the way. He would also check the roads leading into that area to make sure they were in good repair, so that the king would have an adequate way to get into the city.

Mark 1:3 reaches back into the book of Isaiah for the phrase,

"The voice of him that crieth in the wilderness" (Isaiah 40:3).
Again the reference is to the preaching of John the Baptist. John's
voice would go ringing out in the wilderness: "Prepare ye the way
of the Lord, make straight in the desert a highway for our God."

B. Historic Proclamation (1:4-8)

John preached a message of preparation: People were to get their
hearts ready to receive Jesus. In our day too there has to be some
heart preparation for Christ.

Prophecy and history converged in John the Baptist. Seldom
has the world seen a man like he was. John came on the scene
like an Elijah of old; today's media would have loved him.

Mark gives us a snapshot of John, clothed with camel's hair
and with a leather belt around his loins—a camelhair sportcoat
and leather belt, but not from Brooks Brothers. Actually this was
the garb of a guy who had been living in the wilderness. Can you
imagine the impression he must have made? His diet was rather
unusual too: locusts dipped in honey (though I do hope he
picked off the wings and legs).

People eat amazing things. For instance, I am amazed that
anyone can eat raw oysters. I am told they slide right down your
throat. I don't know if you take a bite as they go by or what. But
if people can eat oysters, I guess John could eat locusts.

John was also unusual in his message. He was preaching
about "the baptism of repentance for sins." The word *for*, however, doesn't mean "in order to obtain" forgiveness of sin. He
was not telling people that they had to be baptized in order to be
saved. The word *for* is better understood here as *because of*: a
baptism of repentance because of the forgiveness of sin. When
people had truly repented and God had forgiven them of their
sins, then, as an outward act of obedience and as an indication
that this had taken place in their lives, they were baptized. What
a sensation John caused in the nation when he began preaching
repentance.

The message of repentance is seldom heard in America today.
How many preachers of national stature are calling America
back to repentance? People will never be ready for Jesus until
first of all they become aware of their sins and their need for
repentance.

The word *repentance* means a change of mind about your sin.

It means you see how ugly and terrible your sin is. So you repent. You turn away from that sin. That kind of preaching gets people ready to receive Jesus as savior. Jesus may not look too good to them until their sins start looking bad to them. John the Baptist said, "Repent; Jesus is coming. He can't get into your heart until you straighten out your crooked paths by repenting of your sin." Repentance is the needle that pierces the cloth to make way for the gospel thread. Repentance prepares the way for Jesus to come into your life.

People were repenting. They seemed on the verge of a national revival. Someone has estimated that as many as 300,000 people were baptized by John. Whether that figure is correct or not, we do know that the entire land of Judea and all of Jerusalem poured out to the Jordan River to hear him. John had a message that sin is very serious, that God demands we repent of our sin. That is the only way to be ready for Jesus to come into our hearts. In Luke 13:3 Jesus said, "Except ye repent, ye shall all likewise perish."

Notice that John talked about Jesus when he talked to the people about their sin. The fire flashed in his eyes, but there was also a tenderness and humility about what he said. "There cometh one mightier than I after me, the latchet of whose shoes I am not worthy to stoop down and unloose" (1:7). In John's day, the household slave filled that role. When you went into a home a slave would untie your sandals and wash your feet. John the Baptist was saying that he was not worthy even to take the place of a slave in relationship to his master. When John compared himself to Jesus he realized his own unworthiness.

This is one reason people don't turn from their sin today. Many brag about themselves and see no personal need of Jesus. Probably they are comparing themselves with other people. When you compare yourself with another sinner you may look pretty good. When I was four or five years old, I gained quite a reputation around our block because I had the neighborhood's fastest tricycle. I was the champion tricycle rider. Nobody could beat me. I was king of the block. I could get on my tricycle, speed off, and leave them all. Then one day a boy moved onto our block who had a bicycle with a motor on it. I had never seen one of those before. He said, "You want to race?" I said, "Yeah, nobody can beat me on my tricycle." He had only two wheels; I had three. He had a tank on the front of his, with all that extra weight. We lined up. I got on my tricycle, he got on his bicycle—and I found out how slow my little tricycle was. I had been making wrong comparisons.

John the Baptist realized that Jesus was coming. When the savior was coming, he saw himself as he was. If people would see how wonderful Jesus is, how sinless and holy, they would want to know him as their personal savior. In essence John said, "I baptize with a material element. He is going to baptize with the Holy Spirit, a spiritual element."

John's baptism was ritual baptism. No saving power there. Jesus baptism was the real baptism. When you are saved, the Bible says you are baptized by the Spirit into the body of Christ. Water baptism is a picture of your Spirit baptism. The outside ritual is a picture of what has taken place on the inside.

That's how Jesus was announced—by a preacher baptizing by the river Jordan.

Now we come to a second stage in Mark's description of Jesus as the Son of God.

II. HOW JESUS WAS ANOINTED (1:9-11)

We see next the anointing of Jesus, how Jesus was prepared for service. "And it came to pass in those days, that Jesus came from Nazareth of Galilee, and was baptized of John in Jordan" (Mark 1:9).

Jesus walked on foot to get to that place. He walked approximately seventy miles to be baptized. Since baptism won't save, does it matter whether a Christian believer is baptized or not? Nothing is unimportant if Jesus walked seventy miles to do it. Jesus had only three years to work in his earthly ministry here. He didn't have time for trivia. So we can conclude that there is nothing minor or unimportant about baptism.

Why was Jesus baptized? Two factors are involved, both of which Mark opened up to us in his gospel: Jesus was baptized for human identification and heavenly consecration.

A. Human Identification (1:9)

John's baptism indicated repentance of sin, but Jesus obviously had no sins of which to repent. When Jesus was baptized He was not admitting He was a sinner. Isaiah 53:12 says, "He was numbered with the transgressors." When Jesus came to the baptism of John, though he had not sinned, He had come into the world to bear the sins of others. Jesus was identifying himself with you and me. "The Lord hath laid on him [Jesus] the iniquity of us all" (Isaiah 53:6). When Jesus came to his baptism He got beneath the burden of human sin and bore it all the way to Calvary. Jesus paid the price for our sins. His baptism identified him with our sins.

B. Heavenly Consecration (1:10-11)

Jesus' baptism was also an act of heavenly consecration. God the Son came up out of the water. God the Holy Spirit descended out of the sky. God the Father spoke from heaven. Jesus was acting out what He had come into the world to do. He was consecrating himself. He went into the water, picturing his death. He went under the water, picturing his burial. He came up out of the water, picturing his resurrection.

Like a dove, the anointing of the Spirit came on Jesus. A dove is a symbol of gentleness and sacrifice, so it is interesting to note that a dove was present at the world's first baptism.

The first baptism ever recorded in history was a global baptism, the flood. God baptized the whole world in judgment. But after the flood Noah sent out a dove. The dove came back with an olive branch. Noah sent the dove out again, and the dove never returned. It was as if that dove was looking, so to speak, for some place to land. The dove couldn't land on Abraham, who had lied about his wife. The dove couldn't land on Moses, who had lost his temper and couldn't go into the promised land. The dove couldn't land on David, who had committed adultery and murder. The dove just continued looking for some place to land.

On the day Jesus was baptized in the waters of the Jordan, the Spirit of God like a dove came to rest on him. All of heaven was saying, "There He is, the strong Son of God." God the Father spoke and said, "This is my beloved Son. I claim him. I am well pleased with him." When Jesus acted out in advance what He had come into this world to do, God the Father wanted earth to know that He was pleased with him. It is as if through his baptism Jesus announced ahead of time what He was going to do.

Babe Ruth was a remarkable baseball player. Supposedly one of the most exciting things he did happened during a game in Chicago. Chicago fans had been giving Babe a hard time. Not only was the Babe the home-run king, he was also the strike-out king. He struck out more than any man in the majors. He hit more home runs, but he struck out more. He had struck out three times that day. On his last time up he let two strikes go by. Then he pointed to the fence. He called his shot. The fans went into bedlam. Incensed, the pitcher hurled the ball plateward. Babe caught it and hit it over the fence, exactly where he had pointed. Whether fictitious or not, I love that story. That is what Jesus did. When He was baptized He called the shot. He said, "I am coming into this world. I am going to die on a cross. They will bury me. Three days later I will come up out of the grave."

III. How Jesus was Approved (1:12-13)

Jesus then moved from heaven's testimony to hell's tests. He went all the way from the dove to the devil. First, the blessing, then the battle—that's always the way it is. Right after the moment of blessing is the moment of testing. "And immediately the Spirit driveth him into the wilderness" (1:12).

A. Spiritual Compulsion (1:12)

The Spirit of God compels, drives, Jesus into the wilderness. It's as if the question is raised, "Can He stand the test?" The Holy Spirit seems to reply, "We will send him into the wilderness and He will stand the test."

B. Satanical Persuasion (1:13)

Mark did not dwell on the individual temptations of Jesus, but he did add some details that show us how Jesus was tested for forty days. For instance, notice that Jesus was tested in the wilderness, a place of aloneness. Do you know where a person's character is really tested? It is in the place of aloneness, when nobody sees you. During those forty days alone in the wilderness, the devil must have whispered a thousand times in his ear, "Go on and yield. No one will ever know."

Imagine his hunger. The test of hunger. Those who study such things tell us that after a person has gone without food for a long period of time he or she is especially susceptible to brainwashing and mind control.

Mark alone tells us that Jesus was with the wild beasts. Have you ever heard wild animals in a deserted place at night? Jackals, boars, hyenas, lions. The sound of those animals piercing the darkness of the night is enough to stop the heart, chill the brain, and turn the muscles into jelly. So there was the test of fear. But perfect love casts out fear. There was no fear in Jesus because in him was perfect love.

Then he was tempted by Satan. Heaven and hell and angels and animals—the whole universe was there to see if He could stand the test. The first Adam, in an ideal environment, failed the test. The last Adam, the Lord Jesus, came into a wilderness environment and when the testing was completed He emerged approved. The angels came and had a victory celebration. I wonder if they brought angel food cake.

A tempted Christ can understand a tempted people. Because Jesus understands temptation, when you are on the verge of yielding, hold on. Angels are on the way to deliver you. This is the good news.

Jesus is the strong Son of God. He can meet your needs. He can solve your problems. He can change your life.

2

Jesus Came

Mark 1:14-34

AFTER A FAST-PACED INTRODUCTION, JOHN MARK'S ACCOUNT moves directly into the Galilean ministry of our Lord Jesus. He was something of a reporter. Some believe he was won to Christ by Simon Peter, and there is some evidence that Mark became his companion. Probably Mark wrote down Peter's sermons, eye-witness accounts of what Jesus actually said and did. As has been noted, he showed Jesus Christ on the move. He was less interested in what Jesus had to say than he was in what Jesus did, in the Lord's activities.

A newspaper headline for this particular passage might be two words from Mark 1:4, *Jesus came.* This is the headline in the *Gospel Journal* for this section. As we read these opening sentences, we see Jesus doing what He had come to do (Mark 10:45). Three of his activities arrest our attention.

Jesus came preaching salvation.

I. Preaching Salvation (1:14-15)

After John the Baptist was put in prison, Jesus came into Galilee preaching. John was in prison but Jesus continued to preach. The messenger may be in prison, but the message can't be stopped. Paul once said, "I am in bonds but the Word of God is not bound." Do what you will to the messenger, but the message Jesus came to preach is a message of truth that can never be stifled or bound.

Jesus Christ came as a herald making a gospel proclamation. What a thrill to notice that Jesus Christ was a preacher. John the Baptist was a preacher. The great apostles in the New Testament were preachers. Of course, Jesus was different from other preachers. Other preachers had a message to deliver. Jesus Christ *was* the message. In his own person, in his own life, Jesus Christ was both messenger and message.

"The time is fulfilled, and the kingdom of God is at hand: repent ye, and believe the gospel" (1:15). Whatever else Jesus did, John Mark wanted us to know at the outset that the number-one activity of our Lord was preaching the gospel of salvation. That is the bottom line of the Christian faith. The messengers change from age to age, but the message is the same. In Acts 20:21 Paul detailed the message he delivered. He gave its essence when he said he preached "repentance toward God, and faith toward our Lord Jesus Christ." That's the message the Lord Jesus preached. It's the same message every true Bible teacher, Bible preacher, teaches and preaches. The gospel, the message of salvation, is the same for all people in all ages. It never changes. If you want to be saved, that's exactly how you are saved.

How can I know Christ as savior? How can I be saved? How can I go to heaven when I die? The message is: repent of your sin, and believe in the Lord Jesus Christ.

A. Negative Aspect (1:15c)

Repentance is the negative aspect of salvation. The Greek word for *repentance* means to change your mind. It means a change of mind that changes the direction of your life. You cannot turn to the Lord Jesus Christ unless you turn from your sin. There is a current attitude that people can hold onto their sin with one hand and take Jesus with the other. When the prodigal son made up his mind to go to the father's house, he had to leave where he was and go to his father. The fact of a sinful heart must be faced.

Sooner or later, everyone becomes sick of sin. Eventually sin turns to gravel in your mouth. Before it's over, sin turns to ashes in your hands. But mere sorrow for sin's consequences isn't sufficient. Sinners must be sorry not just for the consequences of sin, not just because of what sin has done to their lives, but sorry because of what sin is and because of what it has done to the heart of God. Sin is like a knife thrust into the heart of our loving God. Sin is what put Jesus Christ on the cross. Sin can't be enjoyed when it is seen in its seriousness and ugliness.

The gospel starts with the negative aspect: Everybody is a sinner. Everybody is guilty of sin. Karl Menninger's book *Whatever Became of Sin?* has as its thesis that we are living in a society where people have refused to acknowledge the fact of human sin in their lives. They have pushed that sin-consciousness down into their subconscious and will not deal with the fact that they need Christ as their savior. Tears of rejoicing can never be experienced until the tears of repentance are experienced.

B. Positive Aspect (1:15d)

Jesus also gave the positive aspect when He said, "Believe in the gospel." The word *believe* is a direction word. The meaning suggests "moving in the direction of." Commitment is involved. This kind of belief is not merely believing something in your head; it's believing someone in your heart. Romans 10:9 says, "If thou . . . shalt believe in thine heart that God hath raised him from the dead, thou shalt be saved."

Some years ago we were having fellowships for young people in our church after football games. One night after a ballgame we had a karate expert. He was a Christian and a karate expert who could do amazing feats of strength. He was cracking concrete blocks with his head. Then he looked around at the young people and asked, "How many of you believe I could chop up a banana on someone's stomach?" All of them raised their hands. He said, "Good, whom would you like to volunteer?" Wouldn't you know it, the young people volunteered me. They all believed it in their heads but when it came to the point of putting their own stomachs on the line, they volunteered me. I didn't believe it in my heart, but they put me up there. I was shaking all over. Suddenly I heard the blade cutting and I had bananas for my cereal right there on my stomach.

Many people have the gospel in their heads, but not in their hearts. Jesus said, "you have to repent and believe the gospel." That means you personally have to receive Jesus into your life and commit your life completely to him.

Repentance and faith are like two sides of a coin. Repentance means you turn away from something, and faith means you turn to the Lord Jesus Christ.

Jesus also came calling soulwinners

II. CALLING SOULWINNERS (1:16-20)

Next we have an account of the call of the first four men who became disciples of Jesus. In 1:16 we see Simon and Andrew. In 1:19-20 we see James and John. In essence the same thing happened to both these groups of men. They were fishermen. The Lord Jesus, as He frequently did in his ministry, was walking around the sea of Galilee and found them mending and casting their nets. Right then and there He called them to follow him.

He was calling people to engage in an activity. It is important to notice that right after preaching salvation He began to call people to be soulwinners. "Come ye after me, and I will make you to become fishers of men" (1:17).

A. The Call (1:17)

Notice the call of the Lord Jesus. He called ordinary men, fishermen, men engaged in a workday task. Abraham Lincoln said that God must love the common people, He made so many of them. God does love the common people. Sometimes we get the idea that in order to be used of the Lord you need to have a PhD degree, or an IQ of 150, or wealth, or social standing. But look at those whom God is using today. For the most part they are ordinary people who have been willing to turn their lives and ambitions over to Christ and allow him to work through them.

I was a sixteen-year-old when God called me to preach. I lived in a little country county seat town in Georgia. I didn't know there was anything beyond Carroll County, Georgia. One Sunday morning I walked down the aisle of my home church. I never dreamed I was going to get to see many people come to know Christ as their savior. I didn't know I was going to have the privilege of standing and preaching the word of God to God's people.

Give God your ordinary life, you as you are now, and God will give you back an extraordinary calling. Jesus Christ came and said to these men, "Come after me, become my followers, and I will make you to become . . ."

We will never be anything unless Jesus makes us something. Some men boast they are self-made men. Most of the time they are self-made messes. The only one who can make something out of a life is the Lord Jesus.

Jesus was talking to them in language they could understand. They understood the terminology of fishing. It is interesting to notice that the first title of his followers was not "bishops," not "pastors," not "deacons," not "apostles." Rather, the first title of the followers of the Lord Jesus was "fishers of men."

This places before us the importance of the soulwinning ministry. When Jesus used this terminology He was stamping his approval on Proverbs 11:30: "He that winneth souls is wise." He was putting his mark of approval on Daniel 12:3: "They that turn many to righteousness shall shine as the stars forever." He was underscoring what the apostle Paul later would write in 1 Corinthians 9:22: "I am made all things to all men, that I might by all means save some." At the outset of his ministry, Jesus called some men and said to them, "I want you to follow me into the great business of catching human beings for me."

The greatest work in this world is soulwinning, leading someone else to know Jesus as savior. There is nothing like it.

B. The Commitment (1:18-20)

We know they had seen Jesus previously. This is not the first time Jesus talked to them (John 1). Here these men were, working at their ordinary jobs. The Lord Jesus came walking by and said, "Come," and "straightway they forsook their nets and followed him." Isn't that amazing? They just turned their backs on their occupations, their businesses. What a testimony to the magnetism of Jesus. What a testimony to these men who wanted more in life than just making money or doing a job.

Multitudes of believers have heard that call. People are still doing what those men did. They are still responding to the invitation of Jesus to become his followers. They are leaving professions and businesses and are going to missionfields to win souls to Jesus. They are giving up lucrative salaries in order to serve the Lord. It is still happening today: people responding to the call of Jesus. The most exciting thing that can happen is to hear the call of Jesus to be a soulwinner. It gives meaning to your life. You will no longer be an insurance salesperson, but a salesperson looking for souls to catch for Jesus. You will continue to be a schoolteacher perhaps, but you will be a schoolteacher looking for young people to catch for Jesus. It can change your whole outlook. It can give purpose to your existence.

Jesus also came healing sickness.

III. HEALING SICKNESS (1:21-34)

Capernaum became the headquarters of the earthly ministry of Jesus. We know that He was accustomed to going to the synagogue, his place of worship, on the sabbath. Jesus was faithful. All his life He attended a dead "church." It was the only church He had to go to, but He was there. On this particular sabbath the Lord Jesus came into the synagogue and taught.

Worship was somewhat different in those days. Often a visiting rabbi passing through would teach. On this particular day Jesus began to teach and "they were astonished at his doctrine." The word *astonished* means to be struck by a blow. Have you ever been hit and it stuns you? That was the impact of the Lord's teaching. What He said dumbfounded them because "he taught them as one that had authority, and not as the scribes" (1:22). Jesus' teaching was definite and different. The scribes were the authorities. They were the ones who were experts in the law. They quibbled about minor matters like the washing of cups and basins. They quoted what Rabbi Daniel had said about what Rabbi Ezra had said.

On their way to the synagogue that day, perhaps the people were expecting Rabbi Dry-as-Dust to speak. Picture them settling in their customary pews, looking forward to their morning nap. Then Jesus began to speak. There was a freshness about it. He didn't have to quote other authorities. He was the authority. There was something alive about it, something exciting and thrilling. He talked about where people lived. He talked about heaven and hell, heart and home, life and death.

Isn't that how church should be? Shouldn't it be interesting? Shouldn't it be gripping? So many years of my life I went to church and it was boring. The music was boring; the prayers were boring; the sermons were boring. When God called me to preach I decided I was going to make church enjoyable. Now Jesus was teaching and the people were astonished.

A. The Filthiness of Sin (1:23-28)

"And there was in their synagogue a man with an unclean spirit; and he cried out, Saying, Let us alone: what have we to do with thee, thou Jesus of Nazareth? Art thou come to destroy us? I know thee whom thou art, the Holy One of God" (1:23-24).

If something like that happened in any church today, I assure you, it would wake up all the sleepers. Can you imagine, right in the middle of the teaching of Jesus, this fellow in the synagogue blurts all that out.

The miracles of our Lord Jesus are intended as illustrations. The parables of Jesus are miracles in words. The miracles of Jesus are parables in works. The diseases Jesus confronted illustrate the effect of sin in life. This man had an unclean spirit.

The word *with* really ought to be *in*—a man *in* an unclean spirit. Not only was the demon in the man, the man was in the demon. He was in the sphere of demonic influence. He was under the influence of an unclean, filthy spirit. He had chosen to immerse himself in the filthiness of sin.

We don't want to see the filthiness of sin, do we? No, we want to dress up sin in the lace and silk of respectability. We want to put it on the television screen and make it look appealing and nice and slick.

When you dabble with sin, you are putting yourself in a position to immerse your life in the filthiness of a sinful lifestyle. Sin will land you into some filthy places. Start playing with sin and before long not only will sin be in you, you will be in sin.

This man filled with an unclean spirit, in the atmosphere of an unclean spirit, cried out, "Let us alone." The unclean spirit recognized the Lord Jesus. He recognized his conqueror. He knew who Jesus Christ was and what Jesus could do. (In the wilderness Jesus had already dealt with "his infernal majesty," the devil.)

There was no question about the power of Jesus over this unclean spirit. "Jesus rebuked him, saying, Hold thy peace" (1:25). Literally, the verb *rebuked* means "to put a muzzle on." An English equivalent of the idea here would be "to shut up": "Shut up and come out of him." The demon convulsed him, cried with a loud voice, and obeyed—and the people were amazed. "What new doctrine is this?" they asked, "for with authority commandeth he even the unclean spirits, and they do obey him" (1:27).

The word got out. "Immediately his fame spread abroad throughout all the region round about Galilee" (1:28). When Jesus comes to any church it will be a source of amazement. When Jesus gets in a church it is the greatest advertisement a church can have. Let the word get out that Jesus is somewhere and people will come to see what's going to happen.

B. The Feverishness of Sin (1:29-31)

After church what do you do? Have Sunday lunch. "And forthwith [that means immediately], when they were come out of the synagogue, they entered into the house of Simon and Andrew, with James and John" (1:29). Here came three uninvited guests, but on this particular sabbath Simon's wife's mother was ill with a fever. Things were not on schedule. The household routine was upset.

We can imagine all this as a kind of picture of the feverishness of sin. Here was a home loved by Jesus, near to Jesus, and yet sickness came. The feverishness of sin gets into our homes sometimes, doesn't it? Maybe it's that old fever of irritability. Are you ever irritable at home? Hot tempers flare and hurtful words flow. When this happens in the home we should do what they did: "They tell him of her" (1:30b). Jesus came, took the sick person by the hand, lifted her up, and immediately the fever left. Jesus can take the feverishness of sin out of our homes too.

Take your home problem to Jesus. We need him in our homes. We need him in our church.

C. The Feebleness of Sin (1:32-34)

"And at even, when the sun did set, they brought unto him all that were diseased, and them that were possessed with devils. And all the city was gathered together at the door. And he healed many that were sick of divers diseases" (1:32-34a).

Here we see the feebleness of sin. Jesus can also deal with it. Around Capernaum were hot mineral water springs. Sick people flocked to Capernaum because there was a famous health resort there. Jesus went where the needs were. Some people in Capernaum could never have gotten to Jesus unless they had been brought.

What a sight this crowd must have been. Here is a father bringing his little crippled daughter to Jesus. There is a man bringing his blind friend to Jesus. Children bring their sick parents to Jesus.

There are people in your area who may never get to Jesus if you don't bring them. We need Jesus in our cities. The only way we are going to get him into our cities is for believers to go where the sin-sick are and bring them to him.

3

The Lord of the Leper

Mark 1:35-45

I.   THE CONDITION OF THE LEPER (1:40)
    A. His Disease (1:40)
    B. His Desire (1:40)
II. THE COMPASSION OF THE LORD (1:41-42)
    A. Personal Compassion (1:41)
    B. Powerful Compassion (1:42)
III. THE COMMAND OF THE LAW (1:43-45)
    A. The Type (1:44)
    B. The Testimony (1:45)

IN THESE VERSES WE HAVE AN INTIMATE GLIMPSE INTO THE LIFE OF THE Lord Jesus. The day had been a long one. Would Jesus sleep a little later this morning?

No, before it was even daylight, while it was still dark, probably between three and four o'clock in the morning, He arose, went out into the stillness of the morning, and in a solitary place poured out his heart to God. Jesus understood that if He was going to give out, He had to take in. A busy day lay ahead of him. People had all kinds of needs that only He could supply. If He would be what He ought to be publicly, He must be alone with God privately at the beginning of the day.

What an example for Christians. If we want to have power to live our lives aright, then we must schedule time alone with God at the beginning of the day. "You must meet God in the morning if you want him through the day." We must follow the example of the Lord Jesus and have a morning time to commune with God. In the morning quiet time, tell him the needs of your life. Draw from the heavenly Father the strength and power you need for that day.

Simon Peter was sleeping late. Rubbing the sleep out of his eyes, he went to the room where the Lord Jesus had been, and discovered that He was not there. Simon Peter then formed a search party to look for the master. They followed after him; the word *followed* really means they hunted him down.

They tracked him down, and eventually discovered where Jesus was. Simon Peter had big plans for Jesus that day. He interrupted Jesus' prayer time and said, "Lord, everybody is looking for you." Was Peter going to have him featured on "Good Morning, Capernaum"? Perhaps the press would come to interview him.

Simon Peter made the same mistake many of us make. He wanted to plan the daily schedule according to the desires of people. He thought he had to plan his day according to what people wanted him to do. There are priorities in life, and the heavenly Father is the only one who can adequately arrange them. So get your orders from him every day. Begin your day getting orders from headquarters and being sure that what you do you are doing because God wants you to do it. Regardless of the demands and pressures that people put on you, be sure that your life each day is in the center of the will of God.

For many years I have been getting up around six in the morning and spending time alone with God in Bible study and prayer. Along the way I have had all kinds of unusual invitations. People have wanted me to do many good things in the morning. What we have to do is follow the leading of the Lord for our lives, be what God wants us to be, please the Lord, and then all these other things will fit into the right place.

The Lord Jesus had a busy day coming up. Just ahead was a man with a hurt that only heaven could heal. Just ahead was a man who had a need in his life that could be supplied only by the power of God.

Reading Mark's gospel allows us to observe as the Lord Jesus moved on to the next cities, healing people, preaching the gospel, doing the things the Father had sent him into the world to do.

I. THE CONDITION OF THE LEPER (1:40)

This passage of scripture can be studied from several points of view.

A. His Disease

Are you familiar with the disease of leprosy? Do you know what people go through when they have it? Luke's gospel says that this man was full of leprosy. He was consumed by the disease.

On the basis of what we know about leprosy, let me describe what must have taken place as it laid hold of this man. Probably it would start with his beginning to feel a little tired. For no reason he would have a feeling of fatigue. Then his joints would begin to get sore. One day he would notice little white spots all over his skin. Later those white spots would begin to harden into nodules. They would turn from white to pink to brown, and then become scaly. Soon nodules would spread all over his body. The appearance of his face would change until he began to resemble a lion. The nodules would ulcerate all over his body, producing a foul odor. They would cover his vocal chords so that when he breathed there would be a wheezing sound. When he talked his voice would be raspy. His eyebrows would fall out. His hair would turn white. Inch by inch this man's body would begin to rot. As he walked he would leave putrid spots where the pus oozed out of his feet. His fingers and toes would begin to fall off.

Leprosy attacks the nervous system in such a way that a person loses all sensation of pain. A man in the grips of leprosy might accidently put his hand in the fire and feel no pain. He would burn himself severely. He would step on a thorn in the path and feel nothing as the thorn ran through his foot. A leper was a walking death that lasted an average of nine years until its victim finally collapsed in a pile of corruption.

Not only would a person suffer unbelievable horror physically, but there was also social rejection. When it was determined that a man had leprosy, he would be banished from the village. He was no longer allowed to have communion with other people. He had to leave family, friends, and tear his garments so people would recognize he was a leper. Over his upper lip he had to wear a cloth so he wouldn't spread contamination. Every time he saw people coming, the leper was required to cry, "Unclean." It would warn them that a leper was nearby. They would sometimes pick up stones to throw at him.

No disease in the Bible pictures the devastating results of sin in a life as does the disease of leprosy. It is believed that the

Israelites first got it when they were in Egypt, from the land of their sin and wanderings. Of course, we know that it actually came out of the garden of Eden. Adam himself became a carrier of the diseases and miseries that have afflicted humankind ever since. When the door of Eden was opened, all kinds of diseases came pouring out into this world like poisonous gasses.

Every time the Israelites saw a leper they saw a walking sermon. They saw miserably portrayed in front of them what sin could do in their lives. It was a picture of the foulness, fearfulness, and devastating nature of sin.

This is how sin afflicts the life of an individual with ugliness. Satan doesn't want you to know sin's true nature. He doesn't want you to understand its results. Worldly advertising paints beautiful pictures of sin. Here is a guy who looks like an all-American. The young woman with him looks like a beauty queen. They are having a grand time. Whenever I see one of Satan's pictures I say inside, "Devil, why don't you turn the picture around? Show the man who has alcohol in him and runs over a little child and kills him. Instead of that attractive girl, show someone who has been robbed of everything good in life." The Bible portrays sin like leprosy—vile, degrading, and terrible.

Sin starts off innocently. It starts small. One day the leper finds a little white spot. It doesn't seem serious.

Do you remember the life of King David? It was a time when kings went forth to war, but he was lazy and decided not to go. He moved from laziness to lust to murder to lying to adultery, and look what came of it. It started off small but it became death dealing. That's the way sin works in a life. A little innocent flirtation on the job. The next thing you know, things have gone further than you ever imagined. The devil has put infatuation in your heart, and before long immorality has been conceived. Sin wrecks your home and someone else's home.

You are at a party and one drink won't hurt—it's the popular thing to do, isn't it? We know how to handle this, how to control it. You take that little social drink so they won't laugh at you and think you're weird. The next thing you know, you are at another party and you drink a little more. Next you get yourself intoxicated and you brag about it. Before you know it, you need a drink each morning and several every night. Before it's over you can't face your job without alcohol. It all started as a little white spot. That is the way sin works.

Sin is also like leprosy in that it is deeper than the skin. It makes its appearance on the skin but it goes deeper than that. A few years ago I had a watch that quit working. I went to the jeweler and told him that something was wrong with my watch: "The hands of my watch aren't working." He took my watch, opened up the back of it, and said, "Your problem is not the hands of your watch; the problem is on the inside." Sin is a problem that gets down into the human heart. No cold cream on the surface of your life is going to solve the problem of sin. No little religion smeared on, no little coming to church on Sunday morning for an hour's dose of religion is going to do. The sinner doesn't need cold cream applied to the outside of his life. What the sinner needs is radical surgery. He needs divine chemotherapy to deal with the sin implanted in his heart.

Leprosy leaves a person feeling worthless and hopeless. The devil will tell a sinner two opposite lies. The first lie sounds like this: "It's just a little thing, it won't hurt anything. Go ahead and try it, it's not serious." When you fall for that, the devil will tell you the next lie: "It's too late. There is no hope. You are absolutely helpless. There is nothing you can do about it. Your case is incurable."

B. His Desire (1:40)

Somehow the word got down to the leper pits that a man named Jesus from Nazareth was healing all kinds of diseases. Hope began to build in the heart of one of those lepers. He crawled out of the leper pit and limped to where Jesus was. When he saw him, he completely disregarded the law of the leper and came running up to Jesus. Falling at his feet he exclaimed, "If thou wilt, thou canst make me clean" (1:40). The leper knew Jesus had the power to do it. Somehow he believed in Jesus' ability. But he wasn't sure if Jesus was willing to do it.

That's the way sin will work in your life. When you see the hope of coming to know Christ as your savior, and of your life being cleansed and changed, the devil will whisper, "You're not worth saving."

Listen, it's not a matter of whether this man was worth being saved or not. It's not a matter of whether we are worth being saved or not. The Lord Jesus saves us not on the basis of *our* worth but on the basis of *his* worth. We are saved, not because we merit salvation but because Christ's merit makes it possible for us to be saved.

This leper had come to the realization that the only hope for his life was a miracle. The only answer to his problem was a miracle from God.

That is the only cure for the sin problem. That is the only answer. Medical researchers have devised cures for many things. We have a cure for TB. We have a cure for polio. We are working to find a cure for cancer. But human beings have never been able to devise a cure for sin. Only a miracle can solve the problem of sin.

II. THE COMPASSION OF THE LORD (1:41-42)

Jesus was moved with compassion. That statement lets us into the heart of the Lord Jesus. Compassion means to be stirred in the inmost part of your being. It's a word that pictures suffering with another person. Can you imagine how it was when that leper came walking up? The crowd must have shrunk back when he came in their midst, but there was one standing there who didn't shrink. The great physician was on the scene.

Jesus Christ never met a disease He couldn't handle. He met the blind and gave them sight. He met the deaf and made them hear. He met the crippled and made them walk. He met a leper and—well, let's see what happened.

A. Personal Compassion (1:41)

The heart of Jesus reached out and he said to that man, "I will" (1:41).

Many people wonder about being saved and having their lives changed. They would really like to know that they could be clean on the inside, but they aren't sure Jesus will do it. Jesus said one time, "How often would I . . . and you wouldn't." He also said, "You will not come to me that you may have life." Jesus is willing. It's our willingness that's at stake. The Bible says, "Whosoever will call upon the name of the Lord shall be saved." "I will," said Jesus.

B. Powerful Compassion (1:42)

Jesus extended his hand toward the leper. There is a psychology behind this that makes it even more meaningful. I don't know how long this man had been in that condition. If he was at the full length of the disease he had been ill for nine years. He was almost at the end of his hope. For eight or nine years he had been ostracized from society. For almost nine years no human had touched him. For almost nine years he had not known what it was to put his arms around his children and draw them to his breast. For almost nine years he hadn't known what it was to kiss his wife.

Now he stood in the presence of the purest person who ever walked on this earth. He stood in the presence of one whose finger had in it enough power to touch and to save every human being who ever lived. He stood in the presence of the holy, righteous Son of God.

Jesus reached out and touched him. The essence of the gospel is that Jesus Christ comes down where we are, reaches out his hands of power, and touches us in our sin. The law forbade a man to touch a leper. But when Jesus touched that leper, the leper did not communicate to Jesus his corruption; instead, Jesus communicated to the leper his cleansing.

Jesus is still touching people. He is still doing what He did for that leper. Here is a man serving out a prison term for what he has done; sin has made wreck and ruin of his life. Sin has isolated him from his family by court order. Sin has him in its grip, yet the wonderful hand of Jesus can go right down into that prison cell and touch him and cleanse him and make him a new man. Here's a teenage boy; sin has wrapped its tentacles around his life and that boy is at the point where he is ready to blow his brains out. Drugs have him; liquor has him. The hand of Jesus can come right down there where that boy is in his degradation and touch him and change him. Here is a rich man who is "up and out"; he has made more money than he knows what to do with. He has made money his god. He has made material things his idol. In the loneliness of his mansion, surrounded by finery, he is as miserable as this leper who came to Jesus. The hand of Jesus can reach right into that mansion and touch him and change him. "I will; be thou clean."

"And as soon as he had spoken, immediately the leprosy departed from him, and he was cleansed" (1:42). I thank God for instant cures. I thank God that when Jesus does it, He does it on the spot. Instantly the man's skin was fresh and clean and whole.

What would you want to do if Jesus had cleansed you like that? This man wanted to tell everybody. Yet Jesus charged him to say nothing to anyone. But what did he do? He went and told everybody about it. Jesus tells us to tell everybody and we tell nobody. I really can't fault this man too much. When someone has been cleansed from leprosy it's hard to keep quiet about it. When your life has been supernaturally changed by Jesus, it's hard to keep quiet about it. In fact, it's wrong to.

III. THE COMMAND OF THE LAW (1:43-45)

The commandments of Moses told this leper what to do. He was to present himself to the priest and get a certificate of cleansing on the basis of a ceremony in Leviticus 14. The leper was to come to the priest. Can you imagine how it was when the leper knocked that day at the door of the priest? There stood this man who was no longer a leper. "I have come for my certificate of cleansing." Can you imagine the shocked look on the face of that priest?

A. The Type (1:44)

The priest was then to go outside the camp where the leper had been. That's what Jesus has done for us. He has come down here where we are. Hebrews 13 says that Jesus suffered outside the gate. On a hill outside the city of Jerusalem Jesus suffered.

The priest was to take an earthen vessel filled with water. He was to take two birds. One of those birds he would kill and let the blood pour into the water. Then the priest was to take the blood and apply it to the wings of the living bird. Next he would take the living bird, with the blood saturating its wings, out into an open field and let it loose. The bird would go flying up in the air. The leper would see that blood sprinkling down from the bird and would understand the price of his cleansing.

B. The Testimony (1:45)

The leper had seen in a dramatic way that he was clean because of the blood. That same thing, only that one thing, cleanses us from our sins: the blood of Jesus.

4

Let's Raise the Roof
Mark 2:1-12

I. THE PARALYZED MAN (2:3-12)
   A. The Seriousness of His sickness (2:3)
   B. The Source of His Sickness (2:5)
II. THE PERSISTENT MEN (2:4-5)
   A. Their Determination (2:4)
   B. Their Expectation (2:5)
III. THE PERFECT MAN (2:5-12)
   A. The Test He Proposed (2:8-11)
   B. The Triumph He Proclaimed (2:12)

SCRIPTURE SAYS THAT JESUS AGAIN ENTERED CAPERNAUM (2:1). According to Matthew 9:1, Capernaum came to be known as his city. It seems to have been the headquarters from which He conducted his greater Galilean ministry. Many of his healing miracles took place there, and people were amazed at what He did. But, however astonished they were, they were not moved to conversion. The Son of God was right there in their midst but for the most part they were unresponsive. It's possible for a city to have miracles take place in its midst yet be indifferent. It's a serious thing when a city has the Lord Jesus presented to it and then that city does not believe in him.

Later on, Jesus pronounced a curse on Capernaum; although that city would exalt itself to heaven, He said that it would instead be plunged down to hell. So now when you come to the edge of the sea of Galilee, they show you the ruins of the ancient city of Capernaum. It's a pile of rubble, brick, and stubble because its inhabitants did not know when their moment of opportunity came. Jesus was in their midst and they rejected him.

But for now, Jesus came back to Capernaum and word got out that He was there. Immediately a crowd gathered and completely filled the house where Jesus was. People were standing in the doorway. People were outside looking through the windows.

The greatest thing that could happen in any church is for word to get out that "Jesus Christ is here." If word got out that the Lord Jesus was in a church, that church would begin to draw people. There is a drawing power about him. He said, "And I, if I be lifted up from the earth, will draw all men unto me" (John 12:32).

It's not so hard to gather a crowd. Lots of people can gather crowds. Strange characters can gather crowds. Artists, jugglers, wrestlers, instrumentalists, singers—they all can get a crowd together. What did Jesus do when He gathered a crowd? The Bible says, "He preached the word unto them" (Mark 2:2b).

Music is fine, but wonderful as it is, it is not the main thing in a church service. The purpose of gathering a crowd in the house of God is that the word of God might be preached to them. In Mark 1 we are told that Jesus came preaching; that is, making a proclamation, a public announcement. But the word used here for the preaching of Jesus means a conversation, or a conversational kind of tone. What it says is that Jesus got the people together. They gathered to listen to him, and in simple, down-to-earth, easy-to-understand language, He was feeding them the word of God.

I think a lot about what takes place when crowds are gathered together. I think a lot about it when people come to church in large numbers. I pray that God will always help the church where I am a pastor to stay on the beam, to understand that the reason for our gathering together is that the word of God might be preached, that people might come to know Jesus as their savior through the preaching.

From this setting, several characters begin to emerge. Many times when I am studying the Bible I wish I were an artist so I could sketch the characters who appear in a passage. For now, I want to sketch some word pictures of the characters who emerge from this scene where Jesus was preaching the word in the house. The first sketch is of the paralyzed man.

I. THE PARALYZED MAN (2:3-12)

On the way to the house where Jesus was preaching were four men carrying a paralyzed man on a little pallet.

A. The Seriousness of His Sickness (2:3)

Five times in this passage the Bible says that this man was sick of the palsy. The word is the one from which we get our word *paralytic*. It means "to be loosed on one side." It indicates that because of some malfunction in the motor area of the brain or spinal cord, his nerves had collapsed and his muscles were incapacitated. This man was crippled. He couldn't walk anywhere on his own. He couldn't get anywhere of his own volition. He was totally dependent on others to carry him wherever he went. To be physically paralyzed is a terrible condition. But it's also a terrible condition spiritually. This man's physical paralysis is a picture of spiritual paralysis.

I think about a man who has a good mind, a responsible mind, and holds an important job in a company. Yet that man is a moral cripple. Sin has crippled his life and makes him ineffective as far as being any benefit in things that matter ultimately in life. Does it surprise you that the Bible says we are all spiritual cripples? In the Old Testament we have the story of one of the grandsons of Saul, Mephibosheth, who was crippled. In a time of war the nurse who was caring for him when he was a baby picked him up in haste and was running and dropped him. So he was crippled because of a fall.

That's the situation with all of us. We are spiritual cripples because of a fall. In the book of Genesis we are told about the sin of Adam and Eve. When they sinned, the whole human race fell, and in their fall we all became spiritual cripples. When we were without strength, when we were crippled, in due season, Christ died for us (Romans 5).

B. The Source of His Sickness (2:5)

The words that Jesus said to this man indicate that he was crippled because of spiritual reasons: "Son, thy sins be forgiven thee" (2:5).

Sickness is not always the result of sin. In John 9 we read about the man born blind. The disciples said, "Lord, who sinned, so that this man is crippled?" Jesus said, "No one sinned." He wasn't sick because he was a sinner. But in another passage, in John 5, when a man was crippled, Jesus said to him, "Sin no more, lest a worse thing come unto thee." Here in Mark 2 this man was physically sick because of sin in his life. He was also a young man, for Jesus said to him, "*Son*, thy sins be forgiven thee."

Do you know that over twenty-million cases of herpes have been reported in this country? When God says that we are to abstain from fornication, keep our lives clean sexually, put sex in the proper context where God has determined it should be, He means what He says. Venereal disease is God's way of saying to the world, "I mean what I say—you can't disobey my moral laws with impunity."

Perhaps you might call this young man a paralyzed playboy. A dread venereal disease may have crippled his manhood. A lot of people today are sowing the seeds of tremendous physical problems for themselves in the future. We can't sin and get by with it. The Bible says, "Be sure your sin will find you out" (Numbers 32:23).

God has given us the right to make choices. He made us with the ability to choose to obey or to disobey his laws; we don't have to obey his laws. But the Bible also is clear that when we disobey the laws of God we can expect to pay the penalties.

Now I want to sketch a second picture, that of the persistent men.

II. THE PERSISTENT MEN (2:4-5)

Four men were coming up the street bringing this paralyzed man to Jesus. They had heard that Jesus was in the house. They had gotten the message.

That's also where we come in. Many people will never come to Jesus unless somebody else brings them. It is our job to go out where lost people are and bring them to Jesus. Sometimes churches get the idea that all they have to do is put up their signs and announce something like this to the world: "Come on in, you lucky sinners, and get saved." The Bible nowhere says that sinners are to come to church. Everywhere in the Bible it is clear that the church is to go where sinners are. Here is a beautiful picture of the responsibility of every child of God to get involved, to be engaged in going out where cripples are and bringing them to Jesus.

A. Their Determination (2:4)

These men were persistent because they were full of determination. We have to keep in mind that the place was absolutely packed. There was no standing room. Then these fellows came with the crippled man on that pallet. Perhaps they moved to the door saying, "Make way for the sick; make way for the sick," yet nobody budged. No room around the door. No room around the windows. Sorry.

But most oriental homes had an outside stairway, where you could go up on the flat roof of the house. So these four men with great effort made their way up that stairway and onto the roof. Then they literally dug it up. These fellows had a man who needed Jesus. Their problem was to get him to Jesus somehow. There they were on top of the roof. What could they do except start dismantling it?

There is something appealing about that, about a group of persons who were so interested in getting someone to Jesus that they went through a great deal of difficulty to get that man there.

It's not easy to get people to Jesus. When you get in the soulwinning business, all the forces of hell will come to work against you. It'll rain on visitation night. Nobody will be home. You'll ride all over trying to find people. I have the feeling that what we need to do is raise some roofs in order to get people to Jesus. We need to do some difficult, out-of-the-ordinary, irregular things. These are not regular times. These are not normal days. The powers of the devil are making their final onslaught before Jesus comes again.

Can you imagine what people thought inside when that started happening? All of a sudden debris and dirt started falling down on their heads.

Don't you like it when the Holy Spirit tears up our plans, our neat little programs, and gets people saved anyhow? I am glad that there is a freedom of the Holy Spirit when the church gets involved in the soulwinning business. It breaks up some old customs. It opens up, digs up, some of our own plans and desires.

They opened up a hole in the roof to get that man to Jesus. They lowered that man down in front of him. I have a feeling that Jesus must have smiled, maybe even had a good laugh. I think He was pleased to see some fellows who were so interested in a friend that they would do whatever they had to do to get him to the Lord. "When Jesus saw their faith, he said unto the sick of the palsy, Son, thy sins be forgiven thee" (2:5).

B. Their Expectation (2:5)

I think they heard that Jesus had done this before. We know that Jesus had already healed one man who had palsy (Matthew 4). I think those four men got together and said, "I heard He did it for one. If He did it for one, He can do it for another."

A saved life is a testimony to every lost person that if He did it for *A* He can do it for *B*. We all should be filled with that kind of expectation. We need a faith that is willing to break through barriers. One of the things I love about our church is that through the years it has been willing to do unusual things to get people to the Lord. The problem with the average church in America today is that it is "business as usual." In an average church on a Sunday morning the service starts at 11:00 sharp and ends at 12:00 dull. There is nothing out of the ordinary; everything has to be in place.

These men were willing to break through barriers. Theirs was a faith that could overcome difficulties. Theirs was a faith that understood what was important. Which is more important, a roof or a man?

Some people believe that this house belonged to Simon Peter. I like to think it was his, for this reason. Can you imagine the face of Simon Peter when they started tearing up his roof? He runs to get his calculator. He is figuring how much it's going to cost. He runs to the telephone and calls his insurance man and wants to know if his homeowners' policy will cover it.

Those four men understood what was important. Too many people are more interested in the place instead of the people. They are more interested in the loveliness of the service than they are in the lostness of people who are or are not there.

I have been doing some archeological investigation and I have come up with an ancient cuneiform tablet that has the names of those four men. The first man's name was Frank Faith. He heard about Jesus healing people and went to his friends and said, "I believe if we can get this man to Jesus, Jesus can heal him." The second man's name was Harry Hope. Harry said, "I believe there is hope for this man. I don't think he's a hopeless cripple. I believe that if we can get him over there to Jesus, there's hope for him." The third man's name was Larry Love. Larry said, "I really love this guy. He's a sinner. I hate his sin, but I love him. Let's get him to Jesus." The fourth man was Dan Determination. He said, "Let's quit talking about it. Let's get on with it." So Frank Faith, Harry Hope, Larry Love, and Dan Determination took action together to get the paralytic to Jesus. They got him on the roof. They tore up the roof. They lowered him right down into the presence of Jesus. And that's as far as they could go.

It's time to paint my third picture. I want to paint a picture of the perfect man.

III. THE PERFECT MAN (2:5-12)

I can picture Jesus. He saw their faith. He looked at this young guy and said to him, "Son, thy sins be forgiven thee." He went right to the problem.

Doctors estimate that fifty percent of all physical sickness comes from emotional and spiritual problems: bitterness in spirit, an unforgiving spirit, holding grudges. The most graphic example of that is ulcers, which are not caused by what you are eating but by what is eating you. God may forgive your sin, but your nervous system won't.

The problem you are facing today is not your wife or husband. Your problem is not your parents. Your problem is not your boss. Your problem is a sin problem. On the basis of the fact that He would shed his blood, Jesus could declare, "I will put away your sins. I will remove the guilt of your sins." A sinner can come to Jesus Christ, and because Jesus shed his blood at Calvary's cross He can take those sins and put them as far away as the east is from the west (Psalm 103:12). He puts them in the depths of the sea (Micah 7:19), covers them with his blood, hides them behind his back, and remembers them no more (Isaiah 43:25; Jeremiah 31:34).

The scribes were the religious leaders of the day, the maintainers of the status quo. Having been sent on an official delegation from Jerusalem to check out this Jesus, perhaps they were squinting their eyes and curling up their noses. Perhaps they were offended by the informality and simplicity with which He was teaching as well as by the way the common people were lapping up everything He had to say. But when Jesus said, "Son, your sins are forgiven," they didn't have the courage to object openly although they were objecting in their hearts. "This man speaks blasphemies; who can forgive sins but God only?" (2:7).

They were asking the right question, but they arrived at the wrong answer. Of course, who can forgive sins but God? No church, no preacher, no denomination can forgive sins. Only God can forgive sins. The problem was that they didn't know who Jesus was.

A. The Test He Proposed (2:8-11)

Jesus proposed a test; He knew what they were thinking.

He is God. He knows what you are thinking as you sit in

church, and everywhere else. Did I turn that roast on at home or not? What time is it? Am I going to get out of this meeting in time to . . . ?

So Jesus, knowing what they were thinking, said, "Is it easier to say, your sins are forgiven, or to say, arise and walk?" (2:9). If you say that someone is forgiven of sin, that's invisible. You can't see it. Forgiveness takes place in the heart. It's a healing in the soul. But to say, "Get up and walk," that's visible. Jesus was taking their own ammunition and shooting with it. The scribes had a doctrine that no sick person could ever get well until he was forgiven of his sins. So in effect Jesus said, "All right, I'll prove my power to forgive sins in the realm of the invisible by showing you my power in the realm of the visible."

B. The Triumph He Proclaimed (2:12)

They couldn't deny the healing if it happened in front of their eyes. In Mark 1:12 we read Mark's favorite word: *immediately*, or on the spot. That's what Jesus brings—on-the-spot healing, forgiveness, salvation.

After a little boy had disobeyed his mother, he got out his slate chalkboard and wrote, "Mom, I'm sorry I was bad. If you forgive me, wipe this out." The next time he came by, his mother had wiped it clean. A sinner comes to Jesus, and says, "Lord, I'm sorry I have sinned. If you forgive me, wipe this clean." Jesus has promised to do that.

The paralyzed man was healed. The bed that had carried him, he now carried. He reached down and picked up that bed—and the bed, once the sign of his sickness, was now the sign of his cure. Here's a man who is hooked on money. All he is interested in is money. He is living for money. That money is the sign of his sickness. Then he gets saved and starts using his money to serve Jesus and get people to Jesus. The sign of his sickness is now the sign of this cure.

In speaking these words, in healing this man, Jesus revealed his identity. Who is He? He is God, the only one who can forgive sins.

Can you picture these four men going back? The one who just was healed has his sleeping bag rolled up under his arm. He's dancing the Jig. Those other four guys are bouncing up and down like rubber balls. Old Frank Faith says, "I believed He

could do it." Old Larry Love says, "I love him so for doing it."
Harry Hope said, "Praise God, He did it." Dan Determination
says, "Let's go find someone else who's sick and bring him to
Jesus."

The Bible says that the man rose and went forth before them
all and they were amazed. His public acknowledgment was a
source of public amazement. It seems to me that if Jesus has
done that for you, the first thing you ought to do is make a public
acknowledgment so you can be a source of public amazement.
It seems to me if you have been forgiven of your sins, the very
first thing you'd like to do is walk down a church aisle saying,
"I have received Jesus as my savior, and I want the whole world
to know it. Though they cannot see the forgiveness in my heart,
I want them to see the change in my life. So here I am, saved. I
want to be baptized; I want to get involved in this church's ministry; I want to live for Jesus from now on."

5

Jesus and Religion

Mark 2:13-28

ONE OF THE STRANGEST, SADDEST FEATURES OF JESUS' LIFE WAS the religious opposition He encountered. As we move through Mark's gospel, we see this rising hostility on the part of the religious leaders of the day. You will recall that at first they objected silently, not out loud. Soon, however, their opposition became more open. They went to the disciples of Jesus and raised a question about his actions. Then they went to Jesus himself and questioned what He had done. Later on, the Pharisees and Herodians joined forces and made up their minds to kill him.

It's amazing that the only sinless one, the one who came into this world to be the fulfillment of the highest hopes and aspirations of their religion, came into their midst and was hated.

Probably nothing is more wicked and cruel than religion. I think about Iran, the people who have been killed, the murder, the turmoil, all in the name of religion.

When Jesus came, He soon encountered the hostility of the religious leaders. As we look at this battle we learn the important distinctions between Jesus and religion. Everybody has religion of some kind, but not everybody has Jesus. Religion is the human attempt to work one's way to God; Jesus is God's attempt to reach humanity. Religion is works; Jesus is grace. Religion is membership; Jesus is relationship. It's possible to have religion and not have salvation. To a man who was very religious, Jesus said, "You must be born again" (John 3:3).

I. RELIGION BRINGS ISOLATION AND JESUS BRINGS INVASION (2:14-17)

First, let us look at three questions that these Pharisees asked Jesus and at his reply. The first question is found in 2:16 when the Pharisees asked the disciples, "How is it that he eateth and drinketh with publicans and sinners?"

We have to set the scene in order to understand why they were asking that question. As Jesus was walking along the seaside, He came to the "receipt of custom." A man sitting there whose name was Levi is the same person who is called Matthew elsewhere. Matthew was a tax collector. He had been appointed by the Roman government to collect taxes from the Jewish people and therefore was considered dishonest. In those days a tax collector charged whatever he thought he could get out of people. Tax collectors became extremely wealthy at the expense of the people. They were also considered traitors to their nation because they were in collaboration with the Roman government. Here was this man, a tax collector, an outcast, and the Lord Jesus came by and said only two words to him: "Follow me" (2:14). Matthew arose from that tax table and followed Jesus. He was willing to turn his back on a lucrative business and follow the Lord.

We can understand that it cost Matthew more to follow Jesus than it did some of the other disciples. Peter and John could always go back to their fishing boats, and they did so on occasion. When Matthew got up from that tax table and walked away from that job, there was no turning back. I can almost imagine Matthew singing, "I have decided to follow Jesus. No turning back. No turning back."

I once heard a joke about a chicken and a pig who were walking by a restaurant one morning, and the restaurant advertised they were putting on a charity, serving a breakfast of ham and eggs. The chicken looked at the pig and said, "Why don't we go in and give to the charity?" The pig said, "Not on your life. For you that would be a contribution. For me that would be total commitment." When Matthew made up his mind to follow Jesus it was total commitment.

A. Levi's Appreciation (2:15)

Matthew then put on a banquet. Luke tells it a little more plainly. Matthew gave a great feast in honor of the Lord Jesus and invited his friends, who were publicans and sinners. We can imagine what must have taken place. I have the idea that when Matthew got his friends there and they were having supper together, Matthew gave his testimony about what Jesus meant to him, and then invited his friends to follow Jesus too.

One of the finest times for you to win others to Christ is when you first become a Christian yourself. After you come to know the Lord, there is a tendency, if you are not careful, to get isolated from your former friends, and then you rarely come in contact with those who do not know Jesus. Sometimes we Christians misunderstand what the gospel is all about; instead of insulation, we get the idea that it's isolation. As a result, we don't have any lost friends. Do you have any lost friends? I don't mean that you participate in whatever wrong things they do, but that you leave open the channels of communication so you can introduce them to the Lord Jesus. Matthew was successful in doing this. "For there were many, and they followed him" (2:15b).

B. The Pharisees' Condemnation (2:16)

The Pharisees (the scribes of the Pharisees, as it literally means in 2:16) saw Jesus eating with those publicans and sinners. Probably in their opinion there wasn't a good one in the crowd. They were all reprobates, sinners. So these religious leaders were upset with Jesus. They went to his disciples and asked, "How is it that he eateth and drinketh with publicans and sinners?" (2:16). Right there we see the difference between Jesus and religion. Religion brings isolation; Jesus brings invasion.

Nowadays churches sometimes get the idea that they are to be so isolated that they just build their buildings and have their services and if any sinner wants to get saved, then he or she can come on over to the church. But churches get so sanctimonious and pious and rigid and formal and uninviting that sinners feel as if they are barred from the premises.

A few years ago I was pastoring in the Chattanooga area. One day I was going to our church and there on the front steps sat a woman. Her clothes were torn. Her face was bruised and beaten. I got out of the car and went to her. To make a long story short, she was a prostitute in Chattanooga. She had been taken out the night before by a group of men and they had abused her through the night. She had literally been beaten with their fists. I told her about the Lord and was trying to win her to Christ, but I wasn't getting anywhere. Finally in desperation I said, "Well, how about coming to our services on Sunday." She said, "Who, me? Oh, no, I wouldn't come to your church." I said, "We would love to have you. We would like for you to come." She said, "Oh, no! I would be like a porcupine in the middle of a bunch of kittens." She believed that she wouldn't fit in.

C. The Lord's Explanation (2:17)

When they raised this question about Jesus associating with sinners, He replied, "They that are whole have no need of the physician, but they that are sick" (2:17). Jesus immediately admitted the condition of those who were at Levi's supper. They were sick and hurting, people in need. He was like a doctor making house calls. He was the great physician. He came into this world not only to heal people of physical illnesses, but primarily to heal them of the sickness and disease of sin. Jesus went among sinners not to be like sinners, but to bring sinners to salvation and to change them by the power and grace of God.

That is what we are supposed to do too. It does not mean we are to become like sinners. I have often thought about the difference between Jesus going among sinners and Simon Peter doing so. Simon Peter went among sinners and warmed himself at the devil's fire. The next thing you know, sin had taken hold of his life. But when Jesus went among sinners, He was not changed by them. Rather, He changed them for the better. Their lives were changed. When Jesus walked away from a group of sinners, they had been infiltrated by the grace of God. They had been claimed by the power of God. They had been touched by the mercy and love of God.

That's the difference between religion and Jesus. Our job is to tell people about a great physician who can heal and change lives.

Jesus said, "I came not to call the righteous, but sinners to repentance" (2:17b). Why did He say that? The answer is simple. There is none righteous. "There is none righteous, no, not one" (Romans 3:10). Jesus was saying that we are all sinners. We are all in need of him.

II. RELIGION BRINGS A FUNERAL AND JESUS BRINGS A FEAST (2:18-22)

The disciples of John and of the Pharisees used to fast. Notice that the disciples of John got themselves in a bad crowd; the language indicates that they were fasting at that particular time. In fact, the Pharisees, the religious people, fasted a lot. The law required that they fast one time a year, but the Pharisees got so rigid and legalistic that they said, "You are to fast two times every week." Monday they fasted and Thursday they fasted. Jesus said, "When you fast, don't make a show of it. Don't be like the Pharisees." They fasted so that others would notice it. They looked as glum and as pious as they possibly could. Here these Pharisees were, with their faces whitened with fasting powder. In contrast, the disciples of Jesus were having a great time, eating and enjoying life, laughing. The problem was that the disciples were too happy.

A. The Accusation (2:18)

Some folks have problems with joy. It is difficult for them to be around people who are happy. These Pharisees looked over there at those disciples having a big time with Jesus and rejoicing. So they went to Jesus and asked a second question, "Why do the disciples of John and of the Pharisees fast, but thy disciples fast not?" (2:18b). Do you see what religion brings? Religion brings a funeral.

B. The Application (2:19-22)

But look at what Jesus brings. "Can the children of the bridechamber fast, while the bridegroom is with them?" (2:19a).

The bridegroom represents Jesus. The children of the bridegroom represent his disciples, those who share in the feast He brings. He said, "As long as they have the bridegroom with them, they cannot fast. But the days will come, when the bridegroom shall be taken away from them, and then shall they fast in those days" (2:19b-20). The Pharisees had misunderstood the fact that outward ceremony must correspond to inward feelings and reality.

There is a time for all things. There is a time to mourn. There is a time to rejoice. Jesus was trying to point out to those Pharisees that a relationship with him was a relationship of joy. There was going to be a time when his disciples would mourn. Jesus was saying, "When I am present in their lives, when I am real in their lives, it's not a time for a funeral; it's a time for a feast."

When I was a boy—it's changed a great deal now—a lot of people had the idea that church had to be as solemn and unenjoyable as possible. You were never allowed to smile in church. In fact you could get your head slapped for smiling. You were one way on the outside of church, but when you came inside the building you were something else altogether. It seemed to me that people made church a funeral instead of a feast.

I want to tell you that, rightly understood, worshiping Jesus is a celebration. We meet together to celebrate the risen Christ. We are not living in the days of mourning; we are living in the days of rejoicing. Christianity is not a sob; it is a song. Christianity is a personal, joyous relationship with Jesus Christ.

Jesus used two illustrations to make his point. "No man also seweth a piece of new cloth on an old garment; else the new piece that filled it up taketh away from the old, and the rent is made worse" (2:21). Jesus was saying, "I have come to bring something altogether new. I did not come to tack something onto Judaism. I have come to bring you to a brand new relationship with God. You can't put new experiences in old forms."

"And no man putteth new wine into old bottles: else the new wine doth burst the bottles, and the wine is spilled, and the bottles will be marred: but new wine must be put into new bottles" (2:22). Wineskins had a tendency to get hard and unyielding. It's kind of the way we are. The older we get, the more we tend to get in a routine.

Do you have a daily routine? Do you have a certain way of doing things? I do. I go to the mirror. I shave. I shower. I have it all planned. As you get older you learn how to do things. You learn what works best and how to do it all in the minimum amount of time.

Before long, breaks in that routine take a toll on us. Did you ever lose anything on the way to church? That's because the devil works harder on Sunday morning than on any other morning. Just at the split second when you have no other choice but to leave, somebody in your family doesn't have something they need. You push the panic button and go back into the house. Finally you stuff all the family in the car like a cage of growling gorillas and you head for church.

We get upset when our routines get messed up, don't we? We are just like those old wineskins. We get hardened into our routines. We don't want them to change. We Christians can get this way, churches can get this way, in our old wineskins of routine, and that's when boredom sets in. But joy comes when the routine is broken, when the out-of-the-ordinary takes place.

When Jesus breaks through, when Christ moves in on the scene and brings a feast instead of a funeral, it breaks the old wineskins. We have to have new wineskins of spontaneous gratitude and joy to receive what Christ comes to bring in our life.

III. RELIGION BRINGS A BURDEN AND JESUS BRINGS A BLESSING (2:23-28)

"And it came to pass, that he went through the corn fields [probably wheat fields] on the sabbath day; and his disciples began, as they went, to pluck the ears of corn. And the Pharisees said unto him, Behold, why do they on the sabbath day that which is not lawful?" (2:23). The Jews had a sabbath day, our Saturday, and on that day the disciples were walking with the Lord through a wheat field. They got hungry, so they just reached out and got some grains of wheat. They shucked the skins, blew them to the wind, and ate the kernels. They were just having a little snack. That's the Bible version of what up in north Georgia we used to call Pepsi-Cola and peanuts. (You haven't lived until you've had a big old Pepsi-Cola and peanuts. It's a delicacy.) That's what the disciples were doing, just taking a break.

A. The Laws of the Sabbath (2:23-24)

Here came those old religious snoops, these detectives. "Oh, look! They're breaking the sabbath. They're doing what is unlawful on the sabbath." The Pharisees had thirty-nine separate rules concerning what work you could and couldn't do on the sabbath. One thing you could not do was pluck wheat. There was nothing wrong with plucking wheat in your neighbor's field. Their problem was they were doing it on the wrong day. Those religious detectives were right on top of them; they had done something wrong on the sabbath day.

They had all kinds of rules about all kinds of things. For instance, on the sabbath day you could spit on a rock, but you couldn't spit on the ground. If you spit on the ground, that was cultivating. That was work. You were helping the ground bring forth a crop. You couldn't carry an orange on the sabbath. You couldn't put an orange in your pocket and carry it. That was bearing a burden. That was work. But you could split that orange in two and carry half an orange. That was not work. The Pharisees had made religion a burden. Jesus came to bring a blessing.

The Pharisees then raised a third question. "Why do they on the sabbath day that which is not lawful?" (2:24).

B. The Limits of the Sabbath (2:25-28)

In reply, Jesus hit them where it really hurt. Remember that they prided themselves on their Bible knowledge. He said—I can almost detect a little dig—"Have you never read what David did, when he had need, and was an hungered, he, and they that were with him? How he went into the house of God in the days of Abiathar the high priest, and did eat the shewbread, which is not lawful to eat but for the priests, and gave also to them which were with him?" (2:25-26). Jesus was referring to the twelve loaves that were on the golden table. According to law, only the priests were allowed to eat those loaves of bread. But David had a need and his men had a need. They were hungry. Jesus was saying that human need took precedent over that law. He was giving it a new interpretation. Jesus was not saying that we ought to abuse the Lord's day. We ought not. He was saying that the Lord's day should not be a burden. It was intended to be a blessing. "The sabbath was made for man, and not man for the sabbath" (2:27).

Here we see the difference between having religion and having Jesus. Having religion is being inhibited by rules; having

Jesus is being inhabited by a redeemer. The Lord's day is an opportunity for rest and refreshment. It's an opportunity to do good. It's an opportunity to worship the Lord. The Lord Jesus Christ is Lord of the sabbath day. Jesus takes these things, changes their meaning, and gives purpose and fullness and joy. Do you have religion? Or do you have Jesus?

I was talking to a young man one time, witnessing to him. He said to me, "I tried religion and it didn't work." I said, "Well, why didn't you just quit it?" He said, "That's exactly what I did." I said, "I quit it too." "You did?" "Yes, I quit religion, and I took Jesus."

You can belong to a church and all you have is religion. You can subscribe to a set of rules and regulations and all you have is religion. But if you will turn from your sin, open up your heart, and invite Jesus to come into your life, you can have Jesus instead of religion.

6

The Sin That Has No Forgiveness

Mark 3:1-35

THE THIRD CHAPTER OF THE BOOK OF MARK CAN BE ORGANIZED around three locations. In 3:1 Jesus entered the synagogue. In 3:13 He went up a mountain. In 3:19 He and his disciples went into a house.

I. CONFRONTING MALICE (3:1-6)

In the synagogue we see the Lord Jesus confronting malice. The opening verses of Mark 3 connect with the sabbath controversy of the second chapter. The Pharisees and the scribes had accused Jesus of violating their sabbath laws and He had responded by saying that the sabbath was made for man and not man for the sabbath. Now, the Lord Jesus was in the synagogue on the sabbath day and a man with a withered hand was there. I believe that this man had been planted there by the scribes; they were watching Jesus to see whether He would heal that man on the sabbath day, that they might accuse him. The word *accuse* means "to bring a formal charge against." They were looking for something to use against Jesus in order to bring a charge against him. They were not interested in the poor man who had the withered hand.

Our Lord picked up their challenge and told the man to stand right out there in the middle of them. Then He asked them a question: "Is it lawful to do good on the sabbath days, or to do evil? to save life or to kill?" (3:4). In those two questions He revealed the motives in the hearts of the scribes and Pharisees. Jesus was there to do good; they were there to do evil. He was planning to save the life of this man; they were planning to kill Jesus.

Now they were silent. Jesus looked around at them, angry and grieved at the hardness of their hearts. Jesus then said to the man, "Stretch forth thine hand" (3:5).

When he did that, the power of Christ was in operation and his withered hand was instantly cured. Jesus Christ had not violated their sabbath by working nor had the man violated it. He merely stretched out his hand. So Jesus did what He intended to do, but also kept them from getting a charge that could be brought against him. He ruined their plans. So, regardless of the fact that the man had been healed, the Pharisees left absolutely furious. "And the Pharisees went forth, and straightway took counsel with the Herodians against him, how they might destroy him" (3:6). The Pharisees and the Herodians were enemies, but hate makes strange bedfellows out of people. So those two antagonistic political parties now joined in a common plot to get rid of Jesus.

II. Choosing Men (3:13-19)

In the second location, on the mountain, we see the Lord Jesus choosing men. He was going to select the twelve disciples who would be his companions and on whom He would place responsibility for carrying his gospel to the ends of the earth.

Luke's parallel account states that Jesus had just spent the night in prayer, an example for us of the importance of giving prayer and spiritual forethought to our decisions. After a night of prayer the Lord Jesus ordained these twelve "that they should be with him," that is, have fellowship with him, "that he might send them forth to preach, and to have power to heal sicknesses and to cast out devils" (3:14-15). Most of us are familiar with the names on the list. There is a story in every one of them. It was a motley crew. If you and I had been selecting the persons on whose shoulders would rest this responsibility, we probably would not have chosen a single one of them.

The Bible says that Jesus ordained them. It's a Greek word that could be translated "he made them." It is related to our word *poem*. You see, the Lord Jesus Christ does not choose us on the basis of what we are, but on the basis of what He can make us. We are not brought to Christ on the basis of our merit, but on the basis of what Jesus can do in our hearts. Many persons have come to the Lord Jesus with broken lives, with little potential for good or for lasting influence. Yet the Lord with his marvelous power has molded and shaped them and turned their lives into a blessing. Do you know that chorus, "All I had to offer him was brokenness and strife, but He made something beautiful out of my life"?

III. CORRECTING MISINFORMATION (3:19-35)

In the third location, we see Jesus and his disciples going into a house correcting misinformation. He corrected some misinformation that his friends had about him, and He corrected misinformation that his foes had about him.

"And when his friends heard of it, they went out to lay hold on him: for they said, He is beside himself" (3:21). The word *friends* probably means relatives. They heard what Jesus was doing. They heard about the miracles and teaching and crowds who were coming to hear him. They decided that He was crazy.

Isn't it amazing how people look at situations? Take a man who completely gives himself to a noble cause. Everybody applauds and says, "Isn't that wonderful for a man to give himself to a cause like that?" Yet, take a fellow who gives himself totally in service to the Lord Jesus Christ and people look at him and say, "He has become a fanatic; something must be wrong with that guy." In one situation it's all right and in another situation it's crazy. Folks go to a ballgame and shout themselves hoarse. People say, "Isn't that great!" They are football fans. Yet let a guy get a little enthused about Jesus and they say, "He's gone off the deep end." Or here's a fellow who gets involved in a successful business deal. He spends his life making money, and folks say, "He's smart." But if somebody gets stirred up and excited about the Lord Jesus Christ, they say, "That guy is crazy." Is the insane person the one who has enough sense to know that this life is temporary, and eternity is forever, and who understands that only what you do for Jesus is going to last? Or is it the person who has somehow decided that this is all the world there is ever going to be, who has shut out of his or her life consideration of those things that are eternal, that really matter, that really count in life? I choose to believe that it is better to be a fool for Christ and to be in eternity with Christ. I would rather be glad I accepted him, glad I served him, than be a fool for this world, a fool for things that don't really count.

So the friends came looking for Jesus and finally found him. But He said, "Who is my mother, or my brethren?" (3:33). Jesus was not denying his earthly family, but rather was trying to teach a lesson. He looked around at all of those people who were sitting there, drinking in everything He had to say, and He said, "Behold my mother and my brethren! For whosoever shall do the will of God, the same is my brother, and my sister, and mother" (3:34-35). He was saying that spiritual relationships are superior to family relationships. Spiritual ties can be closer than physical ties.

Have you found that to be true? Do you have some brothers and sisters in Christ with whom you have more in common than with members of your family? I have found that to be true. Some relationships in the family of God are more meaningful, more important, than blood relationships.

When I was growing up we had family reunions. On a certain Sunday out of the year we always went to the family reunion and all the people would say, "My, how you have grown." (Did they think I was going to shrink?) I always enjoyed it because I got one plate of food and took it to the car and ate it. Then midway in the afternoon I got a second plate of food and ate it. Our family was brought up going to the Lord's house. At family reunions with your cousins and other relatives, when you got right down to it you didn't always have a lot in common. In the family of God, people can experience a relationship that is deeper and more lasting than earthly relationships. So Jesus had to correct his relatives' misunderstanding.

But we also see the misinformation promulgated by his foes. The enemies of Jesus now made a vicious attack against him. They said, "He hath Beelzebub" (3:22). *Beelzebub* was a name for a pagan god. It meant "the lord of the flies" or "the lord of filth." Rather than saying that Jesus was the Son of God, they were saying that He was the son of Satan. They were ascribing the power that He had exercised, changing lives and freeing human beings from the shackles of demon power, to the powers of demons themselves: "By the prince of devils casteth he out devils" (3:22). They were claiming that Jesus had a demon, which was indeed a slanderous accusation.

In his reply Jesus touched on a frequently asked question and dealt with the matter of blasphemy against the Holy Spirit. Jesus pointed to three basic truths.

A. An Unanswerable Premise (3:23-26)

Jesus asked these men, "How can Satan cast out Satan?" (3:23). He was saying that their charge was illogical. It was not sensible. It was incorrect. In order to achieve any goal there must be unity of effort. Regardless of whether that goal is good or evil, there has to be unity in order for it to be accomplished. For Satan to battle against himself, as they have suggested he was doing in the life of Jesus, would have been devastating to the cause of Satan himself. Jesus then gave two illustrations.

First, "And if a kingdom be divided against itself, that kingdom cannot stand" (3:24). You don't find a nation fighting against itself. If that takes place, as it did in the mid-1800s in our country, you have a civil war with internal strife and discord. Satan's kingdom is not divided, because Satan is not fighting against himself.

Second, "And if a house be divided against itself, that house cannot stand" (3:25). We know that's true domestically, don't we? If you start having turmoil on the inside of your home—husband and wife not getting along—that family can't last. Internal division tears a family apart.

The Lord Jesus was saying that the household of Satan is united. The devil is not divided against himself. The devil has more sense than to oppose himself.

Jesus was saying that He was not in collusion with the devil; He was on a collision course with him. He answered their charge with an unanswerable premise.

B. An Undeniable Power (3:27)

Next Jesus used a parable. "No man can enter into a strong man's house, and spoil his goods, except he will first bind the strong man; and then he will spoil his house" (3:27). The strong man here is the devil. The goods represent the souls that the devil has in his power, in his house. The onlookers had witnessed what Jesus had been doing; they had observed his power. Here was a man bound by the power of Satan, so to speak, and Jesus came with power over that situation. In another context in Matthew's gospel we are told about a man who was possessed with a dumb spirit. The powers of Satan had that man bound. Jesus spoke the word and released the man. An undeniable power was present when Christ confronted the demonic world.

Of course we know that the devil is strong and that we must never underestimate him. The devil has his house of plunder; he has those who are in his control. The devil has gone to the bargain counters of life and has taken many a person. Here's a young woman who has sacrificed her purity and placed herself on the bargain counter of life, soiled, reduced in value. The devil has snatched her and put her in his plunder. Here's a man with a keen mind and tremendous potential. Yet he has sacrificed his standards, compromised his convictions. The devil has plucked him and put him into his satanic house of horrors. But the Bible says that there is one stronger than the devil: the Lord Jesus Christ. "Greater is he [talking about Jesus] that is in you than he [talking about the devil] that is in the world." Christ is the stronger. When Jesus Christ came into this world, He had power over the devil; He bound the devil's power in the lives of those who would come to him. That power was bound when Jesus Christ confronted the devil in the wilderness of temptation. That binding commenced there, was continued at the cross of Calvary, and will be consummated when Jesus Christ comes again. I am not saying that the devil is bound today, but a time will come when he will be cast into prison and will be bound there for a thousand years. I am saying that Jesus Christ has power to bind the devil in the life of an individual.

I was out early yesterday morning running . I thought I would try to beat the humidity, but there is no way to do that. So I was out there running, minding my own business, and all of a sudden

I heard this dog bark. I am afraid of dogs; I had a big old dog get hold of me when I was a little kid. I looked out of the corner of my eye and there he came. I said, "This is it. This is the end." That dog was running faster than I could possibly run. No way in the world could I get away from him. He got close to me and all of a sudden the chain that bound him ran out of slack. It reminded me that if you are a believer, the Lord Jesus Christ has power to bind the devil in your life. The devil can't touch you as a believer unless you put yourself in a position near him. That's why the Bible says that believers are to give no place to the devil. Some Christians walk onto the lot where the devil is. They walk into his yard, where they are in a position to be dealt with by the devil.

But Jesus Christ is the strong one. He has power to bind the devil. But don't you go around trying to do it. I hear about people today going around claiming to bind the devil. That's not our business to do. Jesus binds the devil. We just claim the victory of the Lord Jesus. Colossians 2:15 says, "And having spoiled principalities and powers, he made a shew of them openly, triumphing over them in it [in the cross]."

C. An Unforgivable Position (3:28-29)

1. God's Position (3:28-29)

What is God's position in this matter of forgiveness? What does God have to say about it? Sometimes people get the idea that certain sins cannot be forgiven. People sometimes think that the sin of murder cannot be forgiven. But murder is not the unforgivable sin. Others have the idea that adultery is the unforgivable sin. I would say that probably the lowest, the most hurtful, the most damnable sin I can think of is the sin of adultery. To think that some woman would go into the sanctity of another home and steal a father or husband from that home is unconscionable. To think that some man would go into the sanctity of another home and steal a mother or wife from that home is unconscionable, but that is not the unforgivable sin. God will forgive the sin of adultery. The unforgivable sin is not even the sin of blasphemy.

Everywhere I have ever preached, in every church I have ever served, I have run into individuals who fear they have committed the unforgivable sin. Let me say to you, if you are afraid you have committed it, you haven't. Fear you have done so is proof positive you have not. Some people in mental institutions think they have committed the unforgivable sin. One night in a revival meeting a woman came to me greatly troubled. She said, "I am afraid I have committed the unforgivable sin." I asked, "What did you do?" She said, "When I was a young girl, in a fit of anger and temper I cursed the name of God. I am afraid I can never be forgiven." Listen, let me repeat, if you have the slightest fear that you've committed that sin, you haven't committed it. It is highly unlikely that anyone reading this book has committed the unforgivable sin. Because, you see, if you had committed the unforgivable sin, you would have no interest in Jesus. You would have no interest in the church, no interest whatsoever in spiritual things. You wouldn't care, it wouldn't phase you at all, if you had committed the unforgivable sin.

Here is one of the grandest statements about God in the entire Bible. Right in the midst of this solemn warning in 3:28—"Verily I say unto you, All sins shall be forgiven unto the sons of men, and blasphemies wherewith soever they shall blaspheme"—there's a magnificent statement. Do you see what God says? God says to you as an individual, "All sins shall be forgiven." That's God's open offer to you today.

The sin of adultery? David committed the sin of adultery, yet he went to God for forgiveness. Listen to David: "Blessed is he whose transgression is forgiven, whose sin is covered" (Psalm 32:1). God forgave David.

Deny the name of Christ? Deny Jesus? Simon Peter denied he knew the Lord. Yet when he looked at Jesus, Jesus was looking at him as if to say, "Simon Peter, all kinds of sins can be forgiven."

Paul hated the church, hated Christ. By his own admission, he was a blasphemer. Yet when he came to God in repentance God stood there with arms wide open. That's God's position. That's where God positions himself.

2. Your Position

The question is, What is your position? Where do you stand in the matter of forgiveness? Jesus was talking to representatives of the Jewish religion. Here He was not describing what they had done, although they had blasphemed him. In Matthew 12:32

Jesus said, "And whosoever speaketh a word against the Son of man, it shall be forgiven him; but whosoever speaketh against the Holy Ghost, it shall not be forgiven him, neither in this world, neither in the world to come." In Mark's account, they had blasphemed against the Son of God, Jesus. So Jesus was not describing in this warning what they had done. Rather He was predicting what they were in danger of doing.

God gave a threefold witness to the Jewish nation. When John the Baptist came to the river Jordan with a baptism of repentance, calling the people to repentance to prepare for Christ, it was the witness of God the Father. When the scribes and Pharisees showed up, John the Baptist called them the offspring of vipers. They rejected the testimony, the witness, of God the Father.

Then Jesus came on the scene and in every possible way Jesus made his appeal to them by the things He taught, by the miracles He did, and by the life He lived. What was their conclusion? "He's a devil," they said. They rejected the witness of God the Son.

When Jesus Christ died, was resurrected, and ascended to the Father, on the day of Pentecost the Holy Spirit of God came down. Three thousand people received the Spirit-filled witness of those believers, but others said, "These people are full of new wine" (Acts 2:13). They rejected the work of the Holy Spirit giving testimony to Christ. When they did, it was all over for the Jews as a nation.

You see, blasphemy against the Holy Spirit is a sin against the third person of the trinity. That is not because the Holy Spirit is greater than the Father and the Son; it is because He is later than the Father and the Son. The Holy Spirit is God's final call. The Holy Spirit is God going as far as He can go to get an individual saved without violating the will of that individual. The Holy Spirit is God's final witness to the soul. Jesus said about the Holy Spirit, "When he comes he will convict the world of sin, and of righteousness, and of judgment to come" (see John 16:8).

To sin against God's final witness is to place yourself in a position of rejecting God's final invitation. Every time you hear the gospel, every time you realize you need Christ as your personal savior but still reject the Lord Jesus, reject that call of God to be saved, you are sinning toward that sin. There can come a point out there somewhere when a person finally and firmly rejects God's final call, and then God says, "It's all over. I have no other invitation." The sin against the Holy Spirit, blasphemy against the Holy Spirit, is to reject the Holy Spirit's witness to the Lord Jesus finally and firmly.

Aaron Burr, they say, could have been president of the United States, but he betrayed his country. A young preacher witnessed to Aaron Burr when he was an old man. He pressed on him the claims of Jesus Christ. Aaron Burr said, "Young man, when I was a young man, we had a revival at Princeton University. I came very close to committing my life to Christ. I made the decision not to do it. I said to God, 'God, if you will leave me alone, I'll leave you alone.'" "Mr. Burr," the preacher said, "God has kept his part of the agreement."

It's dangerous to hear the gospel and to turn it down. It's dangerous to hear that Jesus loves you and to reject his love. It's dangerous to put yourself in a position of rejection because there comes that final opportunity, that final time, that final appeal to receive Christ as your savior. When you pass over that point, there is no more opportunity. You have rejected the invitation of the Holy Spirit. "There is a time, I know not when / A place, I know not where / That seals our destiny. / There is a line, by us unseen / That crosses the hidden boundary / Between God's patience and wrath." Don't sin against God's call.

A boy from the country was going to the city to get a job. Before he left, his mother said, "Son, I want you to promise me that you will go to church on Sunday." So he promised, and went to the city. He worked the first week, became acquainted with some of the fellows there, and made some new friends. On the weekend his new friends invited him to go horseback riding with them on Sunday. He remembered his promise to his mother and he said, "Sorry, fellas, I can't do it." But they continued to pressure him and after a while he agreed to go. Sunday morning came, and they began their horseback ride. Around 11:00, they rode into the city and as they were passing the church, bells announcing the services began to ring. Our boy could see his parents walking into their little home church in the country. He remembered his promise to his mother but he just kept on riding. The bells grew fainter. When they got to the edge of town, the boy stopped and said, "Fellows, I come from a Christian family. My mother asked me to promise her I'd be in church today. I have noticed as we have been riding that the bells have been getting fainter and fainter. If we ride anymore, I won't be able to hear the bells. I'm going back while I can still hear them."

Have the bells of invitation been ringing in your ears? When you were just a young child, did those bells ring clearly at a vacation Bible school or at a revival? Have those bells kept ringing? Has God's Spirit kept dealing with your heart, and you know you need Jesus as your savior? Maybe today you can still faintly hear those bells.

Come to Jesus while you can. Don't get into an unforgivable position.

7

Are You Listening?

Mark 4:1-34

I.   RESPONSIBILITY OF THE SOWER (4:3, 14, 21-22)
A. We Must Sow Plentifully
B. We Must Sow Passionately
C. We Must Sow Patiently
II. RELIABILITY OF THE SEED (4:14, 26-29)
A. The Seed is Wonderful
B. The Seed is Powerful
C. The Seed is Fruitful
III. RECEPTIVITY OF THE SOIL (4:4-8, 15-20)
A. By the Wayside (4:4, 15)
B. On the Stony Places (4:5-6, 16)
C. Among Thorns (4:7, 18-19)

AT TIMES JESUS CHANGED HIS TEACHING METHODS. IN MARK 4 HE began to teach in parables. There was rising opposition, and He was grieved because of the hardness of their hearts. That expression doesn't mean that Jesus got angry at them because their hearts were hard. It means that his heart was broken; his heart went out to them. Jesus was speaking the truth that could liberate them and change their lives, and they were closing up their hearts, refusing to receive the word of God.

The Lord Jesus then turned to speaking in parables. "And with many such parables spake he the word unto them, as they were able to hear it. But without a parable spake he not unto them: and when they were alone, he expounded all things to his disciples" (4:33-34).

At this juncture the parable became his primary teaching method. A parable is an illustration or a comparison. The Greek word means "alongside" and "to throw." In other words, you have a truth you want to illustrate so you throw alongside it some comparison, some description that people understand, that amplifies and illuminates what you are trying to teach.

A parable, as someone has said, is an earthly story with a heavenly meaning. Jesus began to tell these stories. "And he said unto them, Unto you [talking about believers] it is given to know the mystery of the kingdom of God: but unto them that are without [those who were lost—those who had never received the word in their heart and been saved], all these things are done in parables" (4:11). He said I am giving these things to them in parables, "that seeing they may see, and not perceive; and hearing they may hear, and not understand" (4:12). When you first read that section you might get the idea that Jesus was saying, "I'm putting these things in parables in order to hide the truth from them. I'm putting these things in parables so they will see and yet they won't really see; and so they will hear and they won't really hear." Such an interpretation is contrary to the mission of Jesus. Jesus did not come into this world to hide the truth from people. Jesus came into the world to expose the truth to people. The purpose of Jesus was not to conceal; his purpose was to reveal. What Jesus was actually doing here in 4:12 was paraphrasing a quotation from Isaiah 6:9, a description of the result in the life of people who refuse to hear the word of God. In other words Jesus comes and gives people the truth, but if they won't see it, the time comes when they cannot see. If people won't hear it, the time comes when they cannot hear. As they refuse to know the truth, they lose their capacity to know the truth. Jesus came so that people might have forgiveness of sin, that they might be converted. He was using the parabolic method as a wedge to open up their hard hearts, to give them opportunity to see the truth in picture form, to cause them to get interested, to get their attention again, and to help them move on to find saving truth.

A second reason Jesus told parables is this: "Take heed what ye hear: with what measure ye mete, it shall be measured to you: and unto you that hear shall more be given" (4:24). As you receive the truth, you increase your capacity to get more truth. "For he that hath, to him shall be given: and he that hath not, from him shall be taken even that which he hath" (4:25). Use it or lose it.

I used to play a trumpet when I was in high school. I went to state band and all those kinds of things. Then when I committed my life to the Lord, they didn't have orchestras to play in—all they had were dance bands. So when I got right with the Lord, I laid my trumpet aside. I don't use it now, so I've lost it. I've lost my lip. I probably couldn't make a clear tone now. I remember all the notes, but I can't play the trumpet anymore.

Jesus was saying the same thing about the truth. We either use the truth of God and therefore increase our capacity to get more truth, or we lose what we have.

In this chapter we see an emphasis on the part of Jesus to encourage us to listen to what is being said. Many times He talks about hearing. "He that hath ears to hear, let him hear" (4:9). "If any man have ears to hear, let him hear" (4:23). "Take heed what ye hear" (4:24). "Spake he the word unto them, as they were able to hear it" (4:33). Jesus began the parable of the sower with that word: *harken*, or *listen.*

When I was a boy, our pastor had a habit of saying, "Are you listening?" He had a way of getting your attention. Just about the time you had your eyes on that pretty girl three rows down below you, and were totally oblivious to the message, he would say, "Are you listening?" I would look up. Of course, I had an added incentive to help me listen. My dad was in the choir and I might have my head bowed, writing notes or whatever kids do in the balcony, but I didn't have to look up to know that my dad was looking at me. I could feel two hot spots right on my forehead and they were his eyes.

We have an awesome responsibility to listen to the word of God. Jesus was not just talking into thin air. Jesus was not just piling up words when over and over again He said, "Listen. He who has ears to hear, let him hear."

It is through *hearing* that we understand the word of God and thereby are saved. The Bible says, "Faith cometh by hearing, and hearing by the word of God" (Romans 10:17).

Now, let's look at the parable that Jesus told about the sower.

I. RESPONSIBILITY OF THE SOWER (4:3, 14, 21-22)

"Behold there went out a sower to sow: . . . The sower soweth the word" (4:3,14). When Jesus explained the meaning of this parable, we see first of all the responsibility of the sower. The picture is a common one in Bible lands. One morning the man gets up and walks out of his village into the countryside where the fields are. He has a leather bag of seed around his shoulder. When he gets to the field he reaches into the seed bag and gets an ample handful of seed. He scatters that seed all over the field. That's what a sower did. It was understood. Sowing the seed was a part of his task.

Jesus was the good sower who came into the world. Everywhere He went He was sowing the seeds of the word.

We apply this not only to the Lord Jesus, but to any Christian who is faithful to give out the word of God, to sow the seeds of the word in people's hearts. Jesus said, "As my Father hath sent me, even so send I you" (John 20:21). We as believers are responsible to sow the seed. There are many ways to do that. You can sow the seed preaching sermons. You can sow the seed in personal witnessing, going into homes. You can keep a supply of gospel tracts in your car, in your pocket, and everywhere you go you can drop some of the seed of the word of God. That's our responsibility. That's what God wants us to do. How should you and I as seed sowers go about it?

A. We Must Sow Plentifully

First, we ought to sow the seed abundantly. We ought to sow a lot of seed. Second Corinthians 9:6 says, "He which soweth sparingly shall reap also sparingly; and he which soweth bountifully shall reap also bountifully." If we want a big crop, then we ought to sow a lot of seed. The more seed we sow, the more people we win to Christ. It all begins with the seed-sowing process. So sow the seed abundantly.

B. We Must Sow Passionately

Second, we ought to sow the seed compassionately. Psalm 126:6 says, "He that goeth forth and weepeth, bearing precious seed, shall doubtless come again with rejoicing, bringing his sheaves with him." The picture there is of the sower watering the seed with his tears. I am told that if you take seed and soak it in water overnight it will be more productive. I don't know if that's true or not, but I know that if you will take the seed of the word of God and sow it with a compassionate, loving heart, it will be much

more productive in the lives of lost people. We ought to have tender hearts. We ought to have warmth toward those who are lost
and who need to know Jesus. So sow the seed compassionately.

C. We Must Sow the Seed Patiently

Third, we ought to sow the seed patiently. Galatians 6:9 says,
"Let us not be weary in well doing: for in due season we shall
reap, if we faint not." We don't ever know what God is going to
do with the seed of the word that's sown. I don't know what God
is going to do with this book. I go to every service expecting God
to do something unusual. I look out at the men, women, and
children in the service and they all look pretty much the same.
Some bigger than others, some smaller. Some taller than others,
some shorter. But as far as their receptivity to the word is concerned, I really can't tell. They may sit there and smile and nod
and at the same time be thinking about something else. They
may sit with heads bowed and I don't know whether they are
asleep or are praying for the service.

I never know what happens when the seed goes out, and you
don't know either. We just have to be patient. We just have to sow
the seed of the word, and then, when it gets into hearts, no telling
what God may do with his word. Sometimes the hardest person you
can imagine may turn out to be the easiest person to reach for Jesus.

I was visiting one night in Mobile, Alabama. It was a cold, drea-
ry, drizzly night. I didn't much want to be there. I went and
knocked on this door and the biggest guy you ever saw came to
open it. He just filled up the door. He had bushy hair and a bushy
beard. I started to say, "Oh, I'm sorry, I was looking for the bus sta-
tion." But I was already there and I couldn't lie about it, so I asked
if I could come in. He invited me in. I sat down and took the simple plan of salvation and began to sow the seed in that big old guy's
heart. Would you believe that tears began to trickle down his
cheeks? Before it was over, that mountain of a man got down on
his knees and accepted Jesus as his savior. He had one of the ten-
derest hearts of any guy I have ever witnessed to.

II. RELIABILITY OF THE SEED (4:14, 26-29)

As Jesus began to interpret this parable, instead of saying *seed*
He said *word*. "The sower soweth the word." It really ought to

be capital *W.* "The seed is the word of God" (Luke 8:11).

A. The Seed Is Wonderful

We sing a hymn, "Holy Bible, Book divine. Precious treasure, thou art mine." This word of God is wonderful. It seems to be a rather small, insignificant book. You take a Bible and put it in a library alongside the volumes that other people have written, and comparatively speaking it isn't a very big book. But this Bible has life inside it.

B. The Seed Is Powerful

I remember one time a guy had a little New Testament that was too small to write the words *New Testament* on its spine, so they had just put the initials TNT. I looked at that and thought, "That's exactly right. TNT. The Bible is dynamite." It has the power to produce eternal life. Other books can't do that. Can you imagine what would happen if I started reading Shakespeare every Sunday morning? How many weeks do you think it would take to lose the crowd completely if I started reading the writings of Shakespeare every Sunday morning? Faithful preachers stand on Sunday morning, Sunday night, Wednesday night, week in and week out, month after month, year after year, preaching the word of God, and life and excitement are produced in a church. This book is powerful.

I read sometime ago about the opening up of a pyramid. Inside that pyramid archeologists found many ancient artifacts, one of which was a vase. They found some seeds that had been placed in that vase three thousand years ago and when they planted them, they sprouted in a matter of days. Tremendous life lies inside a seed.

C. The Seed Is Fruitful

You go out into the apple orchard and pick an apple. Do you realize there is an orchard in that apple? Tremendous power lies on the inside.

No other book can do what the Bible does. Hymnbooks can't reproduce themselves; in fact, they have a way of disappearing. We have a way of losing them. Take an old boy, get him thoroughly converted, with a Bible in his hand, and you will be

MARK 4:1-34 MARK 4:1-34   70

amazed what that Bible can do in his life.

The word of God is fruitful. It will bring forth a crop. Notice what Jesus said about that in 4:26-29. He told another parable about the farmer's confidence in the power of the seed to produce fruit. It is God's responsibility to bring forth the fruit, but what does the farmer do? The farmer sows the seed, goes home, and goes to bed. You'll never see a real farmer sitting up in the middle of the night biting his nails because he doesn't know how the harvest takes place.

True, we understand something about the processes of germination, but we really don't know what makes it happen. There is the blade, then the ear, then the full grain. But it's not our responsibility to understand it.

I don't know how a man, a human earthly vessel, can stand in a pulpit and preach from the Bible so that its truth gets into the hearts of people and bears fruit. I don't understand how that happens, but I know that it happens all the time. The seed is reliable.

I have tremendous confidence in the word of God. The word of God spoken two thousand years ago comes with fresh power to the hearts of people in the twentieth century. We are not dealing with some out-of-date, antiquated book. Jesus said, "The words that I speak unto you, they are spirit, and they are life" (John 6:63). This book touches us right where we are. It's amazing how it can get right down here where we live, but it does.

III. RECEPTIVITY OF THE SOIL (4:4-8, 15-20)

Soils differ in their receptivity to the sown seed. The sower is the same, the seed is the same, but the quality of the soil is different. As Jesus said, some falls on the wayside, some on stony ground, some among thorns, some on good ground. Jesus was talking about the human heart. A human heart can become a jungle or a garden. Outside Mobile, Alabama, a family many years ago went into a swamp area. They cleared it out and began to plant beautiful flowers. Now the beautiful Bellingrath Gardens are there for the world to see.

Leave a human heart alone and it will run riot with sin. Unattended, it will degenerate. The human heart has the dread potential of becoming a vacant lot of sin, a junkyard of guilt, a swamp of pollution. What the human heart becomes is dependent on how you listen to the word of God.

As we consider these four kinds of soils, you may be one of them, you may be all four, or you may move from stage to stage.

A. By the Wayside (4:4, 15)

The wayside ground represents the unresponsive heart. That was where the sowers walked on the path down through the field. Many a foot had beaten the ground hard. This soil represents people who have allowed their hearts to be the paths for every dirty foot in this world—every alien thought, every wrong philosophy. They have allowed such things to pound their hearts until it is hard as asphalt on the highway, hard as a slab of cement. They hear, but they really don't hear. They may work in a multistoried building. They may have an office there, look good, and all kinds of important matters may cross their desk, but they don't have any room for the word in their life. It may have been months since they opened a Bible. They may have been coming to church for years, hearing the word with their ears, but not with their hearts. They are not moved, not stirred, not changed.

We all have to be careful that we do not take a constant pounding from the media of our day: television, radio, magazines. If we are not careful we will be infused with violence, pornography, filth, and profanity. Your heart, which was made by God to be tender and receptive to the word, can become unresponsive.

Judas was standing right there while Jesus was saying that. Perhaps at that very moment he was thinking about betraying Jesus.

"Satan cometh immediately, and taketh away the word that was sown in their hearts" (4:15). In other words, the devil comes on the scene and removes the word. God's word makes an impression on your heart and you begin to think about it, but that old heart is hard and here comes the devil. Jesus said in effect, "The birds of the air come and eat up the seeds." The devil has all kinds of birds lined up on the telephone line; the devil whistles and the birds come and gobble the words right out of your heart. Your life doesn't change a bit.

B. On Stony Places (4:5-6, 16)

Jesus also talked about stony ground, where there was a thin layer of soil but right underneath there was a slab of rock. The seed was dropped into that thin layer of soil. "And these are they likewise which are sown on stony ground; who, when they have heard the word, immediately receive it with gladness" (4:16). However, they "have no root in themselves" (4:17). Their root system is inadequate. These are the impulsive hearers. They receive the word with gladness, and they endure for a time. These folks make an immediate response, they come down the aisle with tears, they may come on like gangbusters. This man is going to be the next Billy Graham. He is on fire.

Certainly there is a place for that. I'm not saying that it's all wrong. We ought to get excited about the word of God. We ought to be thrilled. But the problem with these hearers is that they are that way about everything. The latest fad food that comes along, they go buy a case of it. The latest book that is out, they read it and tell all their friends about it. The latest political leader that comes by, they get on his bandwagon and ride with him. They have no depth in their lives. They sprout up quickly, but when the sun comes out—afflictions, tribulations, pressures and persecutions for the word's sake—their enthusiasm disappears. "I heard about you joining that First Baptist Church. Become a holy Joe, have you?" Or, "Well, well, look at goody two-shoes." When the heat is on, the impulsive hearers wilt. Some church folks are like Roman candles—they blaze brightly for about a month, and then they fizzle out.

Do you ever wonder where some members of the church are? I don't know what we would do if everybody came next Sunday. Talk about two services—it would take five services. Where are those folks? Some of them received the word on stony ground.

Any decision is a threefold decision: a heart decision, a head decision, and a will decision. You are not saved until you say, "I will turn from my sin. I will come to Christ as my savior." You can cry buckets of tears. You can traipse down church aisles all you want to. But until the word gets in there where your will is, you are not saved. You may have joined the church, yet your language is still the language of the world. You may have your name on a church roll, yet your lifestyle is identical to the lifestyles of your lost friends. Don't tell me you're saved; you're lost.

C. Among Thorns (4:7, 18-19)

The ones on thorny ground have the destructive hearts, the hearts crammed full of a rival crop. "And these are they which are sown among thorns; . . . And the cares of this world, and the deceitfulness of riches and the lusts of other things entering in, choke the word, and it becometh unfruitful" (4:18). People can get hung up on the cares of this world or the illusions of riches. They want to hold on to Jesus with this hand and onto the world with the other. Thorns choke the word of God.

The seed on the wayside was snatched. The seed on the stony ground was scorched. The seed in the thorns was stifled. The devil, the flesh, the world got those seeds—there was no crop, no fruit.

But then, Jesus said, there is the good ground, the productive crop. That's the heart that says, "Yes, that's the word of God, and I'll take it into my life. Holy Spirit, change me." That person's life is changed.

8

Safety in the Storm

Mark 4:35-41

I. THE JOURNEY OF THE SHIP (4:35-36)
   A. Its Direction (4:35)
   B. Its Destination (4:36)
II. THE ANXIETY OF THE STORM (4:37)
   A. It Came Suddenly (4:37)
   B. It Hit Severely (4:37)
III. THE MASTERY OF THE SAVIOR (4:38-41)
   A. Jesus Was Sleeping (4:38)
   B. Jesus Was Sufficient (4:39-41)

IT HAD BEEN A BUSY DAY. OUR LORD HAD TAUGHT THE PEOPLE THE word of God. Now, in the same boat He had used for a pulpit He pushed out from shore and said to the disciples, "Let's go to the other side." Then He fell asleep. Here was God, the master of this universe, asleep in a little boat.

I have an idea that Jesus did things that Adam could have done if sin had not diminished his power and dominion. I think Jesus did some things in the realm of nature that we will do when we get our new bodies and are in his likeness.

At the end of Mark 4 we see a miracle over the realm of nature. This miracle is real, but it is also a parable of power. It illustrates to us that what Jesus is able to do in the physical realm, He is also able to do in the spiritual realm. It's a wonderful thing when Jesus calms a storm at sea. But it's also a wonderful thing when Jesus calms a storm in a human heart. So this particular miracle is an illustration of life. Here is a picture of life as a voyage on a sea, along with the storms that come up unexpectedly in your life and mine.

Probably some readers of this book could say to me, "Yes, that is exactly my situation today. I'm going through a storm. My life's ship is being tossed to and fro by waves of adversity. I'm in a storm just like Jesus and the disciples were on the sea of Galilee." Because of that, this passage of scripture applies convincingly to your life and mine. Its lessons therefore can be a blessing to us.

I. THE JOURNEY OF THE SHIP (4:35-36)

The journey of the ship is a picture of the journey of life. When I was a boy, I used to hear the old singers sing, "I'm gonna take a trip in the good old gospel ship." It was a picture of life being like a voyage. Many hymns are like that. "Jesus, savior, pilot me over life's tempestuous sea." We sing the song, "Keep me safe 'til the storm passes by."

When the apostle Paul talked about his leaving, his going home to be with God, he said, "The time for my departure is at hand" (2 Timothy 4:6). It was a picture of pulling up anchor and launching onto the great sea of eternity.

Here in Mark we have a picture of your life and my life as we journey through storms and stresses. They were all on the ship and they were all in the sea. In fact, you will notice in 4:36 that other little ships were with him. We are all in this voyage together. There are other little ships besides ours. But there was something especially different about this particular ship: Jesus was on board. If you and I will just get Jesus on board, into our lives as savior and Lord, it will make a critical difference.

A. Its Direction (4:35)

When Jesus is on board, we have a sense of direction. "Let us pass over unto the other side" (4:35). We are going somewhere. We have a destination. I remember a painting I used to see when I was a boy. It was of a young man at the helm of a ship, and right over his shoulder was Jesus. It seemed to teach the lesson that you and I need Christ to be the captain of our ship of life. He was a carpenter, yet now on the ship He was giving orders.

Is Jesus the captain of your ship? Have you invited him to take over the controls of your life? If you do, it gives you some direction. If you do not have Christ, if Jesus is not the captain of your vessel of life, then there is no direction. There is meaninglessness and futility. Without Jesus, life is like a ship tossed to and fro by the waves, with no chart, no compass.

B. Its Destination (4:36)

A lot of folks don't know where they are going. If you interviewed the average person today and said, "Where are you going, what's your purpose, what's your meaning in life?" he or she probably wouldn't be able to tell you. She might say, "I'm going to work on Monday morning." He might say, "I'm going to the mountains on vacation." They may have that temporal sense of direction, but most people have no overall purpose in their lives. It's a terrible thing to be adrift on life's sea and not know why you are here, what the meaning of life really is.

There are three great questions in life. *Who Am I? Where did I come from? Where am I going?* We need to know who we are. We need to know where we are going. Jesus' words here gave a destination. When Jesus comes into your life, He comes in not only as your savior, but also as your security. The presence of Jesus is a guarantee that one of these days your life's ship is going to land safely over on the shore of glory. That's the only real security in life.

You can have stocks and bonds, you can have houses and lands. You can have all the things that people consider security in this world. But if you do not have Jesus in your life, you have nothing that you can ultimately count on. The Bible says, "I am persuaded that he is able to keep that which I have committed unto him" (2 Timothy 1:12). The Bible says, "We are kept by the power of God."

I often think about Noah in that ark. The waves came and the storms beat against it. I suppose Noah must have fallen down in that ark a hundred times with all that rocking and rolling. But no matter how many times he fell down, he never fell out of the ark.

You and I have security in Jesus. We have the promise that one of these days we are going to pass over to the other side. Our future is secure because we know Jesus as our personal savior.

In New Testament times, they tell me, the harbors of various cities would have a sand bar just outside the harbor. So if a boat got there when the tide was out, it couldn't get into the harbor. They would just take the anchor and throw it over into the harbor. It really didn't matter if the winds came and beat against the boat, because you see, they understood that when the tide came in, the ship would follow the anchor right on into the harbor. Jesus Christ is an "anchor of the soul, both sure and stedfast, and which entereth into that within the veil; Whither the forerunner is for us entered, even Jesus" (Hebrews 6:19-20). Jesus Christ is already in heaven and, if you are saved, you are going to heaven one of these days because Jesus is there. Jesus is not going to be in heaven and you not be there. The anchor is the guarantee that one of these days the ship is going on into the harbor.

II. THE ANXIETY OF THE STORM (4:37)

A. It Came Suddenly (4:37)

The storms of life often come upon us suddenly and severely. "And there arose a great storm of wind." Are you in a storm today? A financial storm? A business storm? A professional storm? Whatever kind they are, storms make us anxious. First of all, notice that this storm came up suddenly, as was common on the sea of Galilee. The sea of Galilee was located down between hills, in a kind of basin surrounded by hills. Through those hills were ravines, which made it possible for the wind to sweep down into the sea. From time to time cold air would use those ravines like a funnel. Cold air sweeping down onto the sea of Galilee and hot air rising from the sea would collide and cause a violent storm. The storm would just fall out of the thunder clouds. It could be perfectly calm one moment and the next moment people would find themselves in a furious gale with waves threatening the stability of the ship.

That's the way life is. Things will be just as calm as they can be, and then all of a sudden you are in an emergency, right in the midst of a storm. We never know what a twenty-four day is going to bring, do we? Twenty-four hours can change the course of a life. Just one phone call—"Daddy's dead." Just one doctor's examination—the doctor says, "You have a brain tumor." There you are, devastated by an overwhelming tragedy, flattened with a crushing defeat.

We all need Jesus in our lives because we never know in what moment we are going to find ourselves in the midst of a storm.

There are several reasons why storms come in our lives. Some are the result of our disobedience. Others are caused by the Lord's discipline. And some are demonic in origin.

First, sometimes we cause the storm ourselves. That was true in the life of Jonah. Jonah caused the storm. God said, "You go this way." Jonah said, "No, I'm going that way." God said, "You preach to the Ninevites." Jonah said, "No, I'm not going to do it."

The devil then made it very convenient for old Jonah. A ship was going just when he needed it and he hopped in. He got out there on the ship and the Bible says that the Lord hurled a great wind. When the sailors came to Jonah, Jonah admitted the fact that the storm was his fault. Sometimes by our disobedience we create our own storms.

Second, sometimes the Lord will bring a storm into your life in order to discipline you. Have you ever noticed how, when things are going well, you get too self-confident? You have the world on a string with downhill pull. You're feeling good and everything is great and you have a tendency to neglect your prayer life. You have a tendency not to get in the holy word as you ought. Then God stirs up a little storm in your life. Have you noticed how that gets you back on your knees? Have you noticed how, when a storm comes, you go running back to God? Sometimes God gives you a storm to draw you closer to him.

Third, some storms evidently are produced by the devil. In this passage of scripture, Jesus rebuked the wind (4:39). It's the same word He used when He rebuked the demons. The last two words of "peace, be still," could be translated "be muzzled." The storm is pictured like a wild animal that needs to be brought under control. I have no doubt that at times the devil whips up storms in our lives in order to hinder and harm a child of God. We still have a personal enemy. The devil is alive and active on the scene. Martin Luther was right when he said, "For still our ancient foe doth seek to work us woe."

B. It Hit Severely (4:37)

The Bible says that the ship was now full of water. It looked as if it was going under any moment. The floor boards were beginning to creak and crack.

Sometimes the storms of life are so severe that the strongest of people are afraid they are going under, afraid they are not going to survive. Here's a storm of suffering. Here's a hurricane of heartache. Here's a tempest of turmoil. Here's a squall of sorrow. Oh, the suffering that can come into a life. Do you sometimes say, "I get rid of one ailment and here comes another"?

Sometimes storms of sorrow come into our lives. Remember, "Earth has no sorrow that heaven cannot heal." Sometimes God digs the wells of joy with the spade of sorrow. There is no life where sorrow does not come. There is no human being who doesn't have grief in life.

We must note that the presence of Jesus on the boat did not keep the storm from coming. The Bible says that our Father in heaven causes the rain to fall on the just and the unjust (Matthew 5:45). "Into each life some rain must fall." Anguish knocks at every heart. Pain makes its way into every home.

Sometimes there are the storms of sin too. You may be going through the storm of sin. Sin doesn't start off like a storm, does it? It starts off like a tantalizing, calm breeze. If you don't get Jesus in control of that storm, if you don't get the cleansing power of the blood of Christ in that storm and get his forgiveness, that little breeze of sin will turn into a cyclone in your life.

In all these storms we need to turn to the savior.

III. THE MASTERY OF THE SAVIOR (4:38-41)

Jesus is the sea tamer, the storm tamer. The Bible says about our Lord, "He maketh the storm a calm, so that the waves thereof are still" (Psalm 107:29). No waters can overcome a ship when Jesus is present.

He was on top of this situation. His mastery was evident.

A. Jesus was Sleeping (4:38)

Here we have a beautiful blending of the divinity and humanity of Jesus. He was God, yet He was man. He was man, yet He was God. As man, there He was asleep on a pillow—as much man as if He were not God. Yet there He was—God, about to calm the storm.

Do you see how upset these disciples were? Do you see what frenzy there was in their lives? It was not the fury of the storm that awoke Jesus, it was the panic of the disciples. Those seasoned fishermen said, "We are perishing, we are going to drown." They had lost hope. Gripped with fear, they came running to where

Jesus was. "Master, Master, don't you care that we perish?" (4:38).

Have you ever said that to Jesus? I have, a thousand times. "Lord, don't you care? Aren't you concerned? Don't you know?" I can identify with those disciples. They were going under and, of all things, Jesus was asleep. "Don't just lie there, Jesus. Do something."

Do you know why they questioned Jesus' concern? We find the answer in 4:40. "And he said unto them, Why are ye so fearful? How is it that ye have no faith?" There Jesus put two things in opposition. Fear and faith are mutually exclusive. Fear and faith cannot exist in the same heart. Fear is looking at the storm; faith is looking at the savior. Fear is looking at the circumstances; faith is looking at God.

They had seen so much that Jesus had done. They had seen his miracles. They had heard his words. They had seen demonstrations of his power, yet in the midst of this crisis they allowed fear to take over. They were afraid in the storm.

There was no need for them to be afraid. Jesus had given them his word. He had not said, "Boys, let's go down to the ship and go under," but, "Let's pass over to the other side." Faith is taking Jesus at his word.

It's not enough just to read your Bible, you must claim the promises of the word of God and make them your own. Faith is taking God at his word. You don't have to be afraid when Jesus is on board.

There is one who rules over land and sea. There is one who has power to calm the storms that come up in your life. Do you think for a moment that a puddle of water can stymie omnipotence? Do you think for a moment that a little storm is any problem to the Lord Jesus Christ?

B. Jesus was Sufficient (4:39-41)

"And he arose" (4:39). I like that. When the storm rose up (4:37), Jesus rose up.

When a problem rises up in your life, Jesus will rise up. When I was a boy we used to go to the cowboy pictures on Saturday: Hop-a-long Cassidy, Roy Rogers. On Saturday my daddy would give me twenty cents—he was a very generous man—and nine cents of that would get you in the picture show. A nickel would buy you a bag of popcorn, another nickel would get you a Coke, and then you would have a penny left for bubble gum. If you have seen one of those cowboy movies you have seen them all. The crooks are on top, and as you get right down to the end of the movie it looks as if the bad guys are going to win. About that time the hero in a white hat comes riding up on a white horse. At that point in the picture show we kids would go crazy. We would throw our popcorn, pop our popcorn bags, pour the rest of our Coke down the backs of the girls in front of us, and cheer because someone had come on the scene to save the day.

Now when I read this passage about the Lord Jesus, I want to jump up and cheer and say, "Hurrah for Jesus!" Have you ever had that experience? You were going under and here comes Jesus. You are not going under; you are going up. I would rather be in a storm with Jesus than in a calm anywhere else. Safety is not the absence of the storm; it is the presence of Jesus.

Jesus came on deck, the lightning crackling all around. By the light of the lightning I can see the water spray his beard. Then I hear his words: "Peace, be still." The winds fell as if they were shot with a tranquilizing dart. The sea turned into a mirror of glass.

The disciples looked at Jesus and said, "Who is this man who can calm the seas, and the winds and the waves obey him?" (4:41). That's the question we all have to decide. Who is this man?

He is the God-man. We all need to invite him to come onto our own ship of life.

9

Legion Liberated

Mark 5:1-20

MARK 5 HAS BEEN CALLED THE BIBLE HOME FOR INCURABLES. This chapter describes three cases that are absolutely, humanly speaking, incurable: the demonic man, the diseased woman, and the dead girl. All three were considered impossible cases in the Lord's day, and would be in our day as well. The man would be sent to a mental institution, the woman would be assigned to a terminal care unit, and the girl would be taken out for burial in a cemetery. But there are no incurables with Jesus Christ. In every situation Jesus is more than adequate. To the man who was demonized, Jesus became the great psychiatrist. To the woman with the disease, Jesus was the great physician. To the girl who was dead, Jesus was the great pediatrician.

I. A MISERABLE SOUL (5:1-4)

The man who is commonly referred to as Legion was possessed with demons. His condition was dire. This miserable man is a picture of what it means to be lost and without Jesus. It's a picture of what life is like apart from our Lord.

A. He Was Demented

This man was not in his right mind. He was a candidate for an insane asylum. This is a picture of what sin does to a life. The worse form of insanity is spiritual insanity.

When the prodigal son was in the hogpen, scripture says he came to himself. That means he was not himself, he was away from himself, he was out of himself. He was spiritually unbalanced. A few years ago I was visiting in the home of a couple. On the wall they had a picture of a very handsome young man. I commented on it and then I saw a look of grief come over the face of the mother. She said, "You will meet our son in a day or so, but when you see him he's not going to look like that picture. We don't know what's wrong with him but he is just not himself. He is not like he used to be." That's what sin does in a life. It takes a person and makes him less than he was meant to be. He is no longer himself.

The man possessed with demons was not a maniac, but a demoniac. Scripture makes it clear that demon possession is real. The Bible teaches that the devil is real. The Bible says, "Be sober, be vigilant; because your adversary the devil, as a roaring lion, walketh about, seeking whom he may devour" (1 Peter 5:8).

Jesus talked about the devil. In fact, Jesus even talked to the devil. Probably most of you have the same caricature in your mind that I had when I was a boy when people talked about the devil. I pictured in my mind some grotesque, ugly-looking creature who had on a red union suit with a long tail, carrying a pitchfork, running around trying to scare little children. That is incorrect. The devil transforms himself into an angel of light.

The Bible teaches that demons are real too. When Jesus came into the world there seems to have been an intensification of demonic activity. In the presence of the Son of God, the demons went wild. I think one of the reasons we are witnessing a resurgence of demon activity in our day is because we are nearing the return of Jesus Christ to this earth. The demons know that their days are numbered so they are intensifying their activities.

Here was a man, scripture says, with an unclean spirit. I think it indicates something of the moral filth that sin brings into a life. As I read the newspapers and try to keep up with what's going on in our world, it is clear that what we are witnessing in our day is not normal sin. I think we are witnessing the moral filth that Satan is pouring out on this earth in the last days. Satan has taken our society and opened up the sewers of filth and poured them on it: unthinkable crime, rampant dishonesty, pornography, obscenity. The demons of drink and drugs are taking control of the lives of human beings, ruining and wrecking them.

No wonder Legion was a miserable soul. He was possessed with demons. Of course, everybody is going to be possessed with something. Everybody is going to be occupied by something or someone. God made the human heart, but he never intended for the human heart to be a vacuum. God's plan is that the human heart be occupied by Jesus. God wants his Son, in the person of the Holy Spirit, to occupy your heart and fill it with goodness and beauty and loveliness. Paul prayed that Christ might dwell in our hearts by faith. Yet if we each do not open up our hearts to Jesus, we open up our lives to the influences of Satan and sin.

When Jesus asked this man what his name was, he replied, "My name is Legion: for we are many" (5:9). The word *legion* is a reference to a contingent of approximately six thousand Roman soldiers. This man must have seen the Roman army as it occupied the land of Palestine. He must have seen those Roman legions as they conducted maneuvers over the land. He must have seen their cruelty, the harshness with which they wielded the Roman scepter. So when he thought about his own condition and the misery of his soul and Jesus asked him about it, the word that was most appropriate to him was the word *legion*. The soldiers of Satan were trampling on his heart. Troops of terror were occupying his life. He was completely conquered by the powers of sin.

B. He Was Dead

Legion was a man filled with wild frenzy. His hair was caked with dirt and blood. He had no clothing on; he was stripped naked. His eyes were darting around like flashes of lightning. Can you imagine what a terrible sight he was?

He certainly didn't look dead, yet notice where the scripture says this man was living: "Who had his dwelling among the tombs" (5:3). He was living in a cemetery, and it was not some beautiful memory garden where the grass was manicured and everything was in place. Nor are we talking about a carpeted funeral parlor, where soft music is playing and the flowers have been carefully arranged. When scripture says he was dwelling among the tombs, it was a place where they took dead bodies and left them. Can you imagine the foul odor of decomposing human bodies? Can you imagine a man living in those circumstances? This word *dwelt* means that he had settled down and made his home around the tombs.

I dare say most of us wouldn't want to build a house next to a cemetery. I remember one time when I was a boy, a good friend of mine and I were going to a football game on Friday night. We were just ten or eleven. After the football game I was going to spend the night with my buddy. Between the football stadium and his house was the city cemetery. Of course, we were big, brave boys, we weren't afraid of a little ol' cemetery. So that night we were walking home and the closer we got to that cemetery the faster our legs began to move. By the time we got alongside that cemetery we were running for all we were worth.

The living don't like to be among the dead, but this man's place of living reflected the condition of his heart. In the Bible, *death* basically means separation. There is physical death, which is the separation of the spirit from the body. The Bible says, "It is appointed unto men once to die" (Hebrews 9:27). That's physical death. Then there is the second death, which is the separation of the soul from God for eternity (Revelation 20:6). The Bible also talks about a spiritual death, which is the separation of the soul from God in this life. The Bible talks about being "dead in trespasses and sins" (Ephesians 2:1). Scripture says, "She that liveth in pleasure is dead while she liveth" (1 Timothy 5:6). God said to Adam in the garden of Eden, "In the day thou eatest thereof thou shalt surely die" (Genesis 2:17). Yet after his sin Adam lived over nine hundred years. What did God mean? God simply meant that sin makes you spiritually dead.

Perhaps some persons reading this book are dead. Oh, you're able to walk around and work, your eyes look alert, your body looks strong and healthy—yet without Christ you are just as dead spiritually as a person can be. You are dead to life. You are dead to usefulness. You are dead to blessing. You are like a piece of broken furniture. You have no usefulness.

C. He Was Defeated

This man allowed no restraint. They had often bound him with chains (5:4). No man could bind him (5:3). They put chains on him, bound him with fetters, and like a spiritual Samson he just tore them apart. No one could restrain him.

Isn't that a picture of our society? Isn't that a picture of a generation that says, "If it feels good, do it"? No discipline. No authority. No restraint. We read about ever more terrible crimes in our newspapers.

Here in Mark's gospel we read about a man they couldn't handle. According to Matthew's gospel the people were afraid even to walk by there. He would run them off. "And always, night and day, he was in the mountains, and in the tombs, crying, and cutting himself with stones" (5:5). Perhaps he got some kind of sadistic pleasure from self-inflicted pain. Can you imagine his shrieks, hollering, and screaming in the night? What if you had lived in one of the villages near by? I imagine that many a night some little boy would jump up from his bed, run into his father's bedroom and say, "Daddy, Daddy, is Legion going to get me tonight?" "No, son, I'll take care of you. Legion is not going to get you tonight." When I was going to school at Mercer University, our psychology class went over to Milledgeville where the state mental institution is, about thirty miles away. They were giving us a tour of the place when all of a sudden I heard the most blood-curdling scream I had ever heard. It was a patient in the ward for the criminally insane. They had him in a padded cell, bound hand and foot. It was the cry of a miserable soul apart from God.

One of the saddest men who ever lived was Elvis Presley. By his own admission, he had no peace in his heart. He had wealth untold; he had sold over four hundred million records and he had Cadillacs galore; he had Graceland. Yet he didn't have peace in his heart. The Bible says that the wicked are like the troubled sea. "There is no peace, saith the Lord, unto the wicked" (Isaiah 48:22). You can hang out in every bar in town. You can go to every porno movie house in existence. You can try everything that sin wants to tempt you with, but you will never find peace until you find Jesus.

II. A Mighty Savior (5:5-13)

Jesus and his disciples got off the boat after a rather unsettling trip. Perhaps the disciples were still a bit uneasy. Hadn't they just escaped drowning? They got off the boat and there came Legion running to meet them. No doubt they were scared to death. All except Jesus. He wasn't afraid at all. The devil doesn't scare the mighty savior Jesus.

A. His Perception (5:8)

How did Jesus handle that situation? When Jesus looked at this man He saw his humanity. "He said unto him, 'Come out of the man, thou unclean spirit'" (5:8). Jesus called him a man, though he didn't look like a man. Sin had made him anything but a man.

Jesus sees us not for what we are but for what we can be by his power and grace. It's amazing what Jesus can do with human beings. It's amazing what He can do with a life. If you give yourself to Jesus, just as you are, you'll be amazed at what He'll give you back. Give Jesus your crab apple, and He'll give you back a Golden Delicious. Give Jesus your thorn, and He'll give you back an American Beauty rose. Give Jesus your acorn, and He'll give you back a mighty oak. Give Jesus your Jacob, the schemer, and He'll give you back an Israel, a prince with God. Give Jesus Simon, the cursing fisherman, and He'll give you back a Simon Peter, a mighty preacher. Give him Saul, persecutor of the church, and Jesus will give you back Paul, militant missionary, apostle.

Jesus saw the hesitancy in this man. One minute he was worshiping Jesus (5:6). The next minute he was saying, "What have I to do with thee?" He saw his vacillating spirit. Jesus saw that a spiritual struggle was going on.

Isn't that true of all of us? Do you remember Stevenson's fictional character, Dr. Jekyll and Mr Hyde? There was a schizophrenia about him, and to some extent there is a schizophrenia in every one of us. In our best moments, something in us wants to be the best person we can possibly be. In our worst moments we want to wallow with the hogs.

When the Lord Jesus comes on the scene, the devil starts a battle in your heart. You know you need Jesus as your savior. You know you are miserable in your sins. Christ presses his claims on you.

B. His Power (5:13)

Here was a man who was in the power of the devil, but Jesus had power over the devil. I heard of a little boy who was taught about the devil in Sunday school and came home worried. He said, "Daddy, is the devil stronger than I am?" His dad responded, "Yes, Son, I think he probably is." The little boy said, "Daddy, is the devil stronger than you are?" The father replied, "Well yes, Son, I think he probably is. The little boy said, "Daddy, is the devil stronger than Jesus?" The father answered, "Oh no, Son, the devil isn't stronger than Jesus." The little boy said, "Then I'm not scared of the devil!"

Jesus can command the devil to get out of anyone. That demon said to Jesus, "Send us into the swine" (5:12). Some people have had problems with that. They say that it was unethical of Jesus to kill two thousand swine. That's a pretty good commentary on their sense of values. The townspeople who were raising the swine were more interested in the commodities market than in a soul, in a poor man who needed Jesus—and some church folks are just like them. Some church folks are more interested in the material things of this life than they are in precious souls who need Jesus.

Jesus also had power over death. He broke up the funerals He attended, as He raised the dead. He is the Son of God. He is the word of life. Three times in the scriptures, Jesus confronted funerals. One was of a little girl in this chapter. The second was the son of the widow of Nain. The third, Lazarus, had been dead for four days when Jesus got to the tomb. In the presence of Jesus it wouldn't have mattered if he had been dead for four centuries. Jesus said, "Lazarus, come forth" (John 11:43). An old country preacher said that if Jesus hadn't called him by his first name, every dead person in the graveyard would have come out.

What Legion needed was not reformation, he needed resurrection. That's what we all need. Jesus has the power to give us life today. He can raise us out of the deadness of sin.

III. A Miraculous Salvation (5:14-20)

A. Changes Us (5:15)

From any point of view, salvation is a miracle. It changes lives. Not long afterward, this man was "sitting, and clothed, and in his right mind" (5:15).

We must note that Jesus changed the man before He did anything about his clothes. Jesus didn't start with the outward problem; He started with the inward problem.

Salvation is a heart experience. Salvation is an inside job. Some of you say, "I'd like to get saved. I'm going to give up smoking and get saved." Giving up smoking isn't going to get you saved. Your problem isn't smoke. You say, "If I can give up my beer on Friday night, I'm going to walk down that church aisle and get saved." But beer isn't your problem. It's just one of the outward symptoms. You must be changed in your heart. The Bible says, "It is God who worketh in you" and "He who has begun a good work in you . . ." So get Christ in your life, have your life changed on the inside, and He'll get that outside straightened out. It'll come. The miracle of salvation changes lives.

B. Controls Us (5:15)

The miracle of salvation also controls life. The former demoniac was now under the control Jesus.

C. Challenges Us (5:19)

Interestingly, this man wanted to travel with Jesus, but Jesus had something better for him. Jesus said, "What I want you to do is to go home." "Go home to thy friends, and tell them how great things the Lord hath done for thee" (5:19).

Those people in that area didn't want Jesus around, but He wanted them. So He sent them a witness who could give a personal testimony of what Jesus could do in a life.

Has Jesus done anything for you? Has He saved you? Has He changed you? You say, "Yes, He has." Have you made it public? No? Why haven't you? Are you ashamed of Jesus? Are you afraid? Why haven't you publicly declared what Jesus has done for you? Go home and tell your friends.

"And he departed, and began to publish in Decapolis . . ." *Decapolis* meant a "ten-cities" area. He turned those ten cities into ten bells where he rang out the praises of Jesus. Can you imagine how it was when old Legion got to his home village? The children were playing in the village street. About that time somebody said, "Legion is coming." The streets emptied. Doors closed. Windows were bolted. Then a little boy's voice said, "Momma, it's Daddy, and he's got his clothes on. His hair is combed." The boy walked cautiously out of the house. The villagers began to ease out of their houses. In a moment, the boy was there in his father's arms. He said, "Daddy, you're different. You didn't come running in the house like you used to do, shoving Momma down and turning the table over and beating us up. You're different, Daddy." Then the villagers took it up. "What's happened to you, Legion? You aren't the same man. You have a smile on your face. You're in your right mind." "Dear friends," old Legion replied, "You all know I was a wild man. But a few days ago I met a man named Jesus who cast the devil out of me and filled me with his Spirit. I'm going to spend the rest of my life telling everybody what good things the Lord has done for me."

10

The Touch That Transforms
Mark 5:25-34

I. HER CONDITION (5:25-26)
   A. She Was Diseased (5:25)
   B. She Was Desperate (5:26)
   C. She Was Destitute (5:26)
II. HER CURE (5:27-29)
   A. She Trusted Jesus (5:28)
   B. She Touched Jesus (5:27)
III. HER CONFESSION (5:30-34)
   A. Jesus Requires Confession (5:31-33)
   B. Jesus Rewards Confession (5:34)

AFTER RECOUNTING THE STORY OF THE DEMONIZED MAN, MARK continued with two other incurable cases. Actually, the second miracle, the healing of a woman with a tragic problem, is a kind of parenthesis in the action. Jesus was on his way to heal the daughter of Jairus when this woman of faith came and touched the hem of his garment.

In one sense, all of the miracles of Jesus were parenthetical, sandwiched in as He moved on to his great work on the cross. As He made his way through this world, the cross was always before him, but along the way there were people who were hurting, people with needs. On his way to Calvary Jesus stopped to help people. This is the account of Jesus healing a woman who was burdened and disgraced by a continual flow of blood. Throngs of people were pressing all around him, yet in that crowd there was a discouraged woman who reached out and touched him. When she did that, her life was transformed. Christ did the impossible for her.

As I write, I pray that you too will reach out and touch Jesus.

I. HER CONDITION (5:25-26)

We need to keep in mind that this woman was more than a character on the flat pages of our Bible. She was a real person with a tremendous need.

A. She Was Diseased (5:25)

For twelve years this woman had had a flow of blood from her body. It must have left her very weak. It was a miserable, inconvenient kind of thing. Twice in these verses of scripture her disease was called a plague (5:29,34). In Greek that word has the connotation of "whip." As a whip, this disease drove away her strength as it sapped her life's blood. It deprived her of motherhood. It was embarrassing socially. It ostracized her from other people. It barred her from worship in the temple.

Again, I think this is a picture of what sin does in a life. We need to understand what a calamity, what a plague, sin is in a human life. One of the failures of the modern pulpit, even of the modern evangelists we listen to, is that most of them never really deal with the sin question. The problem of sin is minimized.

But scripture presents sin as a terrible disease, the worst thing that can happen in a human heart. What a tremendous drain there is on the health of human beings because of sin. Sin takes away our life's blood. Sin always does that. Sin never gives; it always takes away. Sin never adds to a life; it always diminishes a life.

B. She Was Desperate (5:26)

"And had suffered [endured] many things of many physicians" (5:26). This woman had done everything in her power to cure her disease. She had gone from doctor to doctor. If you had looked at the shelves in her bathroom cabinet, you would have found all kinds of medicines. She probably had tried cold baths and hot baths, inward cures and outward cures. She had checked in to every clinic available. She had made appointments with every doctor that anyone told her could do anything about her disease, yet none of those physicians was able to help. If you or I had something like that, we would do everything we could to try to find a solution. If I had a disease that was ruining my life, I would do everything in my power to try to find a cure for that disease.

Of course, we can't blame the doctors either. Doctors are human; they are not God. So there are times when even the best doctors can't help. In fact, Dr. Luke, in telling this same incident, indicates that she was humanly incurable.

What remedies are *you* trying, to meet the needs of your life? What doctors are you going to, to try to solve the basic heart problems you face? There are a lot of doctors around proposing a cure. Dr. Pleasure says, "Come to me; I'll cure the need of your heart." Yes, Dr. Pleasure has some sweet-tasting medicines, but I warn you, they are all laced with poison. Then there is Dr. Intelligence. "Come to me, fill your mind with facts, and I'll solve the deep needs of your life." Well, Dr. Intelligence may have something that will swell your head, but he doesn't have a solution to the deep longing in your heart. Some people try Dr. Religion. They go to church and get a little salve of ritual. They go on Sunday to old Dr. Religion and find out, "Oh, how good I am." If that is true, why didn't God tell Adam and Eve that in the garden of Eden? Instead, in the garden of Eden, God said, "There has to be blood shed; you have to have a covering for the sin in your life." A lot of people have tried Dr. Religion, but he has never fulfilled the void in anyone's heart.

Have you ever noticed a sinner as he comes to the end of his quest for heart satisfaction and soul fulfillment? Have you ever noticed how desperate persons become as they go from one pleasure to another? As they go from one addiction to another?

This woman had been everywhere she knew to go, but there was a doctor she hadn't tried: the great physician, Dr. Jesus.

C. She Was Destitute (5:26)

"She had spent all that she had, and was nothing bettered, but rather grew worse" (5:26). Every time the postman came to her house, it was with another bill. Now she had spent all her savings.

That's what sin does too, doesn't it? We are told in the Bible that the prodigal asked for his inheritance in advance from his father, went into a far country, and spent it all, and then a famine arose in the land. Sin will cause you to spend everything you have. Sin will rob you of your health. It will rob you of your home. It will rob you of your happiness. When Saul was slain by the Philistines, after his death the enemies of Saul came and stripped his body. They took from his body the armor; they took the emblems of his kingship. That is the way sin works. It gets its hold on you and takes everything.

There is, however, a note of hope in the account of this miserable woman. She had come to the point where she knew that no man could help her. She was aware that she had nowhere else to turn. She was a prime candidate for the miracle that Jesus can do in a human life.

II. HER CURE (5:27-29)

A. She Trusted Jesus (5:28)

In 5:28 scripture gives the feeling of her heart—I don't think she said these words out loud—"If I may touch but his clothes, I shall be whole." In other words, she trusted in Jesus. Where did she get that kind of trust? How do you generate that kind of confidence in Jesus? We find the answer in 5:27. She gained trust "when she heard of Jesus." Word about what Jesus was doing was getting around. She had heard what He had done in the lives of other people. It's a wonderful thing when word about Jesus gets around. "It is no secret what God can do. / What He's done for others, He'll do for you. / With arms wide open, He'll pardon you. / It is no secret what God can do."

People from all walks of life, of all ages, have come to Christ. They have touched him by faith, and their lives have been changed. Jesus Christ's power is not confined to the walls of anybody's church building. He has the power to save and transform your life anywhere, anytime. Remember that "faith cometh by hearing, and hearing by the word of God" (Romans 10:17).

As we see what Jesus did for this woman, we understand what He is able to do for us.

B. She Touched Jesus (5:27)

Her trust in Jesus caused her to reach out and touch him, just his clothes, the hem of his garment (Matthew 9:20). She didn't touch him on the hand; that would have been too familiar. She didn't touch him on the head; that would have been irreverent.

But real faith reaches out to an object. It is not your faith as

such, it is not your trust per se, that saves you. It is the object of
your faith, the one to whom you reach out in faith.

So this woman was in that throng around the Lord Jesus. They
were pushing against him and against one another, trying to get
near. But she put fingers on her faith and touched the hem of his
garment.

As people throng to services on Sunday, join in the singing of
hymns, and nod approval when Christ is preached, I wonder if
any of them reach out and touch him.

We do not go to heaven en masse. We do not go to heaven in
crowds. We go to heaven one by one. We don't get there because
our parents are saved. We don't get there by belonging to a Bible-
preaching church. We are not saved because we are part of a
crowd of folks who are saved. Each of us has to be saved personally. We have to reach out by faith and touch Jesus.

When she reached out and touched him, the Bible says that
"virtue" went out from him (5:30). Here was a collision. The
flow of her plague was on a collision course with the flow of his
power. When the flow of sin is confronted with the flow of the
power of Jesus Christ, Jesus always comes out the victor.

There is only one solution to the sin problem in your life. That
solution is the power of Jesus Christ generated in his person and
expressed in his death. When Jesus died on the cross of Calvary,
when the spear went in his side, there came out blood and water;
it opened up a cleansing flow that alone can overwhelm the
floodtide of sin in a human heart.

In that moment this woman felt in her body the tremendous
thrill of life, the power of Jesus Christ. The Bible says that "the
fountain of her blood was dried up." Jesus deals not only with particular sins in your life, Jesus Christ is a savior whose power reaches to the fountainhead of sin in your heart. He deals with the sin
problem at its root. Immediately, Mark says, Jesus freely gave her
what she had been paying money to get, what she had been desperately trying to find. She was cured on the spot, "straightway."

III. HER CONFESSION (5:30-34)

A. Jesus Requires Confession (5:31-33)

In spite of the crowd, Jesus knew that someone had touched him.
"Who touched my clothes?" He asked. "And he looked round

about to see her that had done this thing" (5:31-32). One woman in that crowd knew what had happened in her life. Jesus knew what had happened in her life and He called forth her confession. That's important. Notice that Jesus requires confession.

"Whosoever therefore shall confess me before men, him will I confess also before my Father which is in heaven" (Matthew 10:32). "For with the heart man believeth unto righteousness; and with the mouth confession is made unto salvation" (Romans 10:10).

Why does Jesus command public confession of my faith? I think there are several reasons.

One is for your own benefit. Luke 8:47 says, "The woman saw that she was not hidden." Jesus would not allow her to be unnoticed in what He had done in her life. She would have missed so much personal benefit if she had not made that open public confession.

Then, the Bible says, she told him "all the truth," for the benefit of others. When others see what He has done for you, it generates hope in their hearts.

Another reason Jesus wants you to give public confession is to bring glory to him. In Psalm 50:15 the Lord said, "I will deliver thee, and thou shalt glorify me." So when we receive Christ and He changes our lives, we give public confession in order to glorify him.

This woman came forward in fear and trembling. She was scared on the inside, shaking on the outside. In front of everybody, she told him what had happened. "Lord, I touched you and I have been healed." She was timid. It was an ordeal for her to do it, but Jesus required her confession.

B. Jesus Rewards Confession (5:34)

"Daughter [the only time He directly addressed anyone that way], thy faith hath made thee whole" (5:34). He was saying that she was in a new family. He was saying, "You're a child of God."

One of the great things about your public confession of faith, joining a church, and getting into the fellowship of a church, is that you learn who you are in Jesus. You learn you are a member of the family of God, and you have other brothers and sisters.

Jesus wanted her to understand the basis of her cure. It was faith. Another wonderful thing about getting into the fellowship of the local church is that it helps you understand your faith. It helps you understand who Christ is, and what Christian living means. Then Jesus said, literally, "Go *into* peace." He was saying, "You have a brand new life. You have a wonderful life ahead of you." She walked out of her plague into peace.

The Bible says, "Therefore being justified by faith, we have peace with God through our Lord Jesus Christ" (Romans 5:1). I wish I had the vocabulary to help every reader of this book understand the wonderful life ahead if you will choose to reach out by faith and touch Jesus.

> She touched only the hem of his garment,
> As to his side she stole.
> Amid the crowd that gathered round him,
> And straightway she was whole.
> Oh, touch the hem of his garment
> And then thou too shall be free.
> His saving power this very hour
> Shall give new life to thee.

11

A Daughter
Brought Back to Life

Mark 5:22-24, 35-43

I.   THE DESPERATE REQUEST (5:22-24)
A. How It Was Made (5:22-23)
B. How It Was Met (5:24)
II. THE DEVASTATING REPORT (5:35-36)
A. What the Messenger Said (5:35)
B. What the Master Said (5:36)
III. THE DELIGHTFUL RESULT (5:37-43)
A. The Master (5:40b-41)
B. The Daughter (5:42)

W E HAVE NOTED THAT IN MARK 5 JESUS ON THREE OCCASIONS did things that were considered impossible to do. He cured a man who was demon possessed. He cured a woman who had been incurably ill for twelve years. The third miracle, which we will now consider, seems the most remarkable of all. In this miracle the Lord Jesus reversed natural processes by his supernatural power. We all have seen someone take a motion picture projector and run the film backward, so that all the action is reversed. Now we see Jesus Christ in control of the film of life, and He can turn the film backward if He so chooses.

Mark gives the account of a twelve-year-old girl who had died. She was right on the threshold of womanhood, at the beginning of the best years of her life.

Death is an experience common to us all. I remember walking

through a little country cemetery and seeing the burial place of a fifteen-year-old boy. On the tombstone were these words: "Remember, young men, as you pass by, As you are now, so once was I. As I am now, soon you shall be. Therefore prepare to follow me." It was a reminder that death is no respecter of persons; death has no age limit. In cemeteries we can discover graves of all sizes. The young may die; the old must die.

I. THE DESPERATE REQUEST (5:22-24)

A man of prominence named Jairus came to the Lord Jesus in a state of desperation. His little girl, as he put it, was at the point of death.

Of course, all of us will come to that point, and in one sense we are always at the point of death. Who knows but what an accident will snuff us out and we will go into eternity? Who knows but what a cardiac arrest will come later on today and our lives on earth will end? This man was one of the rulers of the synagogue, a man of prestige, a man respected in the community. Now he was in a state of despair. The girl's life was quickly passing away from her. He had heard about Jesus and what Jesus could do. In desperation he came to Christ and made his request.

A. How It Was Made (5:22-23)

First of all, he made his request reverently. He fell at the feet of Jesus (5:22).

Sometimes it is only in an experience of desperation that a person can come to know the Lord. You may have been witnessing to certain friends for a long time and so far they seem totally uninterested. They seem not to have one bit of concern about the things you are saying to them. But it may well be that down the road somewhere they are going to face a crisis and out of that experience you will have the opportunity to tell them about the Lord Jesus. The psalmist said, "Before I was afflicted I went astray" (Psalm 119:67). There is something about affliction, crisis, domestic tragedy, that can bring us to the point where we realize our need for the Lord.

Second, Jairus made his request passionately. "He besought him greatly" (5:23). He was filled with great desire, passionate longing, that something might be done for his child. I don't care how tough a man is, when his little girl has problems, that man can really be upset. He may be a tough-minded corporate executive, but when his daughter gets sick, that man melts just like butter. Every syllable that Jairus spoke indicates his great love for her. We can imagine how it was. She had been the sunshine in their home for twelve years, the delight of his life. Every day when he came home from the job, all of the conflict and burden and turmoil of that day just rolled off his shoulder with one "Hi, Dad, did you have a good day?" Here was a man whose heart was shattered. Here was a man battling to save the life of his child. With great emotion he approached the Lord.

He also made his request prayerfully. "I pray thee, come and lay thy hands on her" (5:23).

It is a great thing when God gives you a child, when there is a birth in your family. It is a greater experience when that child is born again, when that child you brought into the world comes to know Jesus as his or her personal savior. That ought to be uppermost in our prayer lives as parents. We ought to see to it that we pray every day for the salvation of our children until they come to know Jesus.

I believe we can claim family salvation. The Bible says, "Believe on the Lord Jesus Christ, and thou shalt be saved, and thy house" (Acts 16:31). That doesn't mean that our children can be saved because of our faith. Faith is a personal response. But it does mean that we have the right to claim the salvation of our children. It was a wonderful day when my children came to know Jesus, when I saw that answer to my prayers and concern and burden for their salvation.

So here was a man with a desperate request. He came to the Lord Jesus and said, "My little daughter is dying; won't you please come and do something about it?"

B. How It Was Met (5:24)

The response of Jesus to this man's desperation was positive and prompt. Immediately on hearing the request, "Jesus went with him" (5:24). There is a wonderful message for us in that short statement. It is the message that when we have a need, if we will bring that need to Jesus, He will be on his way into our experience to do something about it. We don't always understand how

Jesus meets our needs. We don't always understand which door Jesus will use to come into our lives. But we do know that if we will come to Jesus with that situation, somehow, sometime, in some manner that will afterward be evident to us, Jesus Christ will meet our need.

II. The Devastating Report (5:35-36)

You remember what happened. Jesus was on his way through a crowd of people. It made the journey a bit difficult. It was hard to move while He was encumbered by the multitudes around him. Can you imagine how Jairus must have felt in that situation? Suppose you are in a traffic jam and you have a little girl miles away who may die at any moment. You have a doctor in your car, and you are trying to race home. Can you imagine how you would feel?

Surprisingly, considering the crowded street and the urgency of his mission, the Lord Jesus stopped and said, "Who touched me?" (5:30). It seemed that there was a delay at every point—when there was no time for delay. This little girl was battling for her life.

A. What the Messenger Said (5:35)

Then a messenger from the home of Jairus came with a devastating report. His face was covered with sweat. He was out of breath. "She's dead." Those words had to be the saddest ones Jairus had ever heard. Then the messenger added, "Why bother the master?" (5:35).

But the truth is this: We don't ever annoy Jesus by bringing our circumstances to him. We don't trouble God with our prayers. The Bible says, "If any of you lack wisdom, let him ask of God that giveth to all men liberally, and upbraideth not" (James 1:5). The word *upbraideth* simply means that we don't bug God with our circumstances. We can bring our burdens to Jesus; we can bring our problems to him. He never gets tired of them.

B. What the Master Said (5:36)

Immediately Jesus stepped into the conversation and said, "Be not afraid, only believe" (5:36). Our Lord wanted to lift that man from the depths of fear to the heights of faith.

Where do you turn when you face an emergency in your home? There are the alternatives of succumbing to your fears or turning to your faith in God. The word of Jesus for you is, "Don't be afraid; trust me." Put your confidence in Jesus in times of turmoil and tragedy.

III. THE DELIGHTFUL RESULT (5:37-43)

When Jesus got to the home of Jairus He was met with a typical oriental scene. Still today when a person dies in the Middle East, a group of professional mourners comes to the home.

To us it would have seemed to be a scene of bedlam and turmoil. Jesus would have heard the wailing of flutes. Then as He approached He would have seen mourners actually tearing out chunks of hair from their heads, ripping their clothing, and beating their chests. The air was filled with mournful shrieks and appeals to the dead one to speak again.

The Lord Jesus calmly walked up and said, "Why are you making this racket? This girl isn't dead; she is only asleep" (5:39).

This world laughs at the miracle-working power of Jesus Christ. "And they laughed him to scorn" (5:40a). Was Jesus deterred by their doubt? Not at all. So, let the world laugh at you.

If you know Jesus Christ as your savior, the minstrels of misery may strike up their tune in your heart for a little while, but there will come a time when He will step into the situation and kick those minstrels of misery out again. Although you may think the sun is never again going to shine, a brighter day is ahead.

A. The Master (5:40b-41)

Jesus took Peter, James, John, and the father and mother into the room where the twelve-year-old's body lay. He walked in and confronted death.

Death is a picture of sin. Paul said in Ephesians 2:2, "You hath he quickened, who were dead in trespasses and sins." When the prodigal son returned, the father said, "This [my son] was dead, and is alive again" (Luke 15:32b).

Death is death. There are no degrees of death. There is no such thing as dead, deader, deadest. Dead is dead. Jesus Christ is the only one who has ever died and come back to tell us about it.

I heard about an old slave who was getting ready to die. He said to his family, "I don't fear death. I'm not afraid of going into the land of dying. I know the one who owns the land on both sides of the river." Jesus is the one who knows about the *here* and the *there.* The reason God's people have no need to fear death is because they know Jesus Christ. When Jesus went to the cross, He walked right onto death's turf. He stared death in the face. He stared old death down. He won the victory.

When Jesus died on Calvary's cross, it was the death of deaths. So we don't have to be afraid of death. Jesus took the sting out of death.

Jesus walked into that room, went over to that twelve-year-old girl, took her hand, and spoke to her in Aramaic, the language of the people. It was the kind of thing her mother might say to wake her up to go to school. *Talitha, cumi,* "my little one, get up."

Are you thinking, "I had a sick child and I prayed to Jesus, but He didn't bring *her* back to life." I think that in this particular situation Jesus had compassion on the parents, not on the little girl. For her it was a sad retrogression. If we could just visualize how wonderful heaven is, if we could see how glorious it is for those who have died in the Lord to be in the presence of Jesus Christ, we wouldn't for anything in this world want them to come back to this life.

Jesus had compassion on the parents. In your situation He may have had compassion on the child. Either way, He knows best. We have to leave it up to him.

B. The Daughter (5:42)

What Jesus did for this young girl is a picture of what He'll do for you. First of all, she was living. When Jesus spoke, she arose. Jesus touched her life, she opened her eyes, and a smile crossed her face. She got up.

Everything Jesus touches comes alive. If you open your heart to the Lord Jesus, you'll come alive.

Second, she was walking. She knew who she was.

Last, she was eating. "Give her something to eat," Jesus said. After you receive spiritual life, you can feast on spiritual food.

Parents, pray that your children will come to Christ at an early age. Young people, give your lives to Jesus before you get entangled in sin. Scripture says, "Remember now thy Creator in the days of thy youth" (Ecclesiastes 12:1).

12

Tying the Hands of God

Mark 6:1-6

I. THE REASON FOR HIS VISIT (6:1-2a)
   A. The Patience of God (6:1)
   B. The Persistence of God (6:2a)
II. THE REACTION TO HIS VISIT (6:2b-4)
   A. What the Listeners Said (6:2b-3)
   B. What the Lord Said (6:4)
III. THE RESULT OF HIS VISIT (6:5-6)
   A. The Majority Response (6:5)
   B. The Minority Response (6:5)

THE BEGINNING OF MARK 6 RECORDS THE LAST VISIT OF OUR LORD to his hometown, the little town of Nazareth. It was there, scripture says, that He grew in wisdom and stature, and in favor with God and man (Luke 2:52).

I. THE REASON FOR HIS VISIT (6:1-2a)

The gospel of Luke describes an earlier visit of our Lord to Nazareth. On that occasion Jesus went into the synagogue as He did here. He opened up the scriptures to Isaiah 61, a passage about the messiah. Having read those verses aloud, He closed the book and said, "This day is this scripture fulfilled in your ears" (Luke 4:21). Understandably, the people were surprised—after all, this was a local boy saying such a thing—but after further discussion they became enraged. They grabbed Jesus, took him outside the city to the brow of a hill, and were going to throw him over the cliff. "But he passing through the midst of them went his way" (Luke 4:30). Now He had returned to Nazareth to demonstrate God's patience.

A. The Patience of God (6:1)

Who knows, someone there might believe. Some people in that village now might respond to what Jesus had to say.

Here we learn the wonderful patience of God. He is longsuffering toward us, "not willing that any should perish, but that all should come to repentance" (2 Peter 3:9). A gospel song says, "He was there all the time, waiting patiently in line." That may be an inadequate picture of God, but I do know that God is patient.

How patient has God been with you? How many opportunities has He given you to be what He wants you to be? How many opportunities has He given you to open up your life to him?

Jesus Christ was not moving haphazardly through this world. He was on a mission. He had a purpose and plan: "The Son of man is come to seek and to save that which was lost" (Luke 19:10).

Jesus also demonstrated God's persistence.

B. The Persistence of God (6:2a)

"When the sabbath day was come, he began to teach in the synagogue" (6:2a), as He customarily did. "As his custom was, he went into the synagogue on the sabbath day" (Luke 4:16). Jesus identified himself with a place where the word of God was read. It is wonderful when a man of God takes the word of God and teaches the children of God in the power of the Spirit of God in the house of God for the glory of God. It is wonderful to identify yourself with the place where the word of God, the Bible, is taught.

The synagogues in those days were built in such a way that they pointed toward Jerusalem. So when the Lord Jesus stood to teach in the synagogue that day, He was facing Jerusalem. He was facing Calvary, facing that cross where He was going to die for the sins of the world. In that atmosphere, perhaps with that on his mind, Jesus Christ taught the scriptures. There He was, the summation of everything the Bible had to say, standing in their midst teaching the word of God.

Here we learn about the wonderful persistence of God ("O Love that wilt not let me go"). Jesus persisted in his efforts to find someone in Nazareth who would believe in him.

When I was a teenager we used to have a saying, "So-and-so is carrying a torch." If a girl liked a boy and he didn't like her, we'd say she was carrying a torch for him—or vice versa. God is carrying a torch for us. God is a persistent God. His love will pursue human beings all the way to the gates of hell.

II. THE REACTION TO HIS VISIT (6:2b-4)

What was the reaction when Jesus stood in the synagogue that day and taught the scriptures? "Many hearing him were astonished" (6:2b). The word *astonished* means "to strike by blow." It's a picture of someone being stung by a lick. It means they were amazed, flabbergasted. There is something pathetic about being too familiar with someone. For thirty years these people had seen Jesus. He had walked up and down the town's narrow streets. He had lived a perfect life in their midst, yet they missed it. They had seen him around; it was commonplace.

It makes me think how familiar our land is with Jesus. No other country on earth has had more opportunities to hear the word, to know God, to go to heaven, than the citizens of America. Yet to a large degree we have become a gospel-hardened people. We are too familiar with it all.

That can also happen to a church. We hear so much that the things of God get to be commonplace and we are unmoved. It is a dangerous situation for Christians to get in—when the ideas of the Bible become so ordinary that they don't stir us anymore.

Old Gypsy Smith was a great evangelist. Someone said to him, "Mr. Smith, why is it you have maintained your enthusiasm? How have you been able to stay so excited about the Lord all through these years?" Mr. Smith replied, "It's because I've never lost the wonder of it." For us as believers, John 3:16 ought to be as exciting today as it was the day we first heard it. People getting saved, lives being changed, men and women coming to the Lord: such happenings ought to be as thrilling to us today as the first time we ever saw anybody discover Jesus as their savior.

The people of Nazareth were amazed at what He said. They were startled by the miracles He was doing. But nonetheless they wasted a golden opportunity.

We have to understand the tone of voice in what they said. We have to hear the sarcasm. With cynicism dripping from their words, they asked, "Is not this the carpenter?" Of course, He was the carpenter. Although they didn't mean that as a compliment, it was a great compliment. Jesus had evidently been taught the carpentry trade by his legal father, Joseph. Evidently when Joseph died, Jesus became the village carpenter. It was probably through these means that He supported his mother Mary and his younger brothers and sisters. Many a man in Nazareth would come to that carpenter shop and Jesus would build a yoke, plow, chair or some other article of furniture. Perhaps at the end of the day, having worked with his hands, having identified himself with the working man, He would lay his tools down and relax in the dusk. As the evening sun reflected on the walls of that carpenter shop, perhaps the outline of a cross appeared.

Then perhaps one day they came to the carpenter shop and found the door closed, the lock locked. Perhaps there was a little sign there that Jesus would no longer be in business in the carpenter shop of Nazareth.

Jesus Christ left that shop and walked out into the world, no longer to build plows, yokes, and chairs, but to build lives. He built all over Galilee, He built in Jerusalem, with spiritual hammers and spiritual saws.

One day they took that carpenter and nailed him to a cross prepared by another carpenter. They probably said, "That's the end of him." But it wasn't. If you will listen you can still hear the sound of his hammer. You can still hear his saw. Because Jesus Christ, the carpenter, is still at work. He is building churches where souls are being saved. He is building lives.

If any of us will bring the wreckage of our lives, with its broken pieces, to him, He can put them back together again. He is more than a carpenter.

A. What the Listeners Said (6:2b-3)

They said, "Is this not the son of Mary?" That was a slur. The first time He came to Nazareth they had said, "Is this not the son of Joseph?" Now the common gossip about the origin and birth of Jesus was coming out. The suspicion of illegitimacy was in those words. "Is not this the son of Mary?" Yes, but He was more than the son of Mary. The carpenter, yes, but He was more than a carpenter. He's the savior, the Son of God. As far as they were concerned, Jesus was just one more boy in a crowded house of boys and girls. We must be careful that we ourselves don't miss him in the midst of the ordinary.

"They were offended at him" (6:3). The word *offended* could be translated "a stumbling block." They stumbled at him. They didn't expect anything out of the ordinary from someone so close to home. They didn't expect anyone who had been brought up in their town to know much. You have to be brought up in a small town to understand the mentality and psychology that are involved here. They didn't expect anybody who had been brought up there to rise above what they were.

B. What the Lord Said (6:4)

"Jesus said unto them, A prophet is not without honor, but in his own country, and among his own kin, and in his own house." Jesus' brothers and sisters didn't believe in him. He was without honor in his own home. Familiarity breeds contempt.

Enchantment comes from afar. We normally get much more excited about the person way over yonder than the person right here. An expert is an ordinary person who comes from another town. For example, I think of Adrian Rogers, a great man of God. Folks all over the country get his tapes and read his books. One time I went to his services and he was just preaching the stars down. He was plugged up and wired for sound. I looked over there to one side and there sat an old boy sound asleep. Enchantment comes from afar.

Right now I see some Christians far more enamored with the messenger than with the message. They go from conference to conference, run to speaker after speaker, listen to this tape and that tape. Let me tell you, most of us Christians don't need any more truth. We are not practicing all the truth we know right now. What we need to do is get down to business and practice the truth we already know.

A prophet is not without honor except in his own country. The people of Nazareth were too familiar with Jesus.

III. The Result of His Visit (6:5-6)

Mark 6:5 has to be one of the most amazing statements in the Bible. "And he [Jesus] could there do no mighty work." It doesn't say He wouldn't. It says He couldn't. One of the attributes of God is that He is all powerful. We talk of God as the omnipotent God, the all-powerful God, the almighty. Nothing is too hard for God, scripture says. We know that Jesus Christ was God in human flesh. We also know that when Jesus Christ walked on this earth He was God voluntarily limiting himself to our human nature. Yet He exercised the prerogatives of God. Jesus himself said, "All power is given unto me in heaven and in earth" (Matthew 28:18).

He had demonstrated his power—we have already witnessed his omnipotence—in the book of Mark. Yet Mark also says that Jesus could do no mighty work in Nazareth. Here is a verse of scripture that talks about tying the hands of God, about shackling omnipotence.

Something can place a limit on the power of God. Mark went on to indicate what the problem was: "And he marveled because of their unbelief" (6:6a). Jesus could not work miracles there because of their unbelief. Jesus, although sovereign God, had voluntarily placed a limitation on his power. That limitation was the unbelief on the part of the people. It is an awesome concept. It says to me that God's power can be limited in a church by the congregation's lack of faith. There is no limit to what God wants to do and can do in a congregation of believers, but there is a switch that can either turn on or turn off the power of God. That switch is faith.

Up in the balcony our church has a room with no windows. I go into that room occasionally to study when I am at the church. That room is pitch black right now. Yet that room has the potential to be flooded with light if someone will flip a switch on the wall. If I refuse to turn on the switch, the power of the light never flows into that room. God has connected his power to the belief or unbelief of a human being: He says, "I will not come into a life where I am uninvited. I will not dwell in a heart where I am unwanted."

God has the power to change your life. He has the power to forgive you of your sins. Yet He will not do it unless you ask him to do it. You have to turn on the switch.

A. The Majority Response (6:5)

The majority of the people limited the power of God. They tied the hands of God by their unbelief.

B. The Minority Response (6:5)

There were just a few sick folks on whom Jesus laid his hands and healed them. A few persons said, "I don't care what the rest of them say. I have heard what He has done for others, and I believe He will do it for me."

It may be that the majority of men and women will keep the Lord out of their lives, but *you* don't have to. You don't have to shut the power of God off from your life.

Only one other time in scripture does it say that Jesus marveled (Matthew 8:10). The centurion whose servant was sick of palsy came to Jesus and Jesus said, "I'll go and heal him." "Lord," the centurion replied, "I'm not worthy that you should come under my roof. Just speak the word and he'll be well." Jesus marveled at that response. He said, "Nowhere in Israel have I found such faith." He found faith in a place where you wouldn't expect to find it. Here Jesus marveled because you would expect to find faith in his own town, but He didn't find it.

Which is the bigger marvel? The marvel of belief or the marvel of unbelief?

13

The Death of a Conscience
Mark 6:14-29

THE RECORD OF HOW HEROD THE KING MURDERED JOHN THE BAPTIST in cold blood is one of the blackest episodes in the Bible. Herod, his wife Herodias, and John remind us of the Old Testament triad of Ahab, Jezebel, and Elijah—a wicked king, a she-devil wife, and a courageous prophet.

Herod Antipas, as he was known, was the son of Herod the Great. From his wicked father he inherited a tradition of craftiness and cruelty. Jesus called Herod Antipas "that fox."

One day a message came to the palace about a Galilean magician named Jesus. Opinion was divided about who He was. Some people said, "He is Elijah." Others said, "He is one of the prophets." But Herod said, "You're all wrong; He is John the Baptist, whom I beheaded. He is risen from the dead." That statement from the lips of King Herod gives us a classic statement of what can take place in the human conscience.

All of us have a conscience, though we are not exactly sure what it is. We don't know how to go about defining it. When one little boy was asked what a conscience was, he thought a minute and then said, "Something that makes you tell your mother before your sister does." That's not a bad definition. Someone else said that a conscience is the red warning light that goes off in your soul, or the moral beeper that sounds when you do wrong. The conscience might be compared to a walkie-talkie in your heart by which God speaks to you. Probably the best definition I have seen is in Romans 2:15, where the conscience is described as the inward witness of God to your heart, which either accuses or excuses your actions.

It is important to be attuned to your conscience. It is important to take care of it. The Bible speaks of dulling one's conscience. The Bible warns us not to stifle the voice of conscience. In fact, the scriptures say that it is even possible to sear the conscience with a hot iron and thus murder it. That is how the word of God pictures the death of a conscience. God intends the conscience to drive guilty sinners into the arms of their loving, forgiving, heavenly Father.

In this passage we can trace the steps in the death of the conscience of Herod the king. First, we note that Herod had a troubled conscience.

I. A TROUBLED CONSCIENCE (6:17-20)

The scene took place in a palace on the eastern shores of the Dead Sea. The palace was also a prison. In that palace lived a man who was afflicted with a troubled conscience because a message from God had come to his soul. One day when Herod was visiting his brother Philip, he became infatuated with his brother's wife. He enticed her, and literally stole her from his brother. Thus the marriage of Herod and Herodias violated the laws of God. Whether or not they had ever read it, the scriptures teach that the law of God is written on the walls of the heart of every person. They knew that what they had done was wrong, and Herod's conscience troubled him.

A. The Message of God (6:17-19)

God was faithful to the soul of Herod and sent John the Baptist to him with the message of God. I can imagine how it was on the day when John was going to have his audience with the king. He walked in and with flashing eyes pointed a finger right in the face of Herod. With a voice like thunder, he said, "You two are living in adultery. It is not lawful for you to have her. You have broken the law of God and the wrath of God is going to come pouring down on you." Can you imagine how quickly the king's aides wrestled that troublemaker out of the room? Yet the tense of the verb indicates that John repeatedly said, "It is not lawful for you to have her." Perhaps Herod one day went on a chariot ride with Herodias, and running alongside that chariot was John the Baptist shouting, "It is not lawful for you to have her." Herod decided to go down to the mall to do some shopping one day. Right there in the middle of the mall John was yelling at the top of his voice, "It is not lawful for you to have her."

Herod saw to it that John the Baptist got his own personal cell in a damp and dirty dungeon.

It will cost us to denounce sin. If we want to pay a high price, just denounce sin at the wrong time. Tell the truth in an unpopular place and the sky will fall. So John the Baptist was put in prison because he was faithful in delivering the message of God to a guilty couple.

B. The Man of God (6:20)

It is evident that not only did the message of God trouble the conscience of Herod, he also was troubled by the man of God. But, as scripture literally means here, Herodias too now had it in for John. She had quarreled with him and would have killed him, had that been possible (6:19). Conscience, however, kept on speaking to Herod's heart: "Herod, that preacher is right. You had better do what he says."

So "Herod feared John" (6:20). Isn't that amazing? Here was Herod, a monarch. There was John the Baptist, an imprisoned preacher, yet the king was afraid of him.

Today it seems clear that America has lost its conscience, the voice of its moral conscience, because the preachers of this land have ceased to denounce sin. There was a time when politicians were interested in finding out what the preacher thought about any proposed legislation. God's men who have holy, clean lives need to get into the pulpits of America again and faithfully preach what God says about sin. Every Friday the politicians ought to be meeting and asking, "What are they going to be saying about this in church on Sunday?" Every time the politicians are thinking about doing wrong, somebody ought to say, "We better not do it. Those preachers will tell the world about it, come Sunday."

John caused Herod to be afraid. From time to time Herod would go down to the prison cell and listen to John. Scripture says he heard him gladly; he heard him with pleasure. That was a strange phenomenon. It was a message that Herod couldn't stand to hear, yet there was a fascination about it. A strange contradiction was going on in the heart of Herod. He was disturbed, perplexed, tossed between two alternatives. He alternated between the bed of Herodias and the cell of John the Baptist. He loved the beauty of a holy life, but he loved his sin as well. Herod now had a trapped conscience.

II. A TRAPPED CONSCIENCE (6:21-29)

Sin is like a spider weaving a web. The spider starts with a single thread, and then strand after strand is added until eventually a web is formed. Herod was getting ready to weave a web that would trap his conscience and make it impossible for him to avoid the wrong and impossible for him to do the right.

It was Herod's birthday (6:21) and there was going to be a birthday supper. All of the leaders of the country were invited. That night the palace was lighted; the highways leading to it were ablaze. The guests came into the banquet hall. The table was spread with rich delicacies. Strike up the music. Bring on the wine. We can imagine that later that evening Herod received a note from Herodias: "King, if you desire, I'll be happy to send in my daughter Salome to dance for you." Send for Salome.

A. Passion (6:21-23)

The door opened and in came this beautiful, stunning, attractive teenage daughter of Herodias. The motions of her dance inflamed the guests with lust. There was a time when Salome was a little girl dancing to the tune of "Ring Around the Rosie." Now she was gyrating to the heat of human passion, a sad commentary on a mother who would encourage her daughter to do such a thing. A few weeks ago I was reading an article about one of the young actresses in this nation, a beautiful young woman. Through the years, from the time she was just a child, her mother had posed her nude, making money out of the exploitation of that child. What kind of mother would expose her daughter in that way? This was child abuse of the worst form. There was a time when overt sexual provocation was reserved for display in bordellos, but no longer. In educated America, sophisticated America, it's now on television and in magazines too.

King Herod's mind was inflamed, his brain muddled with wine, his eyes burning with lust. Filled with drunken passion, Herod said to her, "Whatever you ask, I'll give it to you, even to half of my kingdom." Little did he realize it, but the python Passion had wrapped around him and was getting ready to crush his conscience. Salome rushed to her mother. Herodias now had him where she wanted him. "The head of John the Baptist," she replied.

That was a compliment to John, wasn't it? His head was considered to be worth half a kingdom. Rushing back into the presence of the king, Salome made her request. "The head of John the Baptist on a platter."

Scripture says that "the king was exceeding sorry" (Mark 6:26). He had been trapped by his passion.

B. Pride (6:24-28)

Something else trapped Herod: his pride. He knew what he ought to do. His conscience was screaming, "It's wrong, Herod. Don't do it." Then he looked at the invited guests. He was in the midst of his peers. What would they think if he backed out? His pride was getting hold of him.

Perhaps some readers of this book know you are in sin. You know you are guilty. You know you are going to the devil's hell. You also know that Jesus loves you. You know that He will forgive you and save you, but your pride is saying, "What will my friends think? What will my girlfriend say? How will my boyfriend react?"

Herod was on that toboggan slide of sin. He looked over at the executioner, one of his body guards, and gave the nod. The bodyguard pulled out his glistening blade and made his way toward the prison cell where John was. One blow of the blade and John was gone.

Don't feel sorry for John. He got an instant trip to glory. For two thousand years he has been running footraces with the angels on the streets of gold. For two thousand years he has been worshiping the lamb on the throne. Rather, feel sorry for Herod.

The party was over. The lights went out. The disciples of John with tear-drenched eyes took his body and gave it a decent burial (6:29).

Now back to 6:14. We don't know how long it was, but in that period of time Herod had perhaps succeeded in suppressing his conscience. One day, however, a little wisp of a word about the ministry of Jesus came leaking into the palace, just a few words about what Jesus was doing.

III. A TORMENTED CONSCIENCE (6:14-16)

Now a man with a tormented conscience, Herod said, "I know who it is. It's John, whom I beheaded. He has risen from the dead." Herod was tormented because he was aware of personal responsibility. Before he committed it, he could rationalize the situation. "Herodias is putting pressure on me. My peers will think I'm a weakling." But after the deed was done, he was alone with his sin.

A. Personal Responsibility

Sin always looks worse after you commit it than before you commit it. You ought never do anything in your life that later on you would not want to put your hands on and say, "That's mine; I did it. That belongs to me."

Herod was a hounded man. When I was a boy, we had a work farm in our county where convicts were placed. From time to time a prisoner would escape and they would get the dogs after him. They would get one of his shirts or a pair of dungarees belonging to the escapee and give the dogs the scent. That convict would head into the swamps in our rural county. Those dogs would start tracking and hounding him. He'd run through those woods. He didn't have time to eat, no time to rest, no time to sleep. Finally, they would catch him.

We are responsible for what we do. It is just a matter of time until our conscience catches us and we know we are caught.

B. Personal Accountability

Herod may have been a Sadducee. The Sadducees, among other things, did not believe in the resurrection. That was their official theology.

I've got news for you: A tormented conscience will melt many a warped theology. I remember a young mother who proclaimed everywhere that she was an atheist. One night she picked up her baby from the crib and it was turning blue, gasping for breath. She grabbed that child, jumped in the car and rushed to the hospital shouting, "O God, O God, O God!"

A theology of skepticism might do fine a lot of the time, but eventually our conscience will torment us and make us aware that out there in the future, death and judgment await us.

The last biblical picture of Herod is in Luke 23:8-11. In that scene, the Lord Jesus Christ shortly before his crucifixion was brought before Herod. (This is your chance Herod; you can tell it all to Jesus. You can silence the voice of your tormented conscience. Admit your sin. Tell him you want to be saved.) "And when Herod saw Jesus, he was exceeding glad: for he was desirous to see him of a long season, because he had heard many things of him; and he hoped to have seen some miracle done by him. Then he questioned with him in many words" (Luke 23:8-9a).

The Bible says that Jesus answered him not a word. I think there was no need to. Herod's conscience was long dead and buried.

14

Jesus and Human Needs
Mark 6:7-13, 30-56

IN MARK 6:7-13 THE LORD JESUS TOOK THE DISCIPLES, PUT THEM IN teams of twos, and sent them out to teach the gospel, to preach the word, to heal the sick, and to cast out devils. They did as they were told and then returned to report to Jesus. They were excited and thrilled at what God had done. They had been working hard. To those exhilarated disciples, the Lord Jesus said, "Come ye yourselves apart into a desert place, and rest a while" (6:31a).

Every weary Christian worker needs to hear those words. There are times when it is good for God's children to back off a bit, take a rest, renew their spirits, and refresh their bodies. It is not good to neglect one's body. Scripture teaches the importance of rest. We need a balance between work and play. Vance Havn er said, "If you don't come apart, you will come apart." That's true. We need times when we smooth out the wrinkles of our souls, get alone with God, refresh our bodies, and then get ready to serve the Lord again.

This was a busy time, the peak of Jesus' popularity. People were coming and going in a constant flow. So many people were thronging around Jesus and the disciples that they didn't have time to eat (6:31b). Jesus said, "Let's take a break."

They got in a ship, headed for the other side of the shore, but when they got there they found multitudes of people all around (6:32-34a).

I was reading this week about the frustrations of the famous, those who are well known by masses of people. They find it difficult ever to have any time to themselves. How hard it is for Billy Graham to go anywhere or be out on his own or do anything out in the open. Masses of people press in on him. Elvis Presley became a captive of his popularity. He couldn't go to a hamburger stand and buy a hamburger. He would be mobbed. He couldn't go to a theater to see a movie. Similarly, the Lord Jesus Christ found himself constantly surrounded by people.

When He saw those crowds, did Jesus say, "Can't you give us a minute? Don't you see how tired we are?" No, that's not exactly what He said, is it? *I* might have said that and *you* might have said that. I might have expressed my frustration at the crowds that way, but Jesus didn't. He looked at the masses of people and was moved with compassion toward them (6:34a). He loved people. He loved individuals.

All of us look at other people in different kinds of ways. A barber looks at haircuts. A shoeshine man checks to see if you have your shoes shined. A restaurant owner says, "That's a big guy; maybe he'll eat a T-bone steak." When Jesus looked at people, He saw them as sheep who didn't have a shepherd and He began to talk to them. Jesus was a people person. He came into the world for people. He said one time, "The Son of man is come to save that which was lost" (Matthew 18:11). We will learn a great deal about life and about what Christian living means if we will observe Jesus meeting human needs.

The remainder of this chapter gives us three pictures of how Jesus related to people and met their needs.

I. When You're Hungry He Gives His Provision (6:34-44)

The first picture shows Jesus feeding five thousand men (besides women and children) at one time. This miracle is described in all four gospels.

A. The Ministry of the Disciples (6:35-38)

After Jesus had been teaching the people a good long while, the disciples came to him and said, "This is a desert place, and now the time is far passed: Send them away, that they may go into the country round about, and buy themselves bread" (6:34-36). Here we see the attitude of the disciples: The people have been here a long time; they are hungry; send them away. But Jesus looked at them and saw people with needs. They had nothing to eat. They were hungry physically, and physical hunger needs to be satisfied. Our Lord was interested in that.

Our church never turns anybody away who is hungry. Anybody who comes here hungry during the week gets fed. The Bible says that man shall not live by bread alone, but by every word that proceedeth out of the mouth of God (Matthew 4:4). There may be some folks who get hungry physically, but even more people are hungry emotionally. All around us are those with emotional hungers: people who are lonely and need companionship; folks who need a friend, somebody to care; human beings in need of affection and attention. Then there is spiritual hunger, a hunger in the human heart that no material thing—only Jesus Christ—can satisfy.

Jesus said, "Give ye them to eat" (6:37). The *ye* is emphatic. "*You* give them something to eat." I wish that those words could be written over the door of every church in this land. It is the responsibility of the church of the Lord Jesus Christ to provide spiritual food for hungry hearts. It is wonderful to know that in the word of God we have the bread that can satisfy.

The disciples were startled. They didn't have any idea what Jesus was talking about. There was no Wendy's on the corner. They started calculating in their minds. "Shall we go and buy two hundred pennyworth of bread, and give them to eat?" (6:37). That doesn't mean a thing to us, but when you translate it into our categories it would be eight months' salary in those days to buy that much bread.

In their presence was one who created the universe out of nothing, one who had all power. When they left Jesus out of their calculations, they came up short.

B. The Miracle of Jesus (6:39-44)

"Well," Jesus said, "how many loves of bread do you have?" They responded, "We've got five loaves and two fish" (6:38). Then Jesus had the disciples arrange the people in groups of fifties and hundreds. The language here is picturesque. All of those people in their bright clothing, sitting in well-organized patches of people—it was like a picture of well-kept flower beds.

Then Jesus took those five loaves of bread and two fish. When you looked at those thousands of people out there, it wasn't a whole lot of food. But they took what they had and put it in the hands of Jesus.

I don't know what you have—it may be very little—but if you take what you have and put it in the hands of Jesus, He can take your little and make a whole lot out of it. Little is much when God is in it. If you just give God your little, you will be surprised at what He does.

Jesus took the bread, blessed it, broke the loaves, and gave them to his disciples. They gave them to the people, and a wonderful thing took place. I wonder what the expressions on the faces of those disciples was as they were handing out those sandwiches. They started through that first section of fifty and obviously there wasn't enough for even that many. Simon Peter passed his basket of bread and fish down the row and then John got it and passed it back. Simon Peter looked in and it was just as full as when it left his hands. He sent it down another row and John sent it back. Row after row after row. Were the disciples dancing in the Spirit before that thing was over, happy, shouting, carrying on? They were witnessing before their eyes the power of Jesus, the bread of life, to feed people who were hungry.

What is the lesson of this miracle?

When you are hungry, Jesus gives his provision. I don't know what the hunger in your life is, but Jesus can provide. Jesus Christ provides for the hunger needs of our hearts.

Have you ever been hungry for something you didn't have? It happens to me about 10:00 at night. I tell my wife, "I'm hungry for something," so I get a cracker and eat it. That's not it. Then maybe a banana, and that's not it either. I have some "friends" who have a habit of bringing me chocolate-covered donuts with cream in the middle, and that's it!

Are you hungry for something you don't have? Is there a gnawing in your heart? An emptiness in your life? God has created the human heart with a need for Jesus. I believe that people are born with that need. They may not know what it is. They may not know how to define it or where to look for it, but in their hearts there is a hunger.

Our responsibility is to find those people who are hungry and give them Jesus Christ.

II. WHEN YOU'RE HELPLESS HE GIVES HIS PRESENCE (6:45-52)

The second picture shows Jesus walking on the water. "And straightway he constrained his disciples to get into the ship, and to go to the other side" (6:45). The word *constrained* is a strong word. It means that it was the will of Jesus for them to do this. He insisted that they get in the boat and go to the other side. At this point the crowds were so enamored with the miracles of Jesus that a movement to elect him king was taking shape. Because many of the disciples would have been susceptible to that idea, Jesus sent them to the other side. Then He "departed into a mountain to pray" (6:46).

A. The Difficulties of Obedience (6:45-48)

The disciples were obedient to Jesus. They left when He told them to go. Now, later that evening (6:47) "He saw them toiling in rowing" (6:48). The word *toiling* means "tortured." They were battling a storm out there on the sea, their arms were aching, and their bodies were filled with pain.

To obey Jesus is not always easy. Sometimes it's hard to do the will of God. Sometimes it's hard to be faithful to Jesus. Peer pressure can be a tortuous experience. Pressures on your job when you are obedient to Jesus can be agonizing.

But when the disciples were toiling and rowing, He saw them. They didn't have to send up any flares. They didn't have to wave any flags. As the passage reads here, it seems that Jesus saw their dilemma but waited several hours before He got there. He didn't come until the fourth watch of the night (6:48).

Why didn't Jesus go to them immediately? Have you ever wondered that? Have you ever had a problem that Jesus didn't solve quickly? Doesn't He care about you? Isn't He interested in you? Doesn't He know what to do with your problem?

Let me suggest what I think was happening. First, we know that those men knew how to handle the boat. They had been in storms before. It was no big deal when that storm came up. Then it got worse. It was going to be a little more difficult than they had thought, but surely they could handle it. They would be able to cope.

Have you ever had a problem and said, "I can work it out," but then your solution doesn't work?

Then this storm got really bad. Waves were beating against the ship, tossing it to and fro. Water poured into the boat. Finally the disciples got to the point that they were helpless. There was nothing they could do.

B. The Delights of Obedience (6:48-52)

What happened next? "He [Jesus] cometh unto them, walking upon the sea" (6:48). They thought they were seeing a ghost (6:49). He scared them to death. Obviously they weren't looking for him to show up in that particular way.

Sometimes we get afraid because we are not looking for Jesus to come into our lives in the manner in which He comes. But we must remember that whatever the storm may be, Jesus will use it as a passageway into our lives. When we are helpless, Jesus gives his presence. He's right there. He says, "Be of good cheer: it is I; be not afraid" (6:50). Thank God for his presence. I would rather be in the midst of a storm and have the presence of Jesus than be in calm waters and Jesus be nowhere around. It's better to have Christ in a crisis than to have life-as-usual without his presence. He loves us, and when we are helpless, He gives his presence.

III. WHEN YOU'RE HURTING HE GIVES HIS POWER (6:53-56)

A. Hurting People (6:53-55)

When the ship came to the other side and Jesus got out,

> straightway they knew him, and ran through that
> whole region round about, and began to carry about in
> beds those that were sick. And whithersoever he
> entered, into villages, or cities, or country, they laid the

sick in the streets, and besought him that they might
touch if it were but the border of his garment: and as
many as touched him were made whole (6:54-56).

When Jesus came, everyone with sick relatives or friends started
bringing them to him. Here we see our third picture: Jesus helping people.

There are lots of hurting people in this world. They might not
ever tell you that, but down inside they are hurting. Here's a man
going through the trauma of divorce. One day things were great
(he thought) and the next day everything was torn to pieces. His
family is going through all kinds of turmoil. Here's a boy whose
dad came in last night, drunk and fighting. Here's a girl who
thinks she's lost everything worth living for. Here's a couple who
played with fire and got burned. We Christians are responsible
to find those hurting people and get them to Jesus. The church
is in the people business. You can't be like Jesus and not be in
the people business. When people hurt, Jesus hurts. Our job is
to go out there and bring the folks who have hurts to the one who
has power to heal.

B. Healing Power (6:56)

When they brought these people to Jesus, those who touched him
were made whole. But their touch was not what made them
whole.

Some people misunderstand what faith is. Sometimes, for
instance, we say we are "saved by faith and by faith alone."
That's really not right. Faith does not save us. You go to the doctor for surgery and put your faith in that doctor. He cuts you
open; he does the job; he sews you back up. Are you well again
because you had faith in your doctor? No. You had faith, but it
didn't save you. The doctor did. What saves you is the object
of your faith. You are saved not by your faith, but by the one in
whom you trust. They were not saved by their touch, but by the
one whom they touched. It is Jesus who saves us.

15

Jesus and Human Tradition
Mark 7:1-13

MARK 6 AND MARK 7 PROVIDE A STARTLING CONTRAST. IN THE sixth chapter we saw the popularity of Jesus. In the seventh chapter He encounters hostility. Some of the same people who were flocking to hear him would eventually be in the crowd shouting, "Crucify him, crucify him!" It can be a very short step to go from hero to zero.

Five times in this passage Jesus made reference to tradition. There are many kinds of tradition: national public traditions handed down from one generation to another; family traditions, various customs and ways of observing particular holidays for instance; church traditions, using certain symbols of faith or outward expressions of devotion. Tradition is not necessarily a bad thing. "Hold the traditions which ye have been taught" (2 Thessalonians 2:15). There the apostle Paul was talking about teaching the word of God, which is what God wants us to do. In this passage of scripture in Mark, Jesus was dealing with the problem of human traditions taking the place of the authority of the word of God.

The Jews had worked themselves into a system in which the

people observed countless ceremonies and rituals. In the process it was easy to miss personal contact with the God who created them, the God who was their redeemer. It all began with what was known as oral interpretations of the law. In order to help people better understand the word of God an oral interpretation would be given. Those oral interpretations would be handed down from generation to generation and the time came when people didn't know what the law really had said way back yonder. They were more concerned with the diligent observance of those traditions.

We all know how easy it is to get wrapped up in programs. It is easy to get so occupied with what men teach or say that God can't speak to your heart directly from his word.

There is a difference between tradition and truth. Tradition is outward; truth is inward. Tradition has to do with ritual; truth has to do with reality. Tradition is something you keep; truth is something that keeps you.

I. THE ACCUSATION OF THE JEWS (7:1-5)

How did Jesus address the problem of human tradition? We notice first that an official party of Pharisees and scribes had come from Jerusalem (7:1). They had come to find something to criticize. The goal of that committee of critics was not to find out if Jesus was the messiah, but to find something wrong with him. You and I know that if we have it in for somebody, if we really want to find something to indict them for, we can find it. So they were watching Jesus and the disciples, analyzing every little move they made.

A. What They Saw (7:1-4)

Before long they found something to criticize. "Would you look at that?" they said. "Those disciples are eating with unwashed hands." The Pharisees and scribes were shocked, and they were delighted to be shocked. They had wanted to be shocked. They had come down there to be shocked.

B. What They Said (7:5)

"They found fault" (7:2). In every group there are people who are quick to find fault, people who are looking for something to criticize. They disregard all that is good. They can always find a fly in the ointment.

We have to understand that when the Bible says the disciples were eating with defiled hands, it had nothing to do with hygiene. They were referring to a ceremonial cleansing, one of the traditions of the elders. It was a tradition that had built up around an important spiritual truth, but they had lost the truth in the symbol. The tradition said that when you get ready to eat, you've got to be ceremonially clean; you have to go through a rigorous cleansing ritual. Scripture says here that "they washed their hands oft" (7:3). Before they ate, they would take a certain prescribed amount of water, and pour it from the elbow down to the fingers. They would take the fist of this hand and rub it vigorously in the other hand and vice versa. They would rub all the way up to the elbow. It was a ceremony. Further, all the utensils had to be washed in a certain way.

Jesus refused to be bound by man-made rules and rituals. He didn't teach his disciples to observe them either, and that made the Pharisees both uncomfortable and angry. The tradition had started in Old Testament times, when God commanded the priests who were to minister in the temple to wash their hands. The practice was intended to be a reminder that when they went into the presence of God they had to be clean in their hearts. So along the way somebody said, "If it's good for the priests, it's good for the people. Let's have the people do that too." Before long the truth that you have to be clean in your heart was lost and they became occupied with having clean hands. Gradually more and more details were added, even the idea that if you didn't go through the ceremony, a demon would get you.

To bring this into the twentieth century, I think of people who go to church and just go through the motions. Perhaps some people reading this book attend church because it's the thing to do. Perhaps you never make contact with God when you attend a worship service. It has no meaning. It is a ritual, a ceremony. It never touches your heart. If that is true of you, this incident in the life of Jesus will be especially relevant to your situation.

II. THE ANSWER OF JESUS (7:6-13)

How did Jesus respond to their preoccupation with tradition? Jesus took scripture and spoke some of his sternest words.

Sometimes I hear people talk about Jesus and I wonder if they are talking about the Jesus of the New Testament. When I read the New Testament, I see a Jesus who was a real man. He was no namby-pamby, no sissy, and He didn't get cowed by the religious phonies of his day.

Why didn't his disciples keep the traditions? the Pharisees and scribes asked. Jesus looked his critics straight in the eye, the fire of judgment burning in his eyes. "I'll tell you why." Taking Isaiah 29:13, He described what happened when tradition took the place of truth.

A. The Danger of Tradition (7:6-7)

Adherence to tradition can lead to hypocrisy. "Well hath Esaias prophesied of you hypocrites," He began. In the original language there is a definite article right before *hypocrite*: "You, *the* hypocrites." The Greek word means "to pretend" in the sense of being an actor in a play, being on a stage and acting out a part. Jesus was saying, "You folks have turned religion into play acting."

When I was a kid we used to "play like" (I think they call it "make-believe" now, but we called it "play like"). We'd say, "Let's play like we are cowboys." Did you ever ride a stick for a horse? You can tie a rope around the stick, make reins, and have great fun.

The worst form of hypocrite is the religious hypocrite, the religious make-believer. He is the person who pretends to be one thing in his outward behavior, but is altogether different down in his heart. He is the person who comes to church and pretends to be one thing, but is altogether different when he gets back home. His children don't recognize him as the same guy. Jesus said, "You are hypocrites. You honor me with your lips, but your heart is far from me." He was saying, "You are saying the right words, but your heart is wrong. You are right on the outside and wrong on the inside. You say one thing, but you mean something else."

I think about hymns people sing. "My Jesus, I love thee. I know thou art mine. For thee all the follies of sin I resign." Yet some church folks sing that song while they are holding onto all kinds of sin. "Where He leads me I will follow." Yet some folks don't follow the leading of the Lord enough to get back to church on Sunday night and Wednesday night. We had better be careful what we sing with our lips if it's not coming from our hearts.

A lot of people talk about loving but they never love. They

talk about forgiving but they never forgive. They talk about witnessing but they never witness. Jesus says, "Not every one that saith unto me, Lord, Lord, shall enter into the kingdom of heaven; but he that doeth the will of my Father which is in heaven" (Matthew 7:21). The apostle Paul made the same point: "With the heart man believeth unto righteousness; and with the mouth confession is made unto salvation" (Romans 10:10).

You cannot think your way into the kingdom of God. Christianity is a rational faith, a reasonable faith, but you do not get into the kingdom head first. You get into the kingdom heart first.

Jesus was saying, "The hypocrite plays the game. He says one thing with his lips and another thing in his heart. His heart is really far from me."

"In vain do they worship me" (7:7). Jesus was saying, "Your churchgoings don't count. You are going through your ritual, you are going through your ceremonies, but it's doing you no good. It's wasted activity."

Churches today get so wrapped up in their programs and activities that it's difficult for the voice of God to get through. You can look at the average church's order of service and even if you stay home you know what they are doing every minute. Although we criticize some of our liturgical friends, some Baptist churches are just as bad. We get involved in our petty little programs and there is no freedom of the Spirit. We church folks can get so busy in church work that we forget the work of the church. We have our meetings here, our meetings there, and they end up getting in the way of winning people to the Lord Jesus. It is so easy for organizations to build up in a church and become an end in themselves. Any organization is merely a human vehicle that God can use to get out there where lost people are, but that organization has value only if it accomplishes the purpose for which it was created. When it ceases to accomplish that purpose there is no more need for the organization.

B. The Development of Tradition (7:8-13)

"Laying aside the commandment of God, ye hold the tradition of men" (7:8). It's not that we disregard the word of God at the beginning. We put a human tradition alongside it, and then we gradually neglect the word of God. We get wrapped up in our own traditions, in our own agendas. It is a short step to move from neglecting the word of God to rejecting the word of God.

"Full well ye reject the commandment of God, that ye may keep your own tradition" (7:9). A lot of people in the religious world have taken human teaching and put it right alongside the teachings of the word of God. Some groups say that church tradition is just as inspired as the word of God. Many cults are built around the teaching of a prophet or prophetess whose writings essentially replace the word of God. If there is a contradiction between what the divine word says and what a human tradition says, they side up with the human tradition.

Christians can make the same mistake, getting so wrapped up in what some teacher or preacher says that it becomes more authoritative than God's word. Some dear Christians I know just run around from conference to conference getting notes on what this or that teacher said. Don't misunderstand me; I thank God for those who study the word of God and teach it. But no words from any human preacher are inspired. No human teacher's notes are inspired. When you want to find out about a subject, don't go to their notes; instead go to God's word and see what it has to say. I don't care what any person says about it. I want to know what God says. You are under no obligation to believe what I write in this book except when it agrees with what God says in his word.

When human tradition replaces biblical truth, every area of the believer's life is affected, including worship. There are two extremes in worship. When I was a boy, my home church had a rigid form of worship. One of the reasons I don't like the Doxology is because every Sunday of my life for eighteen years, when 11:00 struck, we stood and sang the Doxology. As a little kid I said, "Dear Lord, if you will ever, ever let me have a church of my own, I promise you we will not sing the Doxology." Not that there is anything wrong with the Doxology; it's the rigidity that bothers me, rigid forms of worship.

Then there is the other extreme. I heard someone the other day talking about worship who said, "If you don't raise your hands you are not worshiping." If you want to raise your hands, that doesn't bother me. But you can't require that as worship. I don't care whether you clap or don't clap. Jesus says, "God is a Spirit: and they that worship him must worship him in spirit and in truth" (John 4:24). The church cannot worship for you. It just provides an opportunity for you to worship. Worship is a personal, intimate affair. It is something that goes on in the heart between you and God. We must not build up human traditions and say, "This is right and that is wrong." We must go by what God says in his word.

When you put human tradition ahead of the word of God your compassion is affected. The word of God says, "Honour thy father and thy mother; and whoso curseth father or mother let him die the death" (7:10). Jesus quoted those verses and then pointed out what the Jews had done. They had come up with a system called Corban (which means "a gift") in which a son could take his money to the temple and say, "I declare this Corban; I dedicate this to God." Doing that with his money freed him of the responsibility of caring for his parents. He could just say, "I'm sorry, Dad. This money is Corban, I can't help you." That tradition had quenched human compassion and love.

Don't get so wrapped up in tradition, in programs and outward activities, that you lose the heart of your relationship with Jesus Christ.

16

Jesus and Human Sin

Mark 7:14-23

WE HAVE SEEN HOW THE PHARISEES HAD ELEVATED THEIR ORAL traditions to a position of equal or greater authority than the scriptures. Jesus also pointed out that they misunderstood the nature of human sin. It is difficult at times for us to understand what Jesus was getting at, because we are not accustomed to the kinds of things that the Jews were accustomed to.

I. THE PHARISEES' PHYSICAL FOCUS (7:14-16)

The Pharisees had all kinds of ceremonial practices. If you didn't observe them, it was as if you were a sinner before God and not worthy to come into the presence of God. For example, in the Old Testament, some foods were considered clean foods—it was all right to eat them. Other foods were considered unclean—those foods were not to be eaten. There was a purpose for those ceremonial laws. The Israelites were spending their days among people who didn't know God. But God wanted to educate his people to the fact that He is a holy God and He expects his people to live holy lives. So He gave these ceremo-

nial rituals to impress on the people that they were to be different
from the non-Jews around them. As centuries went by, however,
those laws were extended. At the time of Jesus the average Jew
was a walking set of ceremonies and regulations. Almost every
action of his life had its guidelines of propriety according to the
traditions of the elders.

A. What Is Outside (7:14-15)

It was important that Jesus correct their misapprehension of the
nature of sin. Because they had made sin largely an outward
thing, Jesus wanted them to realize that sin is a much deeper
problem than being obedient outwardly.

We are facing that problem in our day also. Our generation has
just about lost its consciousness of sin. Along with that, many
people have the idea that if they just go to church on Sunday, if
they are sorry for some things they have done through the week,
go through some ceremonies, and repeat some stated prayers,
then they are all right. If they do those things again next week,
come back to church on Sunday, and confess their wrongdoing
all over again, then everything is fine.

We have to understand what Jesus was talking about here. He
was talking about what sin really is, what real defilement is. Man's
opinion of sin and God's opinion of sin are different. Man says that
sin is an accident; God says it's an abomination. Man says that sin
is a blunder; God says it's blindness. Man says it's a chance; God
says it's a choice. Man says it's a defect; God says it's a disease.
Man says it's an error; God says it's enmity. Man says it's failure;
God says it's fatality. Man says that sin is just a trifle; God says it's
a tragedy. Man says that it is a weakness; God says it is wickedness.

When we understand sin as God presents it in the Bible, when
we see its devastating results and the depths of sin in our own
experiences, we will have an altogether different understanding
of sin than we had before.

B. What Is Inside (7:15)

In Jesus' words we can note three characteristics of human sin.
First, human sin is primarily a spiritual matter rather than a
physical matter. He said, "I want you to hear this. I want you
to understand this. Nothing that comes from outside a person

that enters into him can defile him."

Jesus was using the illustration here of the human body and what you put in your body. Keep in mind He was not talking about being healthy; He was talking about being holy. Of course, it is obvious that you can put certain things in your body that will make you unhealthy. You can eat some things that will make you sick. But here Jesus was not dealing with calories or allergies or proteins or carbohydrates. It is not what you take into your body that makes you a sinner before God. It is not something you eat that causes you to need a savior. I think of alcohol, for instance. As a component of certain medicines, it can be helpful. Put it in a beverage and it can be bad. Things are not holy or unholy in themselves.

II. JESUS' SPIRITUAL FOCUS (7:17-23)

A. Sin Is Internal before It Is External (7:17-19)

Jesus said that the things coming out of people are what defile them. Those are what make us sinners. When you look at people and see the things they do, keep in mind that the basic problem is not the outside of their lives; the problem is the inside of their lives. We have noted that the first characteristic of sin is that it is primarily spiritual and not physical.

Jesus then gave a second characteristic: Sin is an internal matter as well as an external matter. "Whatsoever thing from without entereth into the man, it cannot defile him; Because it entereth not into his heart, but into the belly" (7:18-19). When we eat, food goes into our stomachs, our bodies assimilate its nutrient values, and then that particular food passes on through our systems as waste, the unused things we do not need for our bodies.

Jesus' point was that food never touches the heart. The stomach is a pass-through physical organ, a purifying organ. Jesus said that what makes a man a sinner is not the food that gets into his stomach, but rather the sin that originates in his heart. Sin is an internal matter, not primarily an external matter. "It entereth not into his heart" (7:19).

When Jesus used the word *heart* He didn't mean the physical heart that is pumping in our bodies. He was using *heart* in the sense of its being the center of our lives. When the Bible talks about your spiritual heart it is talking about the real you, the core of your existence. For instance, it says, "Keep thy heart with all diligence; for out of it are the issues of life" (Proverbs 4:23). "As he thinketh in his heart, so is he" (Proverbs 23:7). Jesus said, "Out of the abundance of the heart the mouth speaketh" (Matthew 12:34).

So sin is an internal problem. It is something that goes on in the heart. It originates on the inside and not on the outside. Our problem is not primarily the outside sins in our lives; our problem is a heart problem, and the only one who can deal with the problem of sin in the human heart is Jesus Christ.

Suppose tomorrow morning you find your kitchen filled with water. You get a bucket, mop, and you start mopping and squeezing and hauling that water out, but the kitchen just keeps filling up with more water. How much better it would be to go to the source of water and cut off the flow. You can mop, you can carry out water all day long, but you aren't going to solve the problem until you go to the source of the problem.

The Bible deals not only with the fruit of sin, it deals with the root of sin. The Bible talks not only about the flow of sin, it talks about the fountain of sin.

B. Sin Is Potential Before It Is Actual (7:20-23)

Finally, Jesus gave a third characteristic of sin: Sin is a potential within us before it is a reality. In 7:21-23 Jesus gave a sobering catalog of sins. It is like an X-ray of the human heart. "For from within, out of the heart of men, proceed evil thoughts, adulteries, fornications, murders, thefts, covetousness, wickedness, deceit, lasciviousness, an evil eye, blasphemy, pride, foolishness" (7:21-22).

"Evil thoughts" are evil designs. Before we sin, there is the thought of sin, the attitude of sin. Evil thoughts and desires lead to evil choices—we choose to do what we do.

The next six things Jesus mentioned were evil deeds. It is as if the Lord Jesus Christ were quoting from today's newspaper. These are the things that human beings have done in a twenty-four-hour day in America:

—Adulteries, violation of the marriage bond. We are living in a time when adultery is paraded and presented in literature and magazines, on television and in movies, as if it were quite all right. One reason for the fall of the Roman empire was that the marriage relationship and fidelity to that relationship were laid aside; adultery was the course of the day.

—Fornications. That's a more general term which includes all kinds of sexual immorality. Pornographic literature, X- and R-rated movies, lewd songs, premarital sex, and all such things.

—Murders. People are being killed in our country everyday in drug wars—on the streets, in their homes. In America, since abortion has been legal, many millions of unborn babies have been murdered.

—Thefts. Stealing and shoplifting, cheating in school and on one's income tax, stealing from God.

—Covetousness, the greedy desire for more. That's the word which describes the materialism of our day—keeping up with the Joneses as well as wanting more than others have.

—Wickedness. This word describes the individual who is not content to sin himself; he wants to get others to sin as well. He wants others to be as bad as he is. He wants to pull people down with him. This is what's behind the tremendous peer pressure that young people experience in school. Those who do wrong want to cause others also to do wrong.

—Deceit, which means trickery or misrepresentation in order to gain some advantage over a person. A slick business deal, false advertising.

—Lasciviousness, which means open and unashamed sin. It means sin that totally disregards public opinion or public standards of decency. It means outrageous sin, unblushing sin.

—An evil eye, envy or jealousy of other people.

—Blasphemy, slander of God.

—Pride, a lifting up of one's self, a putting down of others.

—Foolishness. This means moral foolishness. It is the attitude of a person who has no interest in God.

Jesus says, "All these things are the sins that come out of the human heart." "For from within, out of the heart of men, proceed ... all these evil things" (7:21-23). Do you get the point? Jesus was saying that all of these sins are potential in us before they become actual. Everyone has the capability of committing any of these sins. The root of all of them is lurking in the heart of each of us. Given the right circumstances, you and I could commit them.

Take marriage, for example. When you get married you make many interesting discoveries. Marriage is the process of getting to know your mate, but not only that. It is the process of getting to know yourself. Marriage creates circumstances that let you see things in your life that you would never have imagined were there. Did you know you were as selfish as you are until you got married? Before you got married, chances are that you were spoiled by Mom and Dad because they thought you were the grandest thing in the world. While you were dating you still probably were treated as if you were the king or queen living in the Taj Mahal. You were *it*. When marriage comes along, that *it* becomes a partnership. You have to share everything with someone else, and you will just be stunned at what this really means. "She makes me so angry," you say. No, she doesn't make you angry. Circumstances have arisen whereby you can see the anger that is already there. Jesus says the problem is on the inside. The problem is a heart problem.

But for the grace of God, the potential for all these thirteen things (and more) is in every human heart. Given the right circumstances, you could murder today. Given the right circumstances, you might steal today. The root of the matter is in you. The Bible says, "The heart is deceitful above all things, and desperately wicked: who can know it?" (Jeremiah 17:9).

What is the solution? How do we solve the problem of sin within? When Jesus died on the cross, He dealt with our sin problem. Now He offers us the possibility for our sins to be cleansed. "If we confess our sins, he is faithful and just to forgive us our sins, and to cleanse us from all unrighteousness" (1 John 1:9).

17

Help for Hurting Parents
Mark 7:24-30

I.   A DESPERATE PARENT (7:25-26)
    A. Her Hurt (7:25)
    B. Her Hope (7:25)
II. A DETERMINED PARENT (7:27-28)
    A. His Strange Refusal (7:27)
    B. Her Satisfying Response (7:28)
III. A DELIGHTED PARENT (7:29-30)
    A. Her Anticipation (7:29)
    B. Her Realization (7:30)

IN MARK 7:24 JESUS FOR THE FIRST TIME STEPPED OUT OF ISRAEL AND went to gentile territory, to the borders of Tyre and Sidon. Those cities were not far from present-day Beirut, Lebanon. By this action Jesus illustrated that He had come to be the savior of the world (John 3:16).

Jesus is a "whosoever will" savior. it doesn't matter who you are, where you have come from, or what your nationality is. Jesus Christ loves you and is willing to save you.

Jesus came into this particular region, went into a house, and didn't want anyone to know He was there. Yet scripture says, "He could not be hid" (7:24). They had already heard about him. In fact, people from that area had come to Jesus before this to hear him and to be healed (Luke 6:17). People immediately began to come to him.

The presence of Jesus Christ can never be hidden—in a church, in a home, in an individual. If Jesus Christ is in your life, you cannot permanently hide that fact. If you have had an experience with Christ, if He is living in your heart and has changed your life, the "truth will out."

One person who came to Jesus is known in scripture as the Syrophenician woman (7:25). She is also called a woman of Canaan (Matthew 15:22). Her language was Greek, her nationality was Syrophenician. Above all, she was a hurting parent, and in that circumstance it may be easy for some readers of this book to identify with her. Perhaps you have a problem with one or more of your children and your heart is breaking.

Tremendous burdens are attached to being a parent. No godly person can bring children into this world and then be dissociated from those burdens. Every parent has problems to some degree. Some folks have especially difficult problems—a rebellious son, a daughter getting in with the wrong crowd—and find themselves almost helpless to do anything to change things. If you are going through burdens with your children, the experience of this Syrophenician woman can help you. Notice first that she is a desperate parent.

I. A Desperate Parent (7:25-26)

This woman came into the presence of Jesus in desperation and agony, falling at his feet. When we hear her problem, we can imagine her concern and anxiety.

A. Her Hurt (7:25)

Her young daughter had an unclean spirit. The term used for *young daughter* is a tender one, meaning her "darling little girl." This child was the apple of her eye. She loved that girl with all her heart. As her mother she felt great responsibility for her well-being.

Before I had children I had four theories about bringing up children. Now I have four children and no theories. Parenting is the process of taking a little life and seeing it pass through your life and disappear into adulthood.

The word here for *unclean spirit* means unclean in a moral sense. Some immorality had taken hold of this girl. It was a frontal assault on her life by the devil. In our day we are experiencing a similar situation. If you are not aware of the fact that there is a frontal assault on the lives of young people today, I don't know where you have been in recent years. Young people are experiencing a frontal assault by the demons of hell. The devil is doing everything in his power to get hold of the lives of our children and wreck them. Further, those parents who really love Jesus, who have sought to bring their children up in the things of God, brought them to the house of the Lord, taught them the scriptures, and prayed for them all the days of their lives—such parents are under more attack than any other group of people on this earth.

The devil is making his last stand. He is doing everything he can to fill the lives of our boys and girls with unclean spirits. There are the unclean spirits of the pressures of school. They are telling our young people that there is no God, that a chance evolution, not divine creation, is in back of everything. They are ridiculing the Christian faith of their students' homes. They are subjecting them to profane and vulgar language. There are the attacks of the music, the ungodly, extreme, utterly degraded kind of music that our children are sucked into listening to. There are drugs and alcohol and peer pressure everywhere. Christian parents are seeing the influence of these things on their children. As with this woman with a hurt in her heart, the devil is doing his best to destroy today's children.

B. Her Hope (7:25)

But she "heard of him" (7:25). Perhaps she had heard about what Jesus did for Jairus, whose daughter had died. Jesus went where that little girl was, spoke the word, and she came back to life again. Maybe this woman said in her heart, "If Jesus could do that for the other little girl, there is hope for my child too." So she brought her problem to Jesus. That is the place to bring any problem. It is the place to bring the problem of children who are being led astray by the devil.

"She besought him that he would cast forth the devil out of her daughter" (7:26). There is always hope for a child when there is a praying mother or father. The first thing I do every morning is have my prayer time, and very high up on my prayer list every day are the names of each one of my children. I call them by name at the throne of God. I claim the blood of Jesus over them.

I pray that God will keep them true and strong and faithful for him throughout that day. I wouldn't dare let my children go out into this kind of world if I hadn't first of all bathed them in prayer.

Parenting is a problematic thing. Someone once said that being a parent is one of those jobs that when you learn how to do it well you no longer have the job. That's pretty true. Parenting is the process of losing control of your children. When they are little things you do everything for them: feed them, bathe them, dress them. Everywhere they go, you have to take them. Then they begin to feed themselves, bathe themselves, dress themselves. They start taking themselves where they want to go. Step by step you lose control of that child. That's the way it is supposed to be. Our children are supposed to develop independence, get to the point that they make their own decisions. With those privileges, of course, come responsibilities.

Sadly, there may come a time when parents may not even be able to talk to a child. If you have come to the point that one or more of your children have wandered away from God, there is one thing you can do. You can pray. Nobody can stop you from calling on God on their behalf. Long after conscious control of your children is over, your prayers can still go with them everywhere they go.

II. A DETERMINED PARENT (7:27-28)

A. His Strange Refusal (7:27)

One of the amazing passages about Jesus in the entire Bible comes next. Look at what happens in verse 27: "But Jesus said unto her, let the children first be filled: for it is not meet to take the children's bread, and to cast it unto the dogs." That sounds brutal, doesn't it? It doesn't sound like Jesus at all. Matthew's account of this same incident sounds still harsher. Matthew gives a fuller account of what was said. (Remember that though directed by the Holy Spirit, humanly speaking the gospel writers pick and choose what they want to record according to the design of their particular book.)

"Have mercy on me, O Lord, thou Son of David; my daughter is grievously vexed with a devil. But he answered her not a word" (Matthew 15:22-23). He wouldn't even answer her? That's not like Jesus. We know that no person coming to him is denied.

Obviously this cannot be what it appears to be on the surface. She said, "Have mercy on me, O Lord, thou Son of David," and He didn't reply. But, farther along in the story, Matthew quotes him as saying, "I am not sent but unto the lost sheep of the house of Israel" (7:24). The answer to his silence can be found in that statement. This woman had heard that Jesus was the Jewish messiah. She, a gentile, was approaching him on Jewish ground, as the Son of David. One of the first big battles in the early church had to do with whether or not you had to become a Jew in order to be saved. Right here Jesus eliminated that argument altogether by refusing to acknowledge a plea that was made on the basis of becoming a Jew before you came to him.

We do not come to Jesus through a Jewish door. We do not come to Jesus through a Baptist door. We do not come to Jesus through a Methodist door. We don't come to Jesus through a Pentecostal door. We come to Jesus through the sinner's door. That's the only way we get to Jesus.

Because this woman had no claim on Jesus as the Jewish messiah, He refused to respond. He made clear that He had come for the lost sheep of Israel. The historical order was the Jew first, then the Greek. The Bible says, "I am not ashamed of the gospel of Christ: for it is the power of God unto salvation to every one that believeth, to the Jew first, and also to the Greek" (Romans 1:16).

But look at how determined she was. She then said, "Lord, help me" (Matthew 15:25). In effect, she was saying, "OK, Lord, I'll drop the Jewish business. I'll come as a poor lost sinner. Lord, help me." Now let's pick up Mark's account: "Let the children first be filled: for it is not meet to take the children's bread, and to cast it unto the dogs" (7:27).

Jews sometimes called a gentile a dog. That's not what Jesus called us. Some statements in the gospels could be better understood by those who heard Jesus' tone of voice and saw the smile on his face. Jesus wasn't insulting her. Rather He was taking an insulting designation and making it a term of endearment. Watch what He did. The word *dogs* here is a diminutive word; He changed the word. We get closer to the original if we read it as *puppies*—the kind of dearly loved puppies that are right there in the dining room with the people.

Look at the battle, the struggle, she was going through. If you have ever had a burden for one of your children, you understand. It is a rugged experience. Praying for our children can be a rigorous process. When you come before the Lord Jesus, you see everything in your own life that's wrong. You see every inconsistency in your heart. You see all the things that ought to be there. So this process of interceding for your child must become a disciplined endeavor in your own life.

B. Her Satisfying Response (7:28)

The Syrophenician woman didn't stop. "She answered and said unto him, Yes, Lord: yet the dogs under the table eat of the children's crumbs" (7:28). She was saying, "Lord, if you want me to be a little house puppy down on the floor, I'm willing to be that. I'll get in whatever position I have to get in, in order to receive what I need from you for my child." When we get serious enough before God in prayer to say to the Lord, "I'll do anything you want me to do. I'll take any position you want me to take, however humble; whatever it takes, Lord, I've got a child who needs you," we are getting close to the ear of God. God will do something for us when we are that determined. Hers was a faith that would not let him go. So she said, "The crumbs from the table will be just fine."

I don't blame her. I'd rather have the crumbs that come from the master's table than to have the feast that comes from the devil's table. Give me the crumbs of Jesus any day. The devil says, "Look here, I'm going to give you all these luxuries if you will live for me. Serve me and I'll do this in your life: I'll make you rich." I repeat, give me the crumbs of Jesus any day.

But when we come to the Lord Jesus, we don't get just the crumbs. He makes us a child in God's family. He seats us at the table and we feast on the good things of the Lord.

"Let the children first be filled" (7:27). With that word *first* Jesus was cracking the door of hope. *First* implies a *second*. So a little ray of light came shining through and that woman saw her chance. That's the way we have to pray for our children too.

III. A DELIGHTED PARENT (7:29-30)

"And he said unto her, For this saying go thy way; the devil is gone out of thy daughter" (7:29). Matthew added that Jesus also said, "Great is thy faith: be it unto thee even as you will." Scripture says that from that very hour her daughter was well

(Matthew 15:28). Jesus gave her a promise. In fact, He said, she is all right now.

If you have a problem with a child, so that you can't even communicate with that child anymore (maybe he or she is hundreds of miles away), get alone with Jesus and stay with Jesus until you receive a promise. Then hold on to that promise.

A. Her Anticipation (7:29)

The Syrophenician woman hadn't yet seen with her own eyes her daughter healed, but she heard it from Jesus and she believed it. On the way home I know that she was a different woman. She had come with a heavy heart; now she had a light heart. She had come with a burden in her soul; now she returned with joy in her soul.

B. Her Realization (7:30)

When she got home she saw firsthand that the unclean spirit had been taken out of her daughter.

I know many godly people who love Jesus but nevertheless they have had the experience of a rebellious child. They did just what this woman did. They "prayed through" until they laid hold of a promise of God. God brought those children back and they are active Christians today, living testimonies to the fact that when parents are disturbed, feeling even desperate about their children's lives, if those parents will be determined in seeking the Lord's help, down the road they will be delighted because their children are serving Jesus.

A friend of mine who is a great Bible teacher told me about his experience with a son who became rebellious. It was an extreme situation. Sometimes they would confine the boy to his room and he would get out through the window. He would get drunk, use drugs, and do all kinds of wrong things. Finally they had to put the boy in a home for delinquents. This Bible teacher said that he and his wife began to pray and fast and memorize scripture, and went before God for the needs of this boy. At times they thought that nothing was going to work. It seemed as if the devil were going to take over that boy—lock, stock, and barrel. One day when they had gone to pick him up, he was sitting in the back of the car, belligerent and rebellious as ever. My friend and his wife began to quote scriptures. Then, he said, just like that, as if something left that boy—in an entirely different tone of voice—their son said, "Dad, I'm hungry. When are we going to eat?" That young man is now on fire for the Lord, serving the Lord.

Parents, don't give up on your children.

And if you are a young man or young woman who has broken your parents' heart by turning away from the Lord, perhaps their prayers and loving concern have now caught up with you. Come home today.

18

He Hath Done All Things Well
Mark 7:31-37

THIS PASSAGE BEGINS WITH A GEOGRAPHICAL NOTATION ABOUT OUR Lord's journey through southern Lebanon. If you look at a Bible map, you see that Jesus was actually taking the long way home. Bible students have speculated about why He took such a long route to get to where He was going.

I think He was taking this period of time to train his disciples. It was a kind of walking seminar. On this long journey, which probably took about eight months, Jesus was teaching and preparing his disciples.

Notice in 7:31 it says that they came "through the midst of the coasts of Decapolis." In Mark 5:20 we learned that Legion, the former demoniac, "began to publish in Decapolis how great things Jesus had done for him: and all men did marvel." There is power in the consistent testimony of a person whose life has

been changed by Jesus. Many people who are otherwise uninterested in Jesus will be drawn to him by the testimony of a
changed life. So Legion had been telling everybody what Jesus
had done for him. It was obvious when you looked at his life
that something had happened.

When Jesus returned to this coast again, the people came.
They were interested in what Jesus had to say.

I. THE MAN'S CONDITION (7:32)

A. A Physically Handicapped Man (7:32)

One of the people who was brought to Jesus was a handicapped
man. He was deaf and he had difficulty in his speaking. Modern
science is making a lot of progress in helping people who have
different kinds of handicaps. They are just now catching up with
Jesus. He is the great physician. He has a well-established practice. No case is beyond his power and control.

The word *deaf* here means "to blunt" or "to dull." Probably
it refers to an injury that had made it impossible for this man to
hear. Probably when he was born he was able to hear, but somewhere along the way an accident had occurred to deafen him.
Along with that he had an impediment in his speech. Perhaps
he stammered when he talked.

So here, a man with a double handicap was brought to Jesus.
This incident points us to those who are physically disabled and
reminds us of their needs. I am grateful that as a society and as
a nation we are becoming more sensitive to the problems of men
and women with physical limitations. I am grateful for the handicapped parking places provided. I'm thankful for all the vehicles
and mechanisms now available to help such persons. I think we
are getting closer to the heart of the Lord. In his ministry Jesus
seemed always to take a special interest in such individuals.

It is interesting to see who gets excited when somebody comes
to town. When an outstanding baseball player or football player
comes to town, the athletes and sports enthusiasts get excited.
When an outstanding musician comes to town, the musicians get
excited. When Jesus came to town, the blind, the deaf, and the
lame got excited.

If you want to be like Jesus, you take time to be with handicapped
persons. If you want to have the spirit of the Lord, you get interested

in those who have physical handicaps. One of the first things I do when I go to a church is look around and see if there are any disabled people there. It tells me a great deal about the heart of that church. Show me a church where handicapped people come and I'll show you a church where Jesus is. Handicapped people are always drawn to Jesus. Many of them can be won to him if somebody with his spirit and love will reach out to them in caring ways.

B. Spiritually Handicapped

This passage points us to those who are physically handicapped, but it goes beyond that. I believe that all of these miracles in the physical realm are illustrations of what Jesus can do in the spiritual realm. You may not be blinded physically. You may not have difficulty walking. You may be able to hear a pin drop a mile away. You may look at people who are physically handicapped and you might feel sorry for them. But if you do not know Jesus as your Lord, if you have never accepted Christ as your savior, you have a spiritual handicap that is far more serious than any physical handicap. Those people who are physically handicapped who know Jesus as their savior—well, one of these days all those limitations are going to be removed. One of these days, when they get to heaven and are on the streets of gold, all of those physical handicaps are going to be corrected. The blind are going to see in glory. Those who are deaf are going to be able to hear. You are not going to see one spastic or paraplegic on Hallelujah Square. Isn't that wonderful to know? Your first day in heaven you will see some fellow jumping up and down, skipping and hopping, and you will remember that he was in a wheelchair down here.

But if you live out your life spiritually handicapped, your misery is yet ahead. If you do not know Jesus as your savior, if you have spiritual eyes that cannot see the things of God, if your spiritual ears are deaf and you have no interest in hearing the word of God, if your spiritual limbs are lame and you do not walk with God, if you die in that condition, you will be a spiritually handicapped person for eternity.

II. THE MASTER'S CURE (7:33-35)

Jesus took that man aside from the multitude, which shows us his tenderness, how considerate He was. Jesus was always sensitive and wise in the way He dealt with people. He dealt with them in a variety of ways. Sometimes He would touch people and they would get well. Sometimes He would just speak the word (even long distance) and they would get well. One time Jesus put clay over the eyes of a man and said, "Go down and wash in the pool of Siloam," and he got well. That tells us we can't restrict Jesus. We can't determine how God does what He does. Jesus Christ is the eternal God. He works as He will. He'll do what He wants to do when He wants to do it.

Sometimes people ask me, "Will God do so and so? Will God do this?" I am always hesitant to say what God will and will not do. He is the sovereign, omnipotent one. When we read the book of Acts we discover infinite variety in the workings of God. The Bible says the Spirit blows where He will; we can't control him. We can't tell God what to do.

There is also consistency in the methods of Jesus, in that some basic principles can be applied to our helping people today. In other words, some ingredients in this cure of Jesus can be transferred into our lives as Christians in order to help people. In this case I see four ingredients in how Jesus helped people.

A. The Touch of Connection (7:33)

When Jesus took this man aside, He put his fingers into his ears, and He touched his tongue. Jesus was acting out what He was getting ready to do. Perhaps it was an aid to faith for this man. I don't know. But when Jesus put his fingers in his ear it is as if Jesus were saying, "I'm going to do something to your ears." The Bible says that Jesus spit. Then He took his finger and touched the tongue of the man, as if He were saying, "I'm going to do something for your tongue." Jesus was acting out his intention, making connection with that man, in a language he could comprehend. Jesus touched him in his need. That's what the gospel is all about.

You and I couldn't go there where He was. Our sins separate us from a holy God. So God said, "I'll go there where they are." One day two thousand years ago Jesus Christ came walking down the ivory steps of glory. The eternal Christ confined himself to the dimensions of a woman's womb and was born into our world. He condescended to identify with us human beings in order to touch us in our humanity, to touch us in our need.

If you want to help people, you have to make connection. If you want to help people, you have to touch them in their need. You have to get right down there where they are. Many Christians are developing a shelter mentality or a fortress mentality. In other words, we are saved, we are Christians, we are going to hang out in our little group over here. We are going to withdraw from the rest of the world, protect ourselves from it.

I do believe that we Christians ought to live separated lives; we must not condone sin. On the other hand, although the Bible teaches that there should be *insulation* on the part of the believer, it does not teach *isolation* on the part of the believer. The way of the scriptures is not isolation, but rather insulation and then *infiltration*. We have to get out there where the sinners are. Do you know any lost people? Do you know some man who is spiritually deaf? He needs that touch of connection. He needs somebody to get down there where he is and love him, express the love of Christ to him, and be a friend to him. I heard a poem one time:

> Some want a church with a steeple and a bell.
> Give me a mission at the gates of hell.

B. The Look of Communion (7:34)

Jesus touched the man and then looked up to heaven. This was his look of communion. When Jesus stood before the tomb of Lazarus, just before He raised Lazarus from the dead, He lifted his eyes to heaven and prayed (John 11:41). Jesus was in touch with the heavenly Father. He spent time in communion with the source of power. The psalmist said, "I will lift up mine eyes unto the hills, from whence cometh my help. My help cometh from the Lord, which made heaven and earth" (Psalm 121:1). Because of that communion Jesus was able to help people. Because of that He had compassion for them. If we are going to help others we have to have that life of communion. There has to be that daily time when we read God's word and let God talk to us. When Jesus looked up to heaven He expected to receive something for that man. You and I, as we go to our quiet time, as we read God's word every day, also get something from God. Communion and fellowship with God will feed our lives, and then we will have something to impart to others.

C. The Sigh of Compassion (7:34)

Jesus sighed. He groaned—an inward groaning, a sigh of compassion. He was "a man of sorrows, and acquainted with grief" (Isaiah 53:3). He was one who sympathized with human beings in their need. Jesus Christ stood before this man, aware that he was one individual out of a mass of hurting humanity. In the midst of a world of woe and sorrow and heartache, Jesus sighed with compassion. The sigh of compassion came right after the look of communion. Because He had looked into the face of the Father, the shock of the needs of humanity was even more dramatic.

The closer we get to God the more aware we are of the needs of people. The secret of compassion is communion with God. The depth of our communion with God will ultimately determine the fruitfulness of our ministry among people. I heard of a preacher in New York City who ran a rescue mission. One day someone saw him leaning against a building in New York City. Tears were flowing down his cheeks and he was praying: "O, God, the sin of this city is breaking my heart."

Have you ever taken a ride through your city or town and seen people who need Jesus? Has it broken your heart? Have you ever prayed a prayer of compassion for them? People all around us have needs beyond our ability to comprehend. Many of them have no homes—and that includes families with children. Many of them have no money whatsoever, and no possessions that they aren't carrying around with them.

One time when I was sick, one of the pre-school departments sent me a little get-well card. They signed their names and then wrote: "When you hurt, we hurt." That's the way God's people ought to be.

A little boy came home from school one day looking melancholy. His mother said, "Was everything all right at school today?" He said, "Billy told us that his daddy died. They buried him yesterday. Billy was crying—he was so sad about his dad dying." The mother said, "Son, what did you do?" He said, "Mama, I put my head down on my desk and cried with him." O God, break our hearts for the lost who need Jesus.

D. The Word of Consummation (7:34-35)

In his mother tongue, the language of his childhood, Jesus said, "Ephphatha," which means "be opened." The speaking of the word opened the ears of that man. The speaking of the word loosed his tongue and he began to speak plainly. Of course you and I do not have the word of God on our lips in the sense that Jesus did. Every time Jesus opened his mouth He was speaking the literal word of God.

But we who know Jesus, who believe the Bible, have in our hands a book containing the powerful word of God. We can walk into the home of lost persons. We can speak that word of God, share the gospel, tell them the way of salvation. I've seen spiritually blind eyes come open with the word of God. I've seen spiritually deaf ears opened with the word of God. I've seen lives changed by the power of the word of God.

III. THE CONFESSION OF THE MULTITUDE (7:36-37)

Isn't this just like human nature? Jesus told the multitude "that they should tell no man: but the more he charged them, so much the more a great deal they published it." Jesus said, "Don't tell," and they told everyone.

There is no such restriction on us today. We Christians ought to get out and publish the name of Jesus. I hear people say, "I witness when I feel led." Let me ask you a question: If you don't feel led to witness, whose fault is it? Our Lord has already given the commission. He has already said, "Go and make disciples." You don't have to feel led when He has already told you to do it. That's just like saying, "I'm hungry; I think I'll pray and see if I'm supposed to eat." You don't have to pray about whether or not to do things you know that God wants you to do.

A. A Conviction about the Past (7:37)

"He hath done all things well," they said. It was an expression of their confidence, their conviction, about the past. And that is the conviction of my heart today. I haven't always known that He was doing all things well. There were times when I didn't understand, when what was happening didn't seem to make sense. But now as I look back on those experiences I can say, "He hath done all things well."

B. A Confidence about the Future (7:37)

Conviction about the past is also a confidence in the future. If Christ has done all things well, He will continue to do all things well. Here are six words that can carry us into the uncertain days ahead.

One of these days, when we close our eyes in death, or lift them in rapture when Jesus returns, and we are carried into the presence of the Lord—there, from the vantage point of glory and the viewpoint of eternity, we will be able to look back over our lives and the dealings of the Lord with us, and we will be able to say, "He hath done all things well." Those times when we felt we were being dealt with severely, when circumstances came in our lives that seemed to be the worst thing that could possibly happen and we raised question marks as high as skyscrapers to the Lord—when we get to heaven we are going to look back at those experiences and say, "Lord, you have done all things well."

19

Curing the Spiritual "Blahs"
Mark 8:1-21

I. REFRESHING THE MULTITUDE (8:1-9)
    A. His Compassion (8:1-3)
    B. His Provision (8:4-9)
II. REFUSING THE PHARISEES (8:10-13)
    A. A Sign Demanded (8:11)
    B. A Sign Denied (8:12-13)
III. REBUKING THE DISCIPLES (8:14-21)
    A. He Cautioned Them (8:14-16)
    B. He Questioned Them (8:17-21)

THE LORD JESUS CONTINUED TO TEACH HIS DISCIPLES BOTH BY ACTIONS and words. He was teaching them who He was and what He was going to do. In the latter part of Mark He would begin to teach them about the cross. He knew they needed to be spiritually alert, spiritually keen, to receive the message of the crucifixion. Sad to say, they were not. It seems that these disciples had a case of the spiritual blahs. So how did the Lord deal with them?

I. REFRESHING THE MULTITUDE (8:1-9)

A great multitude, many thousands of people, had been there for three days and they had no food. Jesus must have been some preacher to keep them listening for three days. Most of us preachers today can't keep folks much past twelve noon, or their stomachs get the best of them and they can't hear the word of God. But for three days Jesus had those people hanging on every word. Then He said, "They don't have anything to eat."

A. His Compassion (8:1-3)

Jesus had a heart for the multitude. He knew what it was to be hungry. For forty days and nights He had been in the wilderness, with nothing to eat, tempted by the devil. He understood what it was to be hungry. When Jesus came into this world, He identified himself with us so that He would know our sorrows and needs, and could perfectly sympathize.

Whatever you are going through, Jesus understands. Whatever the needs in your life are, He sympathizes and cares.

The disciples replied, "From whence can a man satisfy these men with bread here in the wilderness?" (8:4). They were asking, "Lord, where is all this food going to come from?" They had already seen Jesus perform one miracle in the feeding of several thousand people. They knew that the Lord could do it. They were not questioning his power. They were not questioning that it could be done. Rather, the question was, "From whence can *we* satisfy these people in the wilderness? From whence can a *man* . . ."

Well, a man couldn't do it. No man had the power to feed that many people. But we are not dealing with a man; we are dealing with the God-man, with one who had power to take bread in his hands, bless it, break it, and multiply it. When you talk about a problem and get Jesus into the equation, then you have the solution to the problem. I don't care how strained the situation may be—if you put Jesus into the middle of it, the impossible becomes the possible. Jesus is able to spread a table in the wilderness.

So He said to these disciples, "How many loaves of bread do you have?" "Seven," they said. They also had a few small fish. Those loaves were not like our big loaves of bread; rather, they were flat cakes of bread. The fish were mostly bones. They obviously didn't have much food to offer the multitude. But Jesus wanted them to be aware of how limited their abilities were.

When you come to Jesus, you give him what you have. It looks very small when you compare it to the needs of the people in this world. But Jesus wants us to take what we have, put it in his hands, dedicate it to him, and then see what He can do with it.

B. His Provision (8:4-9)

They gave those little loaves and those fish to Jesus. The Lord took them and gave thanks (8:6). The Lord always gave thanks before a meal. That's why we do it. Do you thank God before a meal?

I heard about a group of boys who were sitting in a restaurant in a city. One day a farmer walked into the restaurant, took off his hat, and when his food was brought to him, he bowed his head and prayed. The boys thought that was funny and one of them said, "Hey, does everybody do that where you come from?" The farmer looked up and said, "Yes, sir, everybody except the pigs."

Are you ashamed to pray when you are in a restaurant? I used to be afraid to pray, so I devised ways to do it. I'd get out my handkerchief as if I were blowing my nose. I was in a restaurant one time with a group of preachers. I was just a young preacher and they called on an older preacher to pray right there in the restaurant. When he got through with his long-winded prayer I was almost crawling under the table looking to see if anybody saw us. (I'm long past that embarrassment now, I'm happy to say.)

Then Jesus broke that bread and began to give it to those disciples. It must have been something to see. The Lord just kept on breaking and breaking and there was bread and bread and bread and fish and fish and fish.

You will be amazed at what God can do with your limited abilities and resources if you will put them in the hands of Jesus and let him bless and multiply them. He said, "Take this bread and give it to the multitude."

Do you see how Jesus pulled them in on his work and let them have a part? The disciples were going to Jesus with baskets. The Lord was breaking the bread and fish, filling up those baskets. They were carrying them back and forth to feed the people. They kept coming back to the Lord. He kept giving more. They just kept on feeding the multitude. That's what we do. That's what teaching is. That's what preaching is. That's what witnessing is. You take what God gives to you and deliver it to people.

There is nothing like the bread that Jesus gives to feed hungry souls. So the people were filled and there was lavish abundance left over.

II. REFUSING THE PHARISEES (8:10-13)

The Pharisees were always around. They were like spiritual bloodhounds on the track of Jesus, snooping, trailing. They were like yelping dogs and they never let up until they had driven him to the cross.

A. A Sign Demanded (8:11)

"The Pharisees came forth, and began to question with him" (8:11). They began to argue—"Show us a sign from heaven"—tempting him. They didn't really want a sign from heaven. Instead they were trying to trick him into doing something He couldn't do. They were trying to push him up against the wall. By a *sign* they meant an authenticating miracle, an act that would validate his ministry.

The way we check out messengers now is by the word of God. Does the word of God back up what they say? Is it consistent with the teachings of the Bible? But in those days they didn't have the completed biblical canon and so there would be a sign.

B. A Sign Denied (8:12-13)

Jesus "sighed deeply in his spirit" (8:12). From the depths of his being, in the presence of their hardness and unbelief, He groaned. "There is not going to be a sign," He said. "This generation will have no sign."

Matthew's gospel again gives a qualifying statement, a fuller account. "A wicked and adulterous generation seeketh after a sign, and there shall no sign be given unto it, but the sign of the prophet Jonah" (Matthew 16:4). They were not going to get the kind of miracle they were demanding.

Jesus had been healing the sick, giving hearing to ears that couldn't hear, curing lepers, feeding multitudes, raising the dead. Still, they had the gall to ask for a sign. It was an insult.

The sign was Jesus himself. The greatest sign would be the miracle of his resurrection, of which the prophet Jonah was an illustration. Jonah's three days and nights in the belly of the fish was a picture of the resurrection of Jesus. Jesus said, "For as Jonas was three days and three nights in the whale's belly, so shall the Son of man be three days and three nights in the heart of the earth" (Matthew 12:40). Jesus was saying, "I'm the great miracle."

A generation that is looking for the bizarre, the spectacular, and the out-of-the-ordinary sometimes gets more interested in the miracle than in the miracle worker. These Pharisees wanted the miracles. They didn't want Jesus. The miracle of the incarnation, the miracle of the resurrection, the miracle of the living Christ coming into a life in the twentieth century—that's the miracle.

I'd rather have Jesus than any miracle He is able to do. I'd rather have the Lord in my heart than anything else.

Jesus turned and walked away. It was an act of judgment—refusing the Pharisees (8:13).

III. Rebuking the Disciples (8:14-21)

Back on the ship the disciples realized that they had forgotten to bring along the leftover baskets of bread. "Neither had they in the ship with them more than one loaf" (8:14). They were thinking about that one loaf of bread, and Jesus was thinking about their spiritual condition. He knew they were not getting the message. He realized that they had the spiritual blahs, so to speak. They were thinking about something material.

A. He Cautioned Them (8:14-16)

"Take heed," Jesus said, "beware of the leaven of the Pharisees, and of the leaven of Herod." In the Bible *leaven* is a symbol of corruption, a symbol of false teaching that slips in and permeates and pollutes the gospel. The leaven of the Pharisees was legalism. Beware of the leaven of legalism; that is, trying to live the Christian life by obeying a set of rules. Christianity is not being inhibited by rules; it is being inhabited by a ruler. God have mercy on the legalistic church. It has no joy, no thrill, no excitement, no victory.

The leaven of the Sadducees (Matthew 16:11-12) was the leaven of liberalism. They didn't believe in the supernatural. They didn't believe in the power of God. They didn't believe that God could do miracles. God help the liberal church that does not know his power.

The leaven of Herod represents materialism and worldliness. It is the church that has no dedication. It is the church that has no separated living. It is the church where no observable difference exists between the lifestyles of its members and those of the lost world.

Were they discussing whose fault it was that they didn't have any bread? Here Jesus was, getting ready to teach them about the cross. Here they were, preoccupied with food.

B. He Questioned Them (8:17-21)

Then in rapid-fire succession Jesus drilled them with nine questions. "Why reason ye, because ye have no bread? perceive ye not yet, neither understand? have ye your heart yet hardened? Having eyes see ye not? and having ears, hear ye not?" When Jesus got through, I suspect that all you could hear was those oars in the water. The disciples got the message. Jesus was arousing them from their spiritual lethargy.

What Jesus said to these disciples is what He says to us when we get the spiritual blahs. Use your mind. Use the faculties that God has given you. Use your power to reason. Use your spiritual eyes. Use your spiritual ears. Tune in to the things of God. Start digging in the word and let God speak to you out of it.

I think Jesus also says, "Examine your heart." "Have ye your heart yet hardened?" (8:17). The word *hardened* means to cover with a callus, a hard tough place on your skin. It's easy to get a calloused heart as a Christian. Sometimes your mind may accept it all and even say "Amen" to it, but your heart is cold. Maybe some sin has toughened your heart. Do you know what a backslider is? A backslider is someone who doesn't love Jesus as much as he or she used to love him.

Jesus said, "Remember." When you have a case of the spiritual doldrums, the spiritual blahs, when life has gotten you down, that is the time to remember what God has done.

20

Following Jesus

Mark 8:22-38

IN MARK 8 WE ARE TOLD ABOUT A BLIND MAN WHO WAS BROUGHT to the Lord Jesus. The Lord took him aside, spat on his eyes, laid his hands on him, and asked, "Do you see anything?" The man could see only dimly and said, "I see men as trees, walking." Jesus touched the man a second time and then he "saw every man clearly." This miracle is recorded only in Mark's gospel. It is the only instance in the scriptures where Jesus healed someone gradually.

I think there is a reason why this miracle is placed where it is in Mark's gospel. Just prior to this, the Lord Jesus had chided his disciples for their slowness of spiritual understanding. They were slow to perceive, slow to comprehend what Jesus was saying and doing. I believe the point of the miracle is this: Spiritual maturity is not something that happens all at once. We have to grow and develop.

I'm glad God is patient with us. I'm glad He gives us not only a second touch, but also a third and fourth touch—everything we need to mature in our understanding. As we continue studying Mark, we see God working in the lives of the disciples, step by step opening their spiritual eyes.

I. OUR LORD'S PERSON (8:27-30)

We all need to know who Jesus is. That is the most important question we will ever answer. When we answer that question, it will answer many other questions in our lives.

Jesus had been teaching his disciples for about two years. The number-one lesson He was trying to get over to them was the realization of his identity.

A. Popular Opinion (8:27-28)

"Whom do men say that I am?" Jesus asked his disciples. Of course, people had many opinions about Jesus. Three common ideas were: "He is John the Baptist"; "He is Elijah"; and "He is one of the prophets."

People identified Jesus with John the Baptist because of his preaching. John preached at the river Jordan. He was a street preacher. He preached out in the open. He preached everywhere that people were.

Some people thought that Jesus was Elijah because of his praying. Elijah was a great man of prayer; he had such power in prayer that he could shut up the heavens and it wouldn't rain for years. Then, in response to his prayer, the windows of heaven would open up and rain would come down. Elijah's prayer had the power to call water or fire out of heaven. Jesus came not only as a preaching man but also as a praying man. One time the disciples came to him and said, "Lord, teach us to pray." Jesus was a man of prayer. Sometimes He spent whole nights in prayer.

Other people identified Jesus with one of the prophets; I think it was because of his pathos, because of his heart. When Jesus talked He spoke as no man had ever spoken. The prophets of God were men of great compassion along with great comprehension of God. When Jesus spoke, there was a tear in his voice, there was compassion, there was love.

B. Personal Opinion (8:29)

"But whom say ye that I am?" Jesus then asked his disciples.
That is, what is your personal opinion about me? It's a very
important question. What we believe about Jesus will be the
beginning that will logically lead us to ultimate and life-changing
decisions. We cannot be neutral about the person of Jesus. He
forces us to take a stand about him. We have to come to some
decision about him. No one can be neutral about Jesus. We are
driven to one of four alternatives about his identity:
—Jesus was a legend; He never existed.
—Jesus was a liar; He was lying about whom He claimed to be.
—Jesus was a lunatic; He was crazy and didn't know what He
was doing.
—Jesus is Lord.
Simon Peter climbed the heights of inspiration. He said, "You are
the Christ" (8:29). In Matthew's gospel it says that Peter added, "the
Son of the living God" (Matthew 16:16). When he said that, Jesus
responded, "Flesh and blood hath not revealed it unto thee, but my
Father which is in heaven" (Matthew 16:17). Simon Peter spoke by
divine inspiration. The Spirit of God illuminated his heart and he
was able to say, "You are the Christ, the Son of the living God."
Simon Peter passed the test with flying colors. That's what
Jesus had been saying. That's what Jesus had been trying to get
them to understand. He was not a mere man; He was not just
one of the prophets; he was God come in human flesh. The birth
of Jesus Christ was the most momentous event that has ever
occurred. It was God condescending to be born as a human
being. It was the eternal God confining himself to a single cell
and being born in the womb of a woman in order to be the savior
of the world. That is the most earthshaking, far-reaching event
in the history of this world.

II. OUR LORD'S PASSION (8:31-33)

Having taught them who He was, Jesus also had to teach them
what He had come into this world to do. This is the first time
He clearly alluded to his death. Earlier along the way He had
made vague references to his cross, but now He plainly and
openly began to tell them that He had come into this world to die

"He began to teach them, that the Son of man must suffer many things" (8:31). When Jesus talked about his cross, his passion, his suffering, He emphasized three things.

A. The Necessity of It (8:31)

"The Son of man must suffer many things." The word *must* is a word of necessity. Jesus often used that word *must*. In John 3:14, when He was talking to Nicodemus, He said, "And as Moses lifted up the serpent in the wilderness, even so must the Son of man be lifted up." Why the *must*? Why did Jesus say it had to be? Did Jesus mean He was going to be a victim of circumstances, that He had no choice, and that therefore He had to be crucified? No, He was talking about the plan of God, about God's eternal will. Jesus had to die on the cross for man's sins. It was the only way.

God is love. That is the Bible's basic affirmation about God. If we miss anything else about God, we must not miss that. It is an overwhelming truth, a truth that staggers the imagination, a truth that is difficult to understand.

We also have to remember that God is holy. God is just. The problem becomes this: How can a God who is a loving God love the sinner and at the same time deal with sin? Because God is a holy God, He cannot overlook sin; He cannot fail to deal with it. So how can a holy God deal with sin and yet be a loving God who forgives sinners? That's what I call the "dilemma of deity." Of course, to combine those words, *deity* and *dilemma*, is really a contradiction. But the question remains: How can God love and be just at the same time?

The solution to the divine dilemma was the cross. Back there in eternity somewhere, God the Father, God the Son, and God the Holy Spirit came to understand that there was only one way to be loving and holy at the same time. They would solve the problem in the person of God the Son. So in eternity Jesus understood that there must be a cross. The cross was not divine predestination. It was the divine plan.

When Jesus began to talk to his disciples about the cross, He talked in terms of a "must." When He suffered, bled, and died on Calvary's cross, God was dealing with human sin, but also providing the possibility of forgiveness for the sinner.

God solved his own dilemma. There had to be a cross.

B. The Misery of It (8:31)

"The Son of man must suffer many things." There are volumes in those two words, *many things*. Who knows all that Jesus suffered?

> But none of the ransomed ever knew
> How deep were the waters crossed;
> Nor how dark was the night that the Lord passed thro'
> Ere He found His sheep that was lost.

He would be rejected, Jesus said, by the elders and chief priests and scribes—his own people, the political leaders, the religious leaders, the moral leaders of his day. "Rejected . . . killed." The word for *killed* is not a word used for a normal death. It doesn't mean that Jesus would come and live to be an old man and die of natural causes. It is a word that indicates violent death. He would be slaughtered. Dying on a cross was the most violent form of punishment ever devised. I have never seen a picture of Jesus on the cross that adequately conveys the scene. Most of the pictures have a drop of blood here and a drop there. The Bible teaches that Jesus Christ was so marred that He was unrecognizable. He didn't even look like a human being.

That was the reason for his coming. He came to die on a cross because He loved us. *Love* is why. What held Jesus to the cross? It was not the nails that held him there. It was not the cords that held him there. It was love that held him there. He came to die for our sins.

C. The Victory of It (8:31)

Jesus said He would rise again three days later. He kept referring to his victory over death and, not surprisingly, they always missed it. It went right over their heads.

In particular, the thought of crucifixion was more than Simon Peter could stand. When Jesus started talking about that cross business, Simon Peter wouldn't hear of it. He even took Jesus off to one side and proceeded to rebuke him. Matthew told us exactly what he said: "Be it far from thee, Lord: this shall not be unto thee" (Matthew 16:22). One minute Peter was getting inspiration from heaven and the next minute he was getting inspiration from hell.

That can happen to you and me too. One minute we can be just as spiritual as we can possibly be—on fire for God—and the next minute we can be listening to the voice of the devil.

That's why Jesus later touched that blind man a second time. There are many times I need that second touch. Sometimes I may think I have almost "arrived." I've got my eyes wide open, but all I'm seeing are men as trees walking. I need that second touch.

Simon needed that second touch. He had the nerve to rebuke deity—can you believe it? How can anyone call Jesus *Lord* and rebuke him in the same breath? Jesus whirled around away from Simon Peter. He turned on his heels. With his back to Simon Peter, He said, "Be gone, Satan. Get away from me, Satan. Get thee behind me, Satan. You've got your mind on the things that are of men, not on the things of God." Jesus recognized another voice in the voice of Simon Peter. It was the same old voice He had heard back there in the wilderness temptation saying, "Avoid the cross."

The devil wants people to avoid the cross. Just as he wanted to keep Jesus off the cross, he will try to keep us out of a life of sacrifice.

III. OUR LORD'S PROPOSITION (8:34-38)

The Lord makes a proposition to us in these verses. It's an invitation: "Whosoever will come after me . . . " (8:34). He said it to the people; He said it to the disciples, and He says it to you and me.

Would you like to follow Jesus? Look at the language here. Jesus said, "If any man will come after me," or *whosoever will* come after me. It involves a decision of the will. You've got to decide to follow Jesus. When I was a boy, we used to sing at youth camp: "I have decided to follow Jesus." I hope you the reader have made a definite, willful choice to follow Jesus.

What is involved in this decision to follow Jesus?

A. A Serious Decision (8:34)

First of all, it is a serious decision. "Whosoever will come after me," Jesus said, "let him deny himself, and take up his cross, and follow me." It wasn't, "Follow me and I'll make you popular, a

spiritual superstar." Jesus said, "To follow me, the first thing you
have to do is deny yourself."

What does it mean to deny yourself? Is it to give up some
things? I went to school in New Orleans and I had a preacher
friend who was working in a bank, working his way through
school. One year some of the guys working there in the bank were
talking about what they were going to give up for Lent. One said,
"I'll tell you what. I'm going to give up my beer for Lent this time.
All that alcohol last year nearly killed me." A lot of people think
that to *deny* means to give up something for a while. No, to deny
yourself basically means to say no to yourself. You relinquish all
claims to your life. You renounce your right to run your life.

That is a very serious decision, serious because we are living
in what is known as the "me" generation. Everything revolves
around me. The advertising people have picked up on that
theme. Many ads in essence are saying, "Think of yourself." I
saw an ad yesterday that said something like this: "Who is the
most important person in the world? You. Do something for
you. You deserve a break today." How many times our church
staff members deal with people going through marital problems
and hear words like, "I don't want to hurt the kids, but I've got
to watch out for me." Husbands, wives, you ought to be willing
to tramp through hell for your children.

Jesus said you have to renounce all claims of self. If you are a
Christian you don't belong to yourself. "Know ye not that . . . ye
are not your own? For ye are bought with a price" (1 Corinthians
6:19-20). Jesus Christ has absolute claim to your life. To deny yourself means that you are no longer to live a self-centered life. You
now start living a Christ-centered life. You take up the cross.

The Bible talks not only about the cross of the savior, but also
about the cross of the believer. This is one of those doctrines that
is so prominent in the teachings of our Lord that we have a tendency to neglect it. Not only was there a cross for Christ, but
there is also a cross for his followers.

> Must Jesus bear the cross alone,
> And all the world go free?
> No; there's a cross for ev'ryone,
> And there's a cross for me.

What does it mean to take up the cross? To a lot of people it means that you endure a difficult circumstance. Do you have noisy neighbors who play music really loud? So you say, "Oh, I'm bearing my cross." Do you think of some person as your cross? No, those are trivial examples. A cross is an instrument of death. Jesus was saying, "Be prepared to die for me."

Most of us want to follow Jesus until it interferes with our plans. The level of commitment among average Christians and in the typical church today is very low. "OK, I'll serve you, Jesus, but it's not going to get in the way of my family. I'll serve you, Jesus, but it can't conflict with my job. I'll serve you, but I'm a human being and I've got to do this or that too." Jesus said, "If you don't forsake all that you have, you cannot be my disciple."

B. A Sensible Decision (8:35-37)

Jesus talked about two alternatives in life, with two results. You don't have to follow Jesus. You don't have to deny yourself and take up your cross. You can choose to save your life. But, Jesus said, if you make that choice in life, in the long run you'll lose your life. The other alternative is the way of the cross—you can choose to follow Jesus. In doing that, you will lose your life, but the result will be that you will find your life. That's a paradox.

Make up your mind you are going to keep your life and you will discover that you can't keep it. Set out to have all you want in life and you will discover that you won't want what you have. If you sit down with people who have all kinds of material things in life and ask them if they are happy, most of them (if they are honest) will say that something is missing.

If you decide that you want to follow Jesus and say no to yourself and yes to the will of God in your life, you will make the marvelous discovery of meaning and purpose in life. Jesus said, "You can gain this whole world, but if you lose your soul, what have you got?" The whole world is light as a feather in comparison to your soul. Don't lose your soul.

C. A Satisfying Decision (8:38)

To follow Jesus is a significant decision because we are all living life in relationship to eternity. In the last verse of this chapter Jesus was saying, "Don't be ashamed of me." Are you ashamed of Jesus? This world will try to get us to be ashamed of him, but

we need to develop a wholesome contempt for this world's
ridicule. People who now laugh at us, and make fun of us for
loving and serving Jesus, may secretly envy us. Years later they
may come back and say that our Christian witness meant something to them.

One of these days Jesus is going to return in glory, and our atti-
tudes toward him will determine his attitude toward us then. He
said, "If you're ashamed of me, I'll be ashamed of you." Are you
a Christian, but have just never let anybody know it? Jesus'
words make clear that there are no secret disciples.

21

Mountaintop Experiences
Mark 9:1-10

I. THE HEAVENLY VISION (9:2-3)
   A. The Men (9:2)
   B. The Mountain (9:2)
   C. The Master (9:3)

II. THE HEAVENLY VISITORS (9:4-6)
   A. Their Significance
   B. Their Subject
   C. The Sensation They Caused (9:5-6)

III. THE HEAVENLY VOICE (9:7-8)
   A. Its Source (9:7)
   B. Its Statement (9:7)
   C. Its Sequel (9:8)

THESE VERSES IN MARK 9 COME AT THE MIDDLE POINT IN THE ministry of our Lord. They might be called a great divide or a watershed.

Over the centuries the first verse of Mark 9 has raised a great deal of concern and a lot of questions. Jesus said that some of those standing right there would not taste death until they had seen the kingdom of God come with power. What did that mean? I believe that Jesus was saying that the experience of his transfiguration, which they were going to witness on the mountain, was a preview of how it would be when He came to reign on earth. He was going to give them a glimpse of what the world would be like when He reigned as king of kings and Lord of lords. He was saying that glorious things were ahead for the people of God.

The purpose of this transfiguration experience was to encourage the disciples. They were troubled. There would be days ahead after Jesus had died when it would appear that everything was in vain. So Jesus allowed them to have this magnificent vision to strengthen them in those dark days.

I. The Heavenly Vision (9:2-3)

God gave Peter, James, and John a heavenly vision that day. Heaven and earth were brought close to one another on that mountain and they saw things they had never seen before. It was a mountaintop experience.

Have you ever had an experience when you just seemed to be lifted up above this world and allowed to get a foretaste of the heavenly world? There are times in our lives when we need spiritual refreshment. We need to get on higher ground, get above the mundane, and let God speak to our hearts in a special way. That is what happened to those disciples.

A. The Men (9:2)

Notice that three disciples went with Jesus to a high mountain apart, the same three who seemed to be with him on numerous occasions. When Jesus went to the home of Jairus to heal his daughter, it was Peter, James, and John who were allowed to go into the room with him. Later on, in the garden of Gethsemane, when Jesus prayed and "as it were drops of blood" poured from his forehead, it was Peter, James, and John who were there. Those three seem to have been an inner circle especially close to Jesus. It does not mean that Jesus loved them any more than the rest, but it seems that these three had a capacity that perhaps made them more receptive to his love.

As believers we can be as close to Jesus as we want to be. The Bible says, "Draw nigh to God, and he will draw nigh to you" (James 4:8). His heart is open; He is ready to receive us; He is ready to bless our hearts and speak to our lives today. The real question is: Will we respond to Jesus? Our love must respond to his love.

B. The Mountain (9:2)

Three disciples went with Jesus up on that mountain of transfiguration. I think it was old snowcapped Mount Hermon, about nine thousand feet in height. A place apart. Have you noticed as you read the life of Jesus that He had a way of getting off to the mountains to pray? So He and these disciples went apart to a place to commune with God.

Every Christian needs a place to be alone and talk with the Lord. Do you have a place of prayer? My place of prayer is my study at home, where I have my desk and chair. Sometimes when I'm in there I close my door and get on my knees. It's a place apart from the frustrations and hectic pace of life where I can get into the presence of God.

In 2 Peter 1:18, when Simon Peter later on described this trans-figuration experience, he called this mountain "the holy mount." The high mountain became the holy mountain because he met Jesus on that mountain.

Your place apart can become a holy place. That place where you meet with the Lord to study his word and to pray can become the most sacred spot on this earth for you if you allow it to be.

C. The Master (9:3)

Luke said that this particular experience took place while Jesus was praying. "He was transfigured before them" (9:3). The word *transfigured* here is a translation of the word from which we get our word *metamorphosis.* Metamorphosis is a process in the world of nature in which a caterpillar, a wiggly, fuzzy, squzzy caterpillar, will wrap a cocoon around itself and after a period of time, out of that cocoon, from that old caterpillar, comes a beautiful butterfly. The word *metamorphosis* means a change, an outward change that comes from inside. When the Bible says that Jesus was transfigured, it means that He became on the out-side what He was on the inside. We know that when Jesus came into this world, He appeared to be a human. He wore the peasant clothing of Galilee. He worked as a carpenter in Nazareth. The Bible says that when they saw him, there was no beauty that they should desire him (Isaiah 53:2). That simply means He was an ordinary man, a common man. Yet Jesus Christ was more than a man when He walked on this earth. He was the God-man, the divine Son of God.

When Jesus was on the mountain, as He approached the cli-max of his ministry, He was transfigured. His countenance was altered. His face shone like the sun. His clothing glistened; it was so white, in fact, that no laundryman could have made it any whiter. The glory of God was being manifested in the humanity of the Lord Jesus.

Jesus was absolutely sinless, the only person who ever walked on this earth who never did a wrong thing, who never said a word He shouldn't have said, who never had a thought He shouldn't have had. On that mountain of transfiguration, his glory was no longer able to be confined within him. He radiated glory. It was heaven's attestation to the perfect humanity of the Son of God.

The Bible uses the same Greek word in two interesting verses of scripture. With reference to believers, it says, "And be not conformed to this world: but be ye transformed by the renewing of your mind" (Romans 12:2). The word *transformed* is the same word, *metamorphosis.* In 2 Corinthians 3:18 the word is used again: "But we all, with open face beholding as in a glass the glory of the Lord, *are changed* into the same image from glory to glory, even as by the Spirit of the Lord." That is to say, when God saves us, He puts his glory in our lives. Jesus said, "The glory I have, I have given to them" (see John 17:22). The Christian life is a process by which the glory within us is worked out in our daily lives.

In other words, God wants people to see Jesus in our lives. "Let the beauty of Jesus be seen in me." As we read the word of God, that perfect mirror (2 Corinthians 3:18), God works his glory out into our lives. There should be a radiance about us. Our daily lives ought to remind people of the glory of God.

II. THE HEAVENLY VISITORS (9:4-6)

Luke's account tells us that the disciples were heavy with sleep; they had a problem staying awake. (They've got some descendants in churches today who have the same problem.)

Tremendous things were happening in the garden of Gethsemane and there they were sawing logs, snoring. Here was the greatest Bible conference ever held—the Lord Jesus, Moses, Elijah, the greatest conference speakers of all time—and the disciples were sound asleep. I take comfort in that. If folks went to sleep on Moses, Elijah, and Jesus, then it's not surprising that they also go to sleep on me. But about that time the brilliance of the scene woke them up. Right there in front of them were Moses and Elijah talking with Jesus.

A. Their Significance

Look at them, the representatives of the Old Testament: Moses, the representative of the law, and Elijah, the representative of the prophets. Both of them went to heaven in an unusual way. Moses died in the embrace of God. Elijah went to heaven in a chariot of fire (that is, without dying).

B. Their Subject

What do you think Moses and Elijah were saying? They "spake of his decease [the word is exodus] which he should accomplish at Jerusalem" (Luke 9:31). They were talking about his cross. The cross, the death of Jesus Christ, was not a tragedy, not an accident, not a disaster. Luke said that it was an accomplishment, something Jesus had come into this world to do. The cross was not an afterthought in the heart of God; the cross was written into the warp and woof of eternity. Jesus was "the Lamb slain from the foundation of the world" (Revelation 13:8). Jesus was the fulfillment of Psalm 22 and Isaiah 53.

C. The Sensation They Caused (9:5-6)

Simon Peter woke up and the Bible says he didn't know what to say so he said something. Simon Peter had a way of starting his mouth running before he cranked his brain. He said, "Lord, it's good to be here. It's beautiful. Let's just stay up here. Let's build three tabernacles."

But you can't bring Jesus down to the level of any man. He is the one who is above all. His name is the name that is above every name. You don't build tabernacles and put Jesus in one of them alongside other men.

III. THE HEAVENLY VOICE (9:7-8)

God interrupted Simon Peter; a cloud overshadowed them. That cloud enveloped them, covered them up in brightness. I believe it was the glory cloud that led Israel through the wilderness. I believe it was the cloud that came down on the temple when the sacrifices were made. It was the symbol of the presence and power of God.

A. Its Source (9:7)

Out of that cloud a voice spoke to them, the voice of God the Father.

At the beginning of Jesus' ministry, heaven opened, and God the Father said, "This is my beloved Son, in whom I am well pleased" (Matthew 3:17).

B. Its Statement (9:7)

Now at the climax of Jesus' ministry, God again spoke from heaven: "This is my beloved Son: hear him." Matthew said He added, "In whom I am well pleased."

C. Its Sequel (9:8)

In a moment the cloud passed away. Moses and Elijah went back to heaven and when the disciples looked around there was no man but Jesus only.

God lets us have mountaintop experiences to get our eyes on Jesus and to learn who He is, what He came to do, and what He wants us to do. The sum and substance of what it means to live the Christian life is listening to the voice of Jesus and doing what Jesus tells us to do. Christianity is obedience to Jesus.

When the cloud passed away, when the visitors were gone, and when the voice from heaven was silent, Jesus remained. It is this Jesus whom we take out into a world that is lonely and lost and needy. Jesus is the only one who can save, the only one who can forgive. Only Jesus can change our lives and make us what we ought to be.

22

Valley Experiences

Mark 9:11-29

I. A Difficult Situation (9:14-19)
   A. A Desperate World (9:17-18)
   B. A Defeated Church (9:18-19)
II. A Divine Solution (9:19-29)
   A. He Cultivated Faith (9:23)
   B. He Corrected Failures (9:28-29)

THE PROPHECY CONCERNING THE COMING OF ELIJAH WAS FULFILLED in a sense in John the Baptist. Luke 1:17 says that John the Baptist would come in the spirit and power of Elijah. John was the spiritual fulfillment of that Old Testament prophecy (Malachi 4:5). There would be a literal fulfillment later, when Elijah would precede the return of Jesus to this earth. In Mark 9:12-13, Jesus turned their attention away from speculation about Elijah to what He himself had come into the world to do.

There is a wonderful contrast between the scene on the mount of transfiguration and the scene that met Jesus and the three on their descent to the valley below. There in the valley was a man whose son had tremendous need.

I. A Difficult Situation (9:14-19)

Chaos reigned. The nine disciples who remained behind were being questioned by the scribes. A crowd was milling around. There was a distraught father and a demon-possessed boy.

A. A Desperate World (9:17-18)

The situation reminds me of the kind of world we are living in. Here was a man who was absolutely defeated. His son had a "dumb spirit." The boy was not able to hear or speak. Through demonic power he was experiencing violent convulsions. This was not epilepsy, which could be caused by a brain tumor or a chemical imbalance. Rather, it was a case of actual demon possession. Here was a boy who was dominated by the devil. It is a picture of the devil taking control of the life of an individual, which was common in the days when Jesus was on this earth. When Jesus came He constantly confronted the demon world and released people who were in the power of the devil.

The Bible says that the devil is the god of this world and that the whole world lies in the lap of the wicked one. It is a world where the devil is doing his best to destroy human life. Men and women are made in the image of God, but the devil is determined to take that image and mar it.

The father brought the boy to the Lord Jesus, who like a skilled physician examined the situation and diagnosed the case. The boy had been in this condition since he was a child (9:21).

Yes, the devil wants to get hold of lives while they are young. The devil's plan in our day is to get hold of children and wreck their lives. If you are a parent, he is doing everything he can to get the mind of your child. Sins that used to be the sins of adults are now the sins of young children. Junior high kids are alcoholics. Young teenagers sell dope. Because the devil starts early to do our children harm, we parents had better start early to do them good. It's important to win boys and girls to the Lord, to get them saved at an early age.

I was nine years old when I came to Christ, and today's children know a lot more than I did when I was nine. We sell our boys and girls short. I believe they can come to a Christian understanding; they can be won to the Lord Jesus. If a little boy or girl can be filled with the devil, he or she can be filled with the Holy Spirit. If the devil can claim their minds for sin and shame and wrong, I believe we can claim their minds for Jesus.

We must never minimize the value of teaching the word of God to our little ones. They are barraged by obscene things on television. They are exposed to humanistic philosophy hour after hour, day after day. With some of them the only opportunity God has to get into their lives at a formative age is in church on Sunday morning. I believe that multitudes of children could be won to Christ if we would get a burden for them, pray for them, claim them for Jesus.

I claimed my children for the Lord, each one of them, when they were newborn infants. As soon as I got them home, I took them into my arms, sat down, and said:

"I want to tell you a story. Once upon a time there was a man named Adam and a woman named Eve in the garden of Eden. God put them there. He gave them a wonderful place to live. But sin came into the garden. Dear baby, because of that sin in the garden of Eden, sin has come into this world. You are born with a sinful nature. But God loves you and Jesus died on the cross to save you from your sins. If you will repent of your sins and accept Jesus as your savior, you'll be saved and forgiven and you will go to heaven when you die."

Do you say, "That is really silly; they didn't understand a thing you were saying"? That's right, but I didn't want my children ever to know a time when their daddy hadn't told them about Jesus and how to be saved. You can do that too.

I'm not willing to let the devil have my children. I'm not willing to turn my children over to a devil-dominated society. I'm going to get them to Jesus as soon as I possibly can. The Spirit of God will get hold of those little lives and the word of God will begin to work in their hearts. They can be saved, snatched from this evil world, snatched from the clutches of this demon-possessed planet.

Here was a child of whose life the devil had control. The demon in this boy was tearing at him; the boy was foaming at the mouth, gnashing his teeth, and pining away (9:18). That means he was withering. The devil was ruining that boy's life.

We have young people who are drug addicts before they get out of grade school. We have kids who need to be sent to alcoholic or drug treatment facilities before they are old enough even to think about those kinds of things.

The devil doesn't love people. If you were neck deep in quicksand, the devil would pat you on the head. This old world doesn't love you; it's out to wreck you.

B. A Defeated Church (9:18-19)

No ordinary work was going to do anything in the life of this boy. In those disciples I think we see a defeated church. The father had brought this boy to the disciples of Jesus to cast out the demons. When Jesus commissioned his disciples, He specifically gave them authority over unclean spirits (6:7). In Mark 6:13 it says that those disciples cast out many demons. On many occasions they had done exactly that, but now they were not able to do it.

The scribes just happened to be there and were arguing with them, of course loving every minute of it. Here the disciples were, powerless in the presence of this demon-possessed boy. I can see them now. One of the disciples goes over and says, "There's nothing to this. Demon, come out of him." Nothing happens. Another disciple says, "I can handle this. Demon, come out of him." Nothing happens. About that time the scribes stick the blade of ridicule in and are twisting it. "Well, what's the matter? Is the power of your teacher waning? You can't do it, can you?"

The father said, "I spake to thy disciples that they should cast him out; and they could not" (9:18). What a tragedy.

You could write those words over many a church today—"and they could not." A desperate world and a powerless church. Here we are in a world that's sinking in sin, that desperately needs Jesus, and the world looks at the church and says, "They could not." The problem of the church today is that we are compromised, powerless in the face of the onslaughts of this world, helpless before the media and their pollution.

II. A DIVINE SOLUTION (9:19-29)

About this time, while they were arguing, Jesus came up. The jeering stopped. Jesus Christ took control of the situation.

A. He Cultivated Faith (9:23)

How did Jesus handle the problem in that valley? For the father, Jesus Christ cultivated faith. "O faithless generation, how long shall I be with you? How long shall I suffer you [how long shall I put up with you]?" (9:19).

But the thing that is most amazing to me is how the Lord has put up with *me* all these years. The Lord gets weary of our unbelief. Sometimes He says, "Won't they ever learn? How long shall I put up with them?"

To the father he said, "Bring him unto me" (9:19).

That's what the Lord is saying to us. You have a desperate world out there. You have lives that are being wrecked by sin. Bring them to me, Christ says. I'm the solution to the problem.

Jesus is the answer. Jesus is the cure. If you have had a disappointing experience with a church, if some Christian has disappointed you, come to Jesus. He'll never disappoint you. He'll never let you down. I saw a long time ago that if I were trying to live the Christian life, if I were being a Christian on the basis of what others did, I would end up a defeated, bitter Christian. So I don't put my eyes on people.

Watch how Jesus cultivated the faith of this man. First, He pointed him to the object of faith: "Bring him unto me." The object of faith is important. Then, like a skillful physician, Jesus asked, "How long has he been that way?" "Since childhood," the father answered, describing how the boy would even fall into fire or water. "But if thou canst do any thing" he said to Jesus, "have compassion on us, and help us."

"If thou canst believe," Jesus answered, "all things are possible to him that believeth." The man obviously had the wrong *if*. The problem was not *if* Jesus could do anything. Jesus can do everything. This Jesus created the universe. He upholds all things with the word of his power. He calmed the storm; He walked on the water; He turned water into wine. The problem was not in Jesus. The problem is in us: "If thou canst believe."

Jesus solved the problem by cultivating faith. He spoke the word and said, "Come out of that boy." The Bible says the spirit tore him and he fell down as if he were dead (9:26). Then Jesus went over there, took him by the hand, and lifted him up.

> From sinking sand He lifted me,
> With tender hand, He lifted me,
> From shades of night to plains of light,
> O praise His name, He lifted me!

That's what Jesus can do for a desperate world.

What about the problem of a defeated church?

B. He Corrected Failures (9:28-29)

Like most of us, the disciples didn't want to share their embarrassment with the entire world; they waited until they got back in the house. Have you ever done that? Have you ever had a spiritual flop? Have you ever just really fallen flat on your face spiritually and then waited until you got back to the prayer closet to say, "Lord, why didn't I succeed? What's wrong?" That's what the disciples did. Back in the house they said, "Lord, why could not we cast him out?" (9:28). What's our problem, Lord?

Jesus said, "This kind can come forth by nothing, but by prayer and fasting" (9:29). Matthew gave a fuller account.

> Because of your unbelief: for verily I say unto you, If ye have faith as a grain of mustard seed, ye shall say unto this mountain, Remove hence to yonder place; and it shall remove; and nothing shall be impossible unto you. Howbeit this kind goeth not out but by prayer and fasting (Matthew 17:20-21).

Had a subtle shift taken place in the thinking of those disciples? Had they started putting their faith in themselves and in the process rather than in the one who was the source of the power? It is easy to do that. If we are not careful we will find ourselves putting our faith in the process instead of in the one who causes things to happen. They had cast out demons before. Now perhaps they were resting on their laurels. They were proud of what they had done and they had neglected something. Jesus was not saying that some magical prayer prayed right on the spot, a special prayer, could have done the job. Jesus implied that they were neglecting a lifestyle of prayer.

The reason for our powerlessness is our prayerlessness. The source of power in helping this desperate world does not come from within us. It comes from God, and the only way to get the power of God into a church or into a life is through prayer. We sometimes see twenty or thirty people saved on a Sunday and we praise God for that. But I have a feeling that all of us would

pray the way we ought to pray, would be in contact with God, in communion with God, the way we ought to be, and would bathe our church services in prayer, we might see hundreds saved on a Sunday. I really believe that.

An organist was getting ready to play as the service began. When he put his hands on the keys there was no sound. Everyone knew something was wrong, so the preacher quickly got up and led in a prayer. The janitor was aware of the fact that they hadn't plugged in the organ. So he went over there during the prayer, plugged in the organ, wrote a note, and handed it to the organist. The note said, "After the prayer, the power will be on."

That's right, isn't it? After the prayer, the power will be on.

23

True Greatness
Mark 9:30-50

I T SEEMS AS IF WHENEVER JESUS TALKED ABOUT HIS DEATH, IT BROUGHT out some spiritual flaw in the lives of the disciples. In the present passage we see them arguing with one another about who was going to be the greatest. Probably this particular discussion was precipitated by the fact that Peter, James, and John had witnessed the transfiguration of Jesus on the mountain. You can imagine how they must have felt. Did they come back down the mountain with an air of superiority? I'm sure that all three of them were confident in their minds that they were going to be the greatest. Understandably the other disciples weren't too happy about that prospect.

When they got into the house in Capernaum, Jesus asked, "What were you talking about on the way?" There was an embarrassed silence, a sense of shame. He had been talking about the cross and giving himself for the sins of the world and they were talking about self-glory and self-greatness.

Desire to be great is not abnormal. Ambition to greatness is in every human being to some degree.

Jesus had to answer the question these disciples raised about greatness. He also needed to restore harmony among them. He said, "Have salt in yourselves, and have peace one with another" (9:50).

The world's idea of greatness and the Lord's idea of greatness are different. The world says, "If you want to be great—rule." Jesus says, "If you want to be great—be willing to serve." In this conversation with his disciples, Jesus gave some of the marks of a life of greatness.

A life of greatness is characterized by personal tenderness.

I. PERSONAL TENDERNESS (9:35-42)

Jesus said, "If you want to be first, if you want to be number one, if you want to be truly great, then be last of all; be the servant of all." Then the great Son of God tenderly reached down, took a little boy in his arms, and said to them, "If you receive a little child like this, you receive me." Jesus had time for a little child.

A. Humility (9:38-40)

Tenderness arises from a life of humility. A humble person is interested in the little people. The child in this biblical incident had no influence whatsoever. That child could do nothing for Jesus, yet Jesus took time to relate to him. A lot of people are interested only in what other folks can do for them. They want to associate with people who can help them out in some way. Jesus taught that true greatness means caring for people—regardless. "Whosoever shall receive one of such children in my name, receiveth me" (9:37).

About that time John began to think of something that had happened recently. "Master, we saw one casting out devils in thy name, and he followeth not us: and we forbade him, because he followeth not us" (9:38). John realized they had done the wrong thing in refusing to receive a man who was casting out demons but wasn't in their particular group. Jesus said, "Forbid him not: for there is no man which shall do a miracle in my name, that can lightly speak evil of me. For he that is not against us is on our part" (9:39). Those words of Jesus are a death blow to the intolerant spirit, to the attitude that says, "Our group is the only group that is right."

Also, Jesus here established the basis of fellowship among believers in that little phrase, "in my name" (9:39). It appears again in 9:41. "For whosoever shall give you a cup of water to drink in my name . . . " That's the basis of fellowship. I don't care what group you are in. I don't care what your denomination is. If you have received Jesus as your personal savior, if you have been born again, then you are my sister or brother in Christ. We are in the same family, and we must receive one another. We don't all have to have the same denominational label to be the people of God.

True greatness also expresses itself in ministry.

B. Ministry (9:41-42)

If you want to be first, then be servant of all. The word *servant* there is our word *deacon*. A deacon is a servant. There is no authority in the office of deacon. The office of deacon is a position of service. Jesus illustrated ministry by saying, "Whosoever shall give you a cup of water to drink in my name, because ye belong to Christ, verily I say unto you, he shall not lose his reward" (9:41). Serving can be just a little thing like giving a cup of water to somebody in Jesus' name. Serving others, helping others—that's what greatness is from God's perspective.

II. PERSONAL HOLINESS (9:43-48)

Jesus next brought up a subject that is almost unmentioned in religious circles today. He talked about a place called hell. In fact, He said, it would be better for you to lose one of your hands than to go into this place called hell (9:43). When Jesus used that word (*gehenna*) every Jew knew what He was talking about. It referred to a place south of Jerusalem, the valley of Hinnom. Back during the days of the kings, when the children of Israel had gone into idolatry, it was a place of worship of the god Moloch (Acts 7:43). A figure of that god was heated like a furnace and in their idolatry, they would take their own small children and sacrifice them to Moloch. In that valley of Hinnom you could hear the shrieks and cries of those precious children as they were thrown into the fire. When the godly king Josiah came along, he stopped that pagan practice; he turned the valley of Hinnom or gehenna into a garbage dump for the city of Jerusalem. All of the refuse was carried out there and burned. It was a place of foul odor. Worms crawled around eating the dead bodies of slaves that had been thrown there. The impurity of the city was carried there.

The Lord Jesus used this vivid picture to teach a truth about God's universe, the truth that God hates sin. God loves the sinner, but God hates the sin. Don't ever fail to understand that distinction. God has determined He will purify his universe of sin. He has decreed that "the wages of sin is death" (Romans 6:23). There will be no sin in heaven. God will see that sin is punished.

So Jesus was teaching that there is a place called hell. It is a real, actual, literal place. Those who refuse God's offer of forgiveness of sin, those who choose their sin over the Lord Jesus Christ, will end up there.

In sophisticated congregations in the average church today, nobody wants to hear the truth that there is a hell. But God has not changed his word for our generation. God has not changed his rules, his guidelines, for a sinful society. God says that if people die in their sins apart from the Lord Jesus they go to a place where the fire is not quenched and the worm dieth not. Hell is a terrible place of punishment. It pictures the putrefaction of sin; it is a place where sin attains its full damnable results.

What has this to do with the disciples? With believers? In the midst of the discussion of true greatness, why did Jesus bring up the subject of hell? Why did He use this unusual language saying that it would be better for you to lose your hand or foot or eye than to be whole and go into hell?

A. Sin Must Be Confronted (9:43-47)

Jesus was saying that sin is so serious to God that God has determined to deal with it. The life of true greatness is a life of holiness. Believers must be severe in dealing with any sin that creeps into their lives. Of course you know that Jesus here was using the language of hyperbole in order to teach a truth. He was not saying that you ought to cut off your hand. By this figure of speech, Jesus was saying that there is to be self-judgment. We must take sin seriously.

Your hand (9:43) represents what you do. Is there any action, anything you are doing in your life, that is not pleasing to God? Your foot (9:45) represents where you go. Are you going anywhere that causes you to sin? Are you frequenting any place that brings compromise into your life? You say, "Oh, I like to go there. I enjoy the folks there. I know I do some things I ought not to do, but they're not too serious."

Your eye (9:47) represents what you see, and also your ambitions and desires. Are you looking at anything that brings sin into your life?

B. Sin Must Be Cut Off (9:43-45)

Be sure that nothing in your life is causing you to sin. If it is, get rid of it.

We can't dabble with sin. To dilly-dally with sin is deadly. If we do, it will eat us up like a cancer. It will take control of our lives. We can't tame sin. It would be foolish to try to tame a rattlesnake. Many a man has lost his home because he started going places he shouldn't go, started dabbling in some sins he shouldn't dabble in. He thought he could play with sin.

If you have some habit in your life that's causing you to sin, cut it off.

If you have a boyfriend or a girlfriend who's keeping you from being what God wants you to be, stop seeing that person *now*. Does your boyfriend or girlfriend make you love Jesus more or less? If you cannot say truthfully from your heart, "My boyfriend makes me love Jesus more and makes me want to be everything Jesus saved me to be," check out of that relationship *now*. You say, "Then I'd have to stay home on weekends." Well, it would be a whole lot better to stay home than to make a mistake and marry that guy and live fifty years with the wrong man. To continue in a wrong dating relationship is like saying that God can't provide a husband or wife for you, that you can't trust God to send the right mate into your life, and so you are going to satisfy yourself with one of the devil's substitutes. Regardless of how nice he or she treats you, you are letting a cancer get in your life and it is sapping your spiritual strength. Soon you are not reading your Bible anymore, you are not praying the way you ought to pray. You are compromising as a believer. Yes, it hurts to quit, but you will be better off.

Are you watching shows on TV you ought not be watching? Shut it off. Are you reading literature you ought not be reading? Throw it out. What a tragedy that some people who name the name of Jesus and whose eyes were created to study God's word will expose themselves to the vileness and filth of our day. Stop. What makes you think you can get by with some sin in your life as a believer? I'll tell you what it will become. It will become a worm that dies not. It will become a fire that cannot be quenched in your life. It will consume you. It will burn you up.

III. PERSONAL USEFULNESS (9:49-50)

"For everyone shall be salted with fire" (9:49). The person who goes to hell will suffer eternally in his sin. He will be salted with fire; the fire will continue to burn, yet he'll be there eternally. "Every sacrifice shall be salted with salt." That allusion goes back to the Old Testament, when all of the sacrifices had to be seasoned with the salt of the covenant. Having been salted, a sacrifice was rendered acceptable to God.

A. Pleasing to God

If you as a believer will use self-judgment, if you will deal with sins in your life, if you will apply the salt of the Holy Spirit and the word of God, purging and purifying your life as a believer, then your life will be pleasing to God.

B. Helpful to Others

"Salt is good: but if the salt has lost his saltness, wherewith will ye season it? Have salt in yourselves, and have peace one with another" (9:50). If you exercise self-judgment and get your life clean before God, rendered acceptable to God, then there is that salty nature in your life as a believer. When you come in contact with a lost world there is a flavor in your life that is attractive to those who do not know Jesus.

Do you know why Christians don't attract sinners to Jesus? It's because salt can lose its saltiness.

If we aren't thrilled about serving Jesus, how do we expect our lost world to get excited about him? Our job is to go out and so to magnify Christ that they will be drawn to him.

When you have the choice of either Jesus or hell it seems to me that there is not much choice. And you can't have both.

24

God Hates Divorce
Mark 10:1-16

THESE VERSES IN MARK GIVE US THE TEACHING OF OUR LORD ON the subject of divorce. Probably no subject elicits so much interest and is so important to deal with in our day as this. Over one million people a year experience divorce in America. Five out of nine marriages end up in divorce. In some parts of the country there are more divorces yearly than there are marriages. When we look at these statistics, we know that this subject needs to be addressed by the people of God.

The Bible deals with life right where it is. It comes into our experience; it talks about daily problems. It does not deal merely with the sweet by-and-by; it also deals with the here and now. So, because divorce is a problem among us, God has something to say about it.

When we discuss the subject of divorce, however, we have to be careful that we do not go to one of two extremes: to permissiveness on the one hand, or to harshness on the other. The Bible balances all truths; as we study we must find the balance and see what God has to say.

In the Bible God gives us great overriding principles. Some truths, some principles, are so great that God paints them in broad strokes. The Old Testament sets forth God's attitude toward divorce: "The Lord, the God of Israel, saith that he hateth putting away" (Malachi 2:16); that is, "I hate divorce." God is not saying, "I hate divorced people," which is an important distinction to be made. God is saying, "I hate sin"; He is not saying, "I hate the sinner." God hates alcohol, what it does to people, but He does not hate the alcoholic. God hates lies, but He does not hate the liar.

In this chapter we are going to study the reasons God hates divorce. We are not dealing with those who have been divorced, but primarily with those who have not been divorced. The purpose of this study is not specifically to give help to those who have experienced a divorce; rather, this chapter is intended to be preventive—so that if you have not experienced divorce you will never experience one. I am primarily concerned with young people, with those who hope to be married one of these days. I am going to look at God's ideal, the way God intends for marriage to be.

In the Bible we have God's counsels of perfection. We also have God's counsels of practicality. God's counsels of perfection set the standard right up there where it ought to be. God's counsels of practicality come down to the real world where the problems are, and deal with those problems that occur because of our failure and sin.

God hates divorce because of what causes divorce and because of what divorce causes. God hates divorce because of the reasons for divorce and because of the results of divorce. In answering a question of the Pharisees, Jesus came head on with the matter of divorce and gave us reasons why God hates it.

I. THE PROBLEM DIVORCE DEFINES (10:2-5)

The Pharisees came to Jesus and said, "Is it lawful for a man to put away his wife?" (10:2). "What did Moses command you?" was his answer (10:3). That was the equivalent of our saying, "What does the Bible say?" In other words, Jesus pointed them to the authority of God's word. At that time there were different schools of thought, different positions, about the matter of divorce, but Jesus told them to go back to what the scriptures said about it. The Bible is always the authority, the final word, for

God's people. We don't need a second opinion when we know
what God says in the Bible.

A. The Mosaic Concession (10:4-5)

The Pharisees said, "Moses suffered [permitted] to write a bill of
divorcement, and to put her away [to divorce her]" (see Deuteronomy 24:4). They were accurate in quoting what the Bible taught.
Through Moses in the Old Testament, God had said that when a
man put away his wife, he was to write her a bill of divorcement.
  We have to remember, however, that divorce was never a divine
institution. It was a human device. There is no evidence in scripture that God devised divorce; it was something men devised. So,
in that kind of world, when there was moral laxness among people, God gave some guidelines to regulate divorce. "When a man
hath taken a wife, and married her, and it come to pass that she
find no favor in his eyes, because he hath found some uncleanness
in her: then let him write her a bill of divorcement, and give it in
her hand, and send her out of his house" (Deuteronomy 24:1).
  Controversy arose over what was meant by "some uncleanness." In the time of Jesus it had become a burning issue. People
were getting divorces for all kinds of ridiculous reasons. There
were two schools of thought among the rabbis at that time. The
liberal school said that some uncleanness could mean just about
anything under the sun. If the wife burned the husband's meal
he could give her a divorce. If she served him bad coffee he
could give her a divorce. If she talked too loudly he could give
her a divorce. On the other hand, another school said that some
uncleanness had to do only with immorality.
  The Pharisees were interested in the writing out of a legal document; in other words, in the doing of the paperwork. "Just be
sure you do the paperwork right. Make sure it's legal, and then
you can go ahead and get a divorce." Jesus made clear that this
was a concession made by Moses. If there were a divorce, there
should be a document. Moses was trying to regulate a difficult
problem. He was not encouraging divorce.

B. The Moral Cause (10:5)

Jesus then pointed to the moral cause of the mosaic concession:
"For the hardness of your heart he wrote you this precept" (10:5).

He was saying that divorce among God's people was evidence of moral weakness. The fact that divorce has become such an issue in our society is a reflection of the overall moral temper of our times too. It is evidence that something is wrong. Jesus said it was sclerosis of the heart, hardness of the heart. That's always true. Any time divorce comes in a family, it is because of hardness of heart on the part of one or both persons.

When Moses was leaving Egypt and going into the promised land, we're told that pharaoh hardened his heart and wouldn't let the people go. What did that mean? It meant that pharaoh determined he was going to have his way. He didn't care what they wanted. He didn't care what God said. That is one source of a lot of problems in marriages today. When we determine to have our own way, we create problems. "I don't care what she or he wants; this is what I want." That's hardness of heart.

Every time there is a divorce, it is because a problem has arisen, and God hates divorce because of the sin at the heart of the problem.

In our society we've begun to ask ourselves why so many marriages are in trouble. What's wrong? Why are we having such problems with marriage? In those days a bill of divorcement made public what was going on in private.

Today more has been written about the home than at any other time. When I got married virtually nothing was written on the subject. I didn't know what it meant to be married, what it meant to be a husband, what was expected of me as a husband. Young couples getting married today cannot claim that ignorance. If you are getting ready to get married, hundreds of books by Christian authors are now available to help you not to fail in your marriage. Young people are foolish if they jump into marriage without reading the Bible and perhaps consulting some of these other references.

There is a second reason in these teachings of Jesus why God hates divorce.

II. The Plan Divorce Defies (10:6-9)

Jesus then went back to the original plan, back beyond the book of Deuteronomy and into the book of Genesis. There where the institution of marriage originated, we see what God's plan was for marriage. The seriousness of divorce is due to the sacredness of marriage.

A. A Divine Distinction (10:6)

"From the beginning of the creation God made them male and female." In other words, when God created human beings He made a distinction between the sexes. "Male and female created he them" (Genesis 1:27). I believe that men and women are different not only physically but also psychologically and spiritually. Does that mean the man is superior? Of course not. Does that mean the woman is inferior? Of course not. A man is infinitely superior to a woman at being a man. A woman is infinitely superior to a man at being a woman. *Vive la différence!*

B. A Divine Institution (10:7-8)

"For this cause shall a man leave his father and mother, and cleave to his wife; And they twain shall be one flesh." God instituted marriage.

First, note that word *leave.* If their marriage is going to be what it ought to be, a young couple has to learn to be independent of their parents. They have to learn to make it on their own. They have to make their own mistakes. They have to make their own decisions, and their parents have to allow them the freedom and liberty to fail. It's difficult for us parents to believe that our children are ever mature enough to be out there on their own. But God says, "For this cause shall a man leave his father and mother." Young couples, don't be running back every weekend to see Mom and Dad. Stay home. Go to Sunday school and church where you are; get involved in that young married couples class. Grow up.

God also said that a man is to cleave to his wife. This is the leave-cleave principle. The word *cleave* means to glue together. When you marry that mate, you are stuck to her or him for the rest of your life. That's why it's important to marry the right person. This marriage business is not trial and error. That's not what God says. The husband/wife relationship is intended to be permanent. The parent/child relationship is the temporary relationship. We often get that reversed.

A couple is foolish to put all their energies into the parent/child relationship. Some husbands and wives bring their children up, their children go, and then they look up over the

breakfast table one morning at a stranger. We need to be cultivating our husband/wife relationship. A lot of divorces take
place after the children have gone from the home.

Before you marry, ask yourself, "Will I still love him or her if
. . . ?" We have to understand what marriage means, Hollywood
notwithstanding. We have been so deceived about what marriage
is, about its romantic aspects. That's part of it, but another part
of marriage is just learning to love one another and to live with
one another in spite of failures and faults.

C. A Divine Intention (10:8-9)

God says, "They twain [two] shall be one flesh." Getting married
and becoming one flesh does not happen instantly. Becoming
one is a process. It is not something that happens like magic.
You are to become one physically, yes, but you are also to
become one emotionally and spiritually. One flesh. "What therefore God hath joined together, let not man put asunder" (10:9).

You better not have a wedding if you can't invite Jesus. I
worry about weddings where Jesus can't be invited or where it
would be an embarrassment for the pastor to be at the reception.
Don't start off wrong.

I believe that marriages are made in heaven. I believe that God
has somebody He wants you to marry. I believe that God brings
two people together. I believe that God has a divine plan for each
marriage. And once you're married, don't let some counselor tell
you to get a divorce. That's not what God says in his word.
Don't let anyone talk you into leaving your mate. God says, "I've
joined this couple together, so don't you put it asunder."

God hates divorce for a third reason.

III. The Permissiveness Divorce Demonstrates (10:10-12)

"Whosoever shall put away his wife, and marry another, com-
mitteth adultery against her." The word *adultery* means having
sex with someone other than your mate. We live in a time when
marital fidelity is almost laughed at. One of the main themes of
contemporary songs is the glorification of adultery, immorality,
and promiscuity. This is sexual sin.

Although we are living in sophisticated America, God has not
changed his word concerning adultery. It's still a sin. Hollywood

says it's funny. God says it's deadly. TV says it's comedy. But God says it's tragedy. Marriage is the process of two becoming one. Adultery is a disruptive factor in that process; it violates God's plan of a husband and wife's becoming one. Millions of men and women are shacking up with so many people that they don't know from day to day who their mates are. They are helping to lead this country to debauchery and judgment.

It is not always true when a person gets divorced that sexual immorality was involved. But I am safe in saying that in a great many instances it is a factor. A man leaves the wife of his youth because he has found somebody else who now is more physically attractive to him.

Finally, we come to a fourth reason God hates divorce. I don't believe I'm doing violence to this scripture when I pull Mark 10:13-16 into this context of the Lord's teaching about divorce and adultery. I don't think it was an accident that children are brought into the picture here.

IV. THE PEOPLE DIVORCE DAMAGES (10:13-16)

Almost everyone in our country has been affected either directly or indirectly by divorce. But I think it's children who are hurt the most. They came into this world through no choice of their own. But when a divorce happens, the first reaction of the children is, "I'm to blame. I've done something that's caused Mom and Dad to stop liking each other." Scars that are left on those children's lives because of that divorce take years to get over. Even so, the fact and pain of their parents' divorce remain a lifelong memory.

Jesus said, "Whosoever looketh on a woman to lust after her hath committed adultery with her already in his heart" (Matthew 5:28). What if you're saying, "Look, I've been divorced and I've committed adultery. Is there any hope for me?" Yes, there is.

We have noted that when Jesus gave his teachings on divorce they were his "counsels of perfection." He put the ideal, the divine standard, where it ought to be. When He did that, his disciples said, "If the case of the man be so with his wife it is not good to marry" (Matthew 19:10). They meant if it's that way, it would be better not to marry at all. But then Jesus said, "All men cannot receive this saying, save they to whom it is given" (Matthew 19:11). He was saying that you have to take every sit-

uation, bring it to the great principles of God's word, and then, on
the basis of those broad principles, deal with your situation as
best you can. One of the broad principles is this: "Though your
sins be as scarlet, they shall be as white as snow" (Isaiah 1:18).

The Bible talks about committing adultery, but you don't have
to live in adultery. You can ask God to forgive you. You can tell
a lie, but you don't have to live as a liar. God will forgive you of
your sin if you will ask him to. There may be consequences. Difficulties may linger on, but you can be forgiven.

Jesus said, "Let the little children come unto me and forbid
them not." And "Whosoever shall not receive the kingdom of
God as a little child, he shall not enter therein" (10:15). That's
how we have to come to God: like a little child, whatever we've
done. Jesus can forgive all sin.

25

One Thing Thou Lackest

Mark 10:17-31

I. THE MAN (10:17)
   A. His Quest (10:17)
   B. His Question (10:17)
II. THE MASTER (10:18-21)
   A. Jesus' Inquiry (10:18-20)
   B. Jesus' Invitation (10:21)
III. THE MISTAKE (10:22)
   A. Remorse Rather than Repentance
   B. The Material Rather than the Eternal

I N THIS PASSAGE OF SCRIPTURE WE SEE A CONTRAST BETWEEN TWO young men. One of them is the rich young ruler; the other is our Lord. The rich young ruler had a lot in this world, but nothing in eternity; the Lord Jesus had nothing in this world, yet everything in eternity. The rich young ruler had earthly position; the Lord Jesus Christ left a throne of glory, made himself of no reputation, to come into this world and have no position here at all.

This scripture is one of the Bible's tragedies. So much is right about this story. For instance, the young man came at the right time. There is no better time for people to come to Jesus than when they are young. He came to the right person, the Lord Jesus. He asked the right question, a question about the eternal destiny of his soul. He received the right answer; Jesus told him how to go to heaven.

He came at the right time, he came to the right person, he asked the right question, he got the right answer—yet, tragedy of tragedies, he did the wrong thing. Instead of becoming a member of the Bible *Who's Who*, he wound up in *Who's Not*. He came close to being a Christian, he came close to being saved, yet he turned and walked away.

I. THE MAN (10:17)

Combining the accounts of Matthew, Mark, and Luke, we discover that this person who came running to Jesus (10:17) was a rich young ruler. His name is not given.

A. His Quest (10:17)

This young man came to Jesus and knelt in respect before him. He came to Jesus because his heart was searching.

The young man already had many things. He had youth, a wonderful thing, a wonderful time to give one's life to Jesus. The Bible says, "Remember now thy Creator in the days of thy youth" (Ecclesiastes 12:1). If you are a young person reading this book, if you have not already done so, I urge you to give your life to Jesus today. Don't give the flower of your life to the devil, and then give the decapitated stem to Jesus. Don't burn the candle of your life for the devil, and then blow the smoke of a wasted life in the face of God. Come to Christ when you are young and live for Jesus all your life.

He was a wealthy man. Wealth in and of itself is not wrong, if you get it honestly and use it wisely.

He was a religious young man. He said he had kept the commandments from his youth up and Jesus did not repudiate that statement. Obviously he was a very moral young man who had avoided the danger that wealth brings to a lot of people: Wealth tends to gnaw away at one's morals, but this young man had avoided that problem. He was a fine, upstanding, morally pure person.

Yet for all of the good things to be said about him, something was missing. There was something that his money, youth, and morality had not been able to give him. This young man had made the discovery that every man or woman makes sooner or later in life. He had discovered that there are some things which money cannot buy.

I think we are learning this in our generation. Money can buy a bed, but it cannot buy sleep. Money can buy food, but it cannot buy an appetite. Money can buy medicine, but it cannot buy health. Money can buy a house, but it cannot buy a home. Money can buy a diamond, but it cannot buy love. And, most important of all, money cannot buy salvation. Don't make the mistake of thinking that, because you have material things, because you are young, because you are a morally good person, you have everything you need in this life.

This young man was aware of the fact that he needed something, and he was searching for that missing ingredient.

B. His Question (10:17)

"Good Master," he asked, "what shall I do that I may inherit eternal life?" Certainly he was on the right track. Certainly he was getting down to the basic question. I think any person would be interested in that question, because this life at its longest is really not very long. So, "What do you have to do to go to heaven when you die?" It was a tremendous admission of ignorance on the part of this young man. He admitted by his question that he didn't know the answer to life's most important question, how to be saved and go to heaven.

Isn't the spiritual ignorance of people today amazing? We are living in one of the most intellectually advanced and sophisticated ages of all times. We know how to put astronauts on the moon, yet we don't know how to get to heaven.

There is, however, a little flaw, a problem, in the question which the young man asked. That is, he had the idea he had to *do something* in order to be saved. But salvation is not something we earn; salvation is something God gives us. The Bible says, "The wages of sin is death; but the gift of God is eternal life through Jesus Christ our Lord" (Romans 6:23). We don't do something in order to get to heaven. Salvation is not based on what a person does; salvation is based on what God does. Salvation is a gift, given to us in the Lord Jesus Christ. In order to get eternal life we have to receive Jesus.

"This is the record, that God hath given to us eternal life, and this life is in his Son. He that hath the Son hath life; and he that hath not the Son of God hath not life" (1 John 5:11-12). If you want to go to heaven when you die, there is only one way. Jesus is the only way of salvation.

II. The Master (10:18-21)

First, I am impressed with how delicately our master dealt with this young man.

A. Jesus' Inquiry (10:18-20)

"Why callest thou me good?" (10:18). Why did Jesus ask that question? The young man came with enthusiasm, filled with optimism, bubbling over with interest. But instead of answering his question, Jesus asked a question in return. Jesus wanted to see if the young man really knew to whom he was talking: "There is no one good but one, that is, God."

We have a way of throwing adjectives around and applying them to anything: great, tremendous, wonderful, precious, neat, cool, awesome. But the Bible is careful in its use of adjectives. When the Bible uses the word *good* it uses it carefully. The Bible says that only one is good and that is God. Jesus was asking, "Do you realize who I am? You can't call me good unless you call me God. If you don't call me God you can't call me good."

What a person believes about Jesus is at the heart of salvation. If you believe that Jesus Christ is God and if you receive Jesus as God, it will have life-changing effects. You will never again be the same.

Jesus also inquired about the young man's understanding of the purpose of the commandments. The first four command-ments have to do with our relationship to God. The last six com-mandments have to do with our relationship to other people. Jesus quoted these six (10:19) and said in effect, "If you want to have life, these are the commandments." The young man replied, "Master, all of these have I observed from my youth" (10:20).

Outwardly that was probably true. He had lived a good moral life. But the young man's problem was this: he had made only a shallow examination of his heart. Most people make that mis-take. Most of us have a tendency to look at the superficial good-ness in our lives. We look at our external respectability and con-clude that we are OK ("I'm a good person. I don't beat my wife. I don't abuse my children. I pay my bills"). The purpose of the law is to serve as a probe, to help us go down into the depths of our hearts and see ourselves as God sees us. The Bible says, "By the law is the knowledge of sin" (Romans 3:20). God did not give the ten commandments so that his people could keep them and go to heaven on the basis of keeping them. In other words, God didn't say, "I'm going to give you these ten commandments so you can go to heaven by checking them off." God gave the ten commandments to serve as a mirror in order to show us ourselves as we really are. Paul said that the law was a schoolmaster to bring us to Christ (Galatians 3:24).

We cannot be satisfied with superficial goodness. Human goodness is dangerous because it is deceptive. Let me explain. If you look at your life on the outside and say, "I'm a pretty good person," you do not allow God to take the searchlight of the Holy Spirit and shine down deep in your heart. Outward goodness can lull you to sleep and you can go to hell thinking you are too good to need Jesus Christ as your savior.

B. Jesus' Invitation (10:21)

Jesus was helping the young man see his sin and his need. "Then Jesus beholding him [looking right into his soul] loved him" (10:21). Jesus saw what that young man could become if he would receive him as his savior. Perhaps He could see another Paul right there, or another Timothy. With love for the young man, Jesus said, "One thing thou lackest." In other words, Jesus said, "There is one thing missing in your life." That word *lackest* is the same verb that is found in Romans 3:23 where the Bible says, "For all have sinned, and *come short* of the glory of God." Jesus put his finger on the problem that was keeping that young man from being saved. It was like a doctor putting his finger on the sore spot. Jesus said, "Go sell everything you have, give it to the poor, and follow me." This young man's wealth had taken the place of God in his life. That's one of the dangers of affluence, one of the problems of the overprivileged.

There are dangers in wealth. There are problems attached to material prosperity. After the young man turned sadly away, "Jesus looked round about, and saith unto his disciples, How hardly shall they that have riches enter into the kingdom of God!" (10:22-23). Those words shocked the disciples. They were astonished. "Children," Jesus went on, "how hard is it for them that trust in riches to enter into the kingdom of God!" (10:24).

Why is it hard for the rich to be saved? Because they get to
trusting in their riches. That's our tendency, isn't it? We get
material things and we start depending on them. We have the
idea that they are the solution to every problem in life. Those
material things can build walls around rich people so that it is
hard for anyone to get into their hearts and tell them about Jesus.
It makes it hard for them to come out from behind those walls
and confess their need of Jesus Christ. In order to go to heaven,
a person has to get to the point of admitting that he or she is a
poor, lost, hell-deserving sinner.

"It is easier for a camel to go through the eye of a needle, than
for a rich man to enter into the kingdom of God" (10:25). What
did Jesus mean? Was He talking about a little narrow gate? No,
He meant just what He said. He was talking about the eye of a
needle. He was saying that it is absolutely impossible for a camel
to go through the eye of a needle. Here is this big old camel and
there is that little bitty eye of a needle. Jesus was saying that it
is easier to take that camel—humps and all—and drive it through
the eye of a needle than to try to get to heaven without Jesus.
You had just as well try to ride a Georgia mule to the moon as to
get to heaven without Jesus. An elephant on roller skates could
get to the moon faster than you will get to heaven without Jesus.

They said, "If that's so, who can be saved?" "With men it is
impossible," our Lord replied, "but not with God: for with God
all things are possible." He is saying there are two ways men try
to go to heaven: man's way and God's way. He is saying that it
doesn't matter what man's way may be; it doesn't matter whether
a man tries to buy his way with his riches or tries to earn his way
with his good deeds. With men salvation is impossible. There
is only one way to be saved: God's way, made possible in his Son
the Lord Jesus.

Does that mean for me to be saved I have to sell everything I
have and give it to the poor? Was Jesus teaching that you have
to choose a life of poverty in order to be saved? No, the great
physician does not treat every disease with the same medicine.
The great physician knows the problem in the heart of every person and prescribes the medicine accordingly. He might say if
you want to be saved you have to turn your back on that
boyfriend or girlfriend and come to Jesus. He might say you have
to let go of that business deal. He might say you have to turn
loose that secret sin.

What is keeping you from Jesus? What is the problem in your life? Jesus knows what it is.

What it boils down to is this. You can't have your sins—and heaven too. John Bunyan said, "Wilt thou have thy sins and go to hell or leave thy sins and go to heaven?" It's that simple.

Jesus dealt with the main problem in the young man's life and then said, "You will have treasure in heaven; come take up your cross and follow me."

After the young man had gone, Simon Peter spoke up and said, "Lo, we have left all, and have followed thee" (10:28). Jesus said, "You will find out that it will be worth it to you now and it will be worth it to you then."

It pays to serve Jesus, though there is a cost involved. But when you follow the Lord Jesus Christ, whatever you turn your back on, He will make it up to you in ways you could not imagine.

I feel so sorry for people who don't have Jesus. It's worth it to live for Jesus right now. If there weren't any heaven, I'd still be glad I was living for Jesus now. Ten thousand years into eternity you will be glad you followed Jesus. It will be worth it.

III. THE MISTAKE (10:22)

Let's back up for a minute. It was decision time. Here was the man. Here was the master. Was the young man breathing hard, wiping the perspiration from his brow, biting his lip? I think that the demons of hell crawled to the edge of the pit to watch; the angels stopped what they were doing in heaven.

A. Remorse Rather than Repentance

Then the young man made a mistake. He was remorseful instead of repentant. "He was sad at that saying" (10:22). He was grieved, but it was not a godly sorrow that leads to repentance.

B. The Material Rather than the Eternal

He wanted God, but not at the price of his gold. He wanted eternal life, but he couldn't give up his luxury. He walked away. He chose the material over the eternal.

I've often wondered what happened to him. Was he ever

saved? The Bible doesn't say. But I'm more interested in what you, the reader, are going to do—if you have not yet accepted Jesus as your personal savior and Lord. Don't walk away from Christ.

26

On the Way to Jerusalem

Mark 10:32-45

I.   A SORROWFUL PREDICTION (10:32-34)
     A. Hostility (10:33)
     B. Severity (10:34)
     C. Victory (10:34)
II. A SHAMEFUL AMBITION (10:35-41)
     A. The Request (10:35-37)
     B. The Reply (10:38-40)
     C. The Reaction (10:41)
III. A SACRIFICIAL REDEMPTION (10:42-45)
     A. His Coming (10:45)
     B. His Living
     C. His Dying

THE LORD JESUS NOW TURNED HIS FACE TOWARD JERUSALEM. IT WAS just about a week before He would be hanging on a cross, dying for the sins of the world. There is a tense atmosphere in these verses, a sense of foreboding on the part of the disciples.

Although Jesus had told them He was going to die on the cross, they weren't prepared for that message. They didn't want to hear him say such things. They had visions of a present kingdom, an earthly reign. They could see themselves with Jesus ruling and dominating this earth. For Jesus to talk about going to the cross disturbed that hope.

On the way up to Jerusalem, as they made their journey, we see Jesus alone with his thoughts, and the disciples both amazed and afraid. In that atmosphere Jesus needed to speak some words of encouragement and help.

I. A SORROWFUL PREDICTION (10:32-34)

First, for the third time Jesus predicted his death. He had already told them He was going to die (Mark 8). A word He used there that catches our attention is the word *must.* Jesus talked about the necessity of his cross. Later Jesus again talked about his cross (Mark 9), but the word that hits our minds there is the word *shall.* Jesus dealt with the certainty of the cross. Here, in Mark 10, He emphasized the cruelty of the cross, giving minute details about what was going to take place.

We have to keep in mind that when Jesus made predictions about the cross He was totally in charge. Jesus did what none of us is able to do. We cannot predict the time or the manner of our death. That is not in our power. The Bible says, "Boast not thyself of tomorrow; for thou knowest not what a day may bring forth" (Proverbs 27:1). When Jesus thought, He was thinking the mind of God. When Jesus spoke, He was speaking the mind of God. So He knew everything about his death at Calvary. He was not a victim of circumstances. He was not a martyr for a cause. One time He said to the disciples, "No man taketh it [my life] from me, but I lay it down" (John 10:18).

A. Hostility (10:33)

Jesus predicted that He would "be delivered unto the chief priests, and unto the scribes." He was predicting that He would be betrayed, turned over to the religious leaders, and they would assign him to die.

Isn't it amazing how "religion" always is hostile to the Lord Jesus Christ? It is not all that different in our day. Religion is the effort of man to work his way to heaven. Religion says, "I'll be good enough; I'll do enough good works in order to earn or merit my entrance into heaven." The coming of Jesus was God's testimony to man that he could not save himself. God had to break through into human history and provide a way for us to be saved.

Jesus said, "They are going to deliver me up into the hands of the Jewish leaders, and the Jewish leaders are going to turn me over to the gentiles." That's exactly what took place.

B. Severity (10:34)

Jesus went into detail about the cruelty of what they were going to do to him.

"They shall mock him." They would make fun of him. Here was the Son of God, the Lord of glory come down to be the savior of the world, and what did people do? They ridiculed and jeered at him.

"They shall scourge him." We read that word and the impact and severity and pain of it don't really get to us. Jesus was predicting that they would whip him—and we know that's what they did.

"They shall spit upon him." Have you ever had anybody spit on you? One time when I was down in New Orleans for many months I preached right off Bourbon Street in the French quarter. We had a little portable organ, one or two fellows had guitars, and we would hand out gospel tracts and sing. Then one of us would preach. I was handing out tracts there one night and a drunk man came by and saw that tract I was getting ready to hand out. He spit right in my face. Can you imagine doing that to the Lord Jesus Christ? Yet folks are still doing it today. They are still trampling on the wonderful Son of God.

C. Victory (10:34)

"And the third day he [talking about himself] shall rise again." That statement just went over the heads of the disciples. They never seemed quite to catch the message that He was going to rise again. People haven't really caught that message yet. It hasn't really dawned on a lot of Christians today that Jesus is alive. Jesus Christ is just as alive now, twenty centuries later, as He was the day He came forth from the tomb. To realize that fact changes your outlook.

Jesus Christ is alive. You can have fellowship with him on a daily basis. He can be real in your life. He can answer prayer. He can walk with you and talk with you.

> I serve a living Savior,
> He's in the world today.
> I know that He is living
> Whatever men may say.

II. A SHAMEFUL AMBITION (10:35-41)

Get the picture? Once again we note that when Jesus talked about the cross it revealed another spiritual flaw in the lives of these disciples. The cross reveals the human heart. The message of the cross shows us just how filled with ambition and self-centeredness we are.

A. The Request (10:35-37)

This time two of the disciples named James and John came up to Jesus. Matthew's gospel says that they came with their mother and she was the one who made this request. "Lord, we want you to do for us whatever we ask you to do." If you are a parent, you may have heard that kind of language. One of your children wants something and doesn't want to tell you what it is. "Daddy, would you do what I want you to do?" That's the way children are. That's the way these disciples were. They already had in their minds something they wanted Jesus to do for them, but I think they knew they really shouldn't ask what they were going to ask for. I hear a little guilt there. So in order to nail that thing down, they were trying to get Jesus committed to do it. But Jesus was too smart for that; He's smarter than we parents are. Sometimes we get caught in that vise, but Jesus didn't.

"And he said unto them, What would ye that I should do for you?" (10:36). They said, "In your kingdom, Lord, we want you to give us special seats of honor, on your right and left hand." They were going for the number one and two spots, the two most important positions. "We want to be Secretary of State and Secretary of Defense. We want to be right up there on top."

Jesus had referred to his coming glory (8:38). Note that although they were slow to hear what He said about the cross, they had caught on to the glory aspects. That's like us too, isn't it? We are slow to get the message of suffering and sacrifice, but we latch onto the good stuff.

B. The Reply (10:38-40)

Jesus said to them, "You don't know what you are asking. Are you able to drink of the cup I'm going to drink of? Can you be baptized with the baptism I'm going to be baptized with?" Jesus talked about this "cup" on several occasions. One time he said to the disciples, "The cup which my Father hath given me, shall I not drink it?" (John 18:11). In the garden of Gethsemane Jesus said, "O my Father, if it be possible, let this cup pass from me" (Matthew 26:39). Jesus was talking about the suffering of his cross, all that He would endure at Calvary for the sins of the world. "Drinking a cup" means to experience a matter fully. When Jesus used the word *baptism* here, He was talking about being fully immersed in, or overwhelmed by, an experience. He called his cross a baptism.

"And they said unto him, We can" (10:39). "Sure, Lord, we can handle it." That's the way we are. Many churches want the glory of numbers, the glory of national recognition, but they don't want to pay the price of the labor involved.

The pathway to glory is always the pathway of suffering. There is no glory apart from suffering. That is an inevitable truth taught in scripture. Jesus said, "Yes, you are going to suffer all right, but those places of honor are not mine to give." When you start serving Jesus the way you ought to serve him, you are not going to be worried about who gets the honor. In fact, it is amazing what God's people can accomplish when they really don't care who gets the praise and recognition for it.

C. The Reaction (10:41)

When the other ten disciples heard about that request, what do you think they thought? They were much displeased (10:41). The ten were angry at James and John; they wanted those positions themselves.

III. A SACRIFICIAL REDEMPTION (10:42-45)

"But Jesus called them to him" (10:42). This is how to solve disagreements among believers. Get them to Jesus. You cannot be out of sorts with your brother or sister and be in fellowship with Jesus at the same time.

Then Jesus contrasted greatness in this world and in his kingdom. "Ye know that they which are accounted to rule over the Gentiles exercise lordship over them" (10:42). In this world's system of things, the more important you are, the more people serve you. In this world's system of things—pomp, authority, grandeur, splendor, who gets to sit where, who gets the chief appointments—all those kinds of things are what count. The world's attitude is: the higher you get, the more you can look down on everyone who is below you.

"But so shall it not be among you" (10:43). That's not the way God's people are to do business. Rather, Jesus said, "Whosoever will be great among you, shall be your minister: And whosoever of you will be the chiefest, shall be servant of all" (10:43-44). In this world's economy, the higher up you get, the more you are served. But in God's economy, the higher up you get, the more you serve others.

See the difference? In the Lord's work here, maybe you become a Sunday school teacher. You are not a teacher in order for the class to serve you, but you serve the class. Maybe you become a deacon or a pastor, and then you serve a congregation. They don't serve you. Jesus said if you want to be great, be a servant.

A. His Coming (10:45)

Jesus' own life illustrates that principle. Now we come to a key verse in Mark's gospel: "For even the Son of man came not to be ministered unto, but to minister, and to give his life a ransom for many" (10:45). Almost never did anyone else call Jesus the Son of man, but He called himself that. It seems to have been his favorite self-designation. He was the Son of God, but when He came into this world, He called himself the Son of man.

He was saying that his coming was a voluntary coming and that He came to identify with us, to know us and be a part of us, to know our fears, tears, and anxieties. He came and walked among us.

B. His Living

He came not to be served but to serve. Everywhere Jesus went He was helping others and doing things for others.

C. His Dying

He came to give his life a ransom for many. The word *ransom* means to release by the payment of a price. It is a word taken from the world of slavery. We all stand before God as slaves—and

God, by the payment of the price (the blood of Jesus), releases us from the slavery of sin. Jesus said, "I have come to give my life as a redemption price for many."

Sin makes a slave out of you. You start playing with sin and like a boa constrictor it will wrap itself around you. The next thing you know, it has you in its grip. Here you are in the slave market of sin. The cruelty and misery of sin have taken their toll on you. One day the Lord Jesus Christ comes walking into the slave market of sin and with his blood pays the purchase price for your redemption. "Forasmuch as ye know that ye were not redeemed with corruptible things . . . But with the precious blood of Christ, as of a lamb without blemish and without spot" (1 Peter 1:18-19).

Do you wonder if you're included? How many people did Jesus pay the ransom for? "For there is one God, and one mediator between God and men, the man Christ Jesus; Who gave himself a ransom for all, to be testified in due time" (1 Timothy 2:5-6). For how many? For all. "For therefore we both labour and suffer reproach, because we trust in the living God, who is the Saviour of all men, specially of those that believe" (1 Timothy 4:10).

The Lord Jesus has paid for your redemption. If you believe in him, turn from your sins, and invite him into your life, you will become one of the ransomed.

27

Blind Bartimaeus
Mark 10:46-52

I. THE CONDITION OF THE MAN (10:46)
   A. A Blind Man (10:46)
   B. A Beggar (10:46)
II. THE CRY FOR MERCY (10:47-48)
   A. It Was Insistent (10:47)
   B. It Was Persistent (10:48)
III. THE COMMAND OF THE MASTER (10:49-52)
   A. Jesus Called the Man (10:49-50)
   B. Jesus Cured the Man (10:51-52)

ON THIS FINAL JOURNEY TO JERUSALEM JESUS WENT THROUGH THE city of Jericho. The name *Jericho* means to smell; it was given that unusual name because of the rose gardens all over the city as well as the balsam, cypress, and other fragrant bushes. It was in Jericho that a little man named Zacchaeus climbed a tree, the Lord spoke to him, and Zacchaeus was saved that day. After that experience, as they were leaving Jericho, the Bible tells us about blind Bartimaeus.

When Jesus was on this earth He healed many different sicknesses and diseases. He healed people with palsy. He cleansed lepers. He raised the dead. But the New Testament records more cases of Jesus' healing those who were blind than of any other disease. The most familiar account is the story of Bartimaeus.

I. THE CONDITION OF THE MAN (10:46)

Bartimaeus is a picture of the condition of people outside the Lord Jesus, a reminder of what it means to be lost.

A. A Blind Man (10:46)

Bartimaeus was the son of Timaeus (*bar* means "son"). He had never known what it was to see a sunset, trees, the rolling flow of a river. He had never seen the stars at night. He lived in a narrow world of darkness.

It is terrible to be blind physically, but another kind of blindness that is even worse is spiritual blindness. The Bible talks about the blindness of the mind. "The god of this world hath blinded the minds of them which believe not" (2 Corinthians 4:4). Ephesians 4:18 describes those without Christ as having their understanding darkened. Not to know Jesus as savior is to be spiritually blind, unable to see.

People all around us see quite well with their physical eyes, but not with their spiritual eyes. They have no apprehension of the horror of sin. They cannot see where sin is going to lead them or what sin will do to them. They have no vision of what it means to face the wrath to come. The Bible says there is a judgment. The wrath of God is revealed from heaven against sin. But the spiritually blind have no perception of that. Of course, they don't see the loveliness of Jesus either.

Bartimaeus would be in constant danger. At times he might get to the edge of a precipice and wouldn't know that it was there. Those who are blind spiritually are in danger of spending eternity apart from the Lord Jesus Christ. The Bible warns of everlasting darkness.

B. A Beggar (10:46)

Blindness had lowered Bartimaeus to poverty. But there is more to poverty also than just physical poverty. The Bible talks about the poverty of the soul. It is possible for someone to be physically and materially well off yet be spiritually bankrupt, in the moral poorhouse. When Adam sinned in the garden of Eden, humankind fell to the spiritual poverty level. So those without Jesus Christ are spiritually poor today. Their lives are like an empty pocket, a ragged pocket that has been turned inside out, emptied of everything of worth and value. To be lost means to be spiritually sightless, spiritually penniless.

II. The Cry for Mercy (10:47-48)

"And when he heard that it was Jesus, he began to cry out" (10:47). Bartimaeus had probably heard a lot about Jesus. That day when Jesus passed by, hope must have risen in his heart. Here was a man who had been begging for money; now he was begging for mercy.

A. It Was Insistent (10:47)

"He began to cry out, and say, Jesus, thou Son of David, have mercy on me." When Bartimaeus called Jesus the Son of David, it showed he had insight that some people who had eyes with 20-20 vision did not have. Jesus Christ indeed was the Son of David and the messiah. So he addressed Jesus by his royal name. The Bible had predicted that the messiah would give sight to blinded eyes: "Then the eyes of the blind shall be opened" (Isaiah 35:5).

When John the Baptist was in prison he began to wonder if Jesus were the messiah. He sent some of his followers to ask Jesus if He were the one. Jesus sent back a message describing what He was doing. "Go tell John that the blind are receiving their sight" (Matthew 11:5).

Bartimaeus cried out for mercy. He didn't demand his rights. We are living in a day when people are demanding their rights—women's rights, civil rights, senior citizens' rights, children's rights. I have news for you. I don't want my rights. If I got my rights, I would be in hell, and you would too. Every one of us deserves the wrath of God. We have no right to God's forgiveness, no right to heaven, no right to salvation. What you and I need is not our rights, but the mercy of God. I don't come to God demanding my rights. I don't come to God demanding justice. David said, "Have mercy upon me, O God, according to thy lovingkindness" (Psalm 51:1).

I'm so glad that Bartimaeus asked for mercy. That happens to be one of the things God has plenty of. "God . . . is rich in mercy" (Ephesians 2:4). "Not by works of righteousness which we have done, but according to his mercy he saved us" (Titus 3:5).

B. It Was Persistent (10:48)

Bartimaeus's insistent cries caused an uproar. His persistence in calling out to Jesus disturbed people. I can imagine that the authorities in town were honored that Jesus was passing through and wanted everything to go well. But here was that public nuisance, blind Bartimaeus. I can almost hear them say, "Be quiet. You are always interrupting things. Would you please be still? Jesus is passing by." That putdown didn't bother blind Bartimaeus.

If you want to be saved, don't let anybody talk you out of it. The devil will try to stifle your cry for mercy. He will damn your soul if he can. This old world will mock you and try to drown you in its pleasures. The religious world will try to quench your search lest you disturb its ceremonies and rituals. If you want to be saved, don't let anybody or anything keep you from coming to Jesus.

You say, "Somebody will laugh at me." Let them laugh.

Bartimaeus saw his opportunity and he wasn't going to let it pass by. He just kept on calling.

III. THE COMMAND OF THE MASTER (10:49-52)

"And Jesus stood still" (10:49). The cry for mercy will stop deity in its tracks. God's ear is in tune to the cry of that one lost sinner who wants to get saved.

A. Jesus Called the Man (10:49-50)

"Jesus commanded him to be called" (10:49). "Be of good comfort [good cheer], rise; he calleth thee." Bartimaeus must have been thrilled. I don't think many people cared anything about him; he was not the kind of person a lot of folks wanted to be around. He couldn't do much for them. He wasn't outstanding. Not many people paid attention to him. Yet the Lord of glory came through his town one day, he cried to Jesus for mercy, and Jesus said, "Come on over here, Bartimaeus." The word of God went out to Bartimaeus. I can see him as he got up. To think that Jesus was interested in him, to think that someone was really concerned for him. "And he, casting away his garment, rose, and came to Jesus" (10:50). I like that. There is an important truth about salvation there. He had to remove anything that hindered him from getting to Jesus.

We have to abandon some things to come to Jesus. We have to give up sin. We have to turn our backs on sin.

One day a little boy got his hand caught in a vase. Try as they would, they could not get that child's hand out of that vase. They pulled and pulled and finally they had to break the vase to get his hand loose. When they broke the vase they found his little fist balled up with a nickel inside. Some people hold on to that nickel, to that sin in their life, and won't let it go. Jesus says, "I'll forgive you and save you, but you have to cast aside the sin and the weight that so easily beset you and come to me."

B. Jesus Cured the Man (10:51-52)

I see Jesus as He called the man. I see him as He cured the man. "What wilt thou that I should do unto thee?" (10:51). Bartimaeus knew exactly what he wanted: "Lord, that I might receive my sight." He had come to the one who specialized in that.

"Go thy way, thy faith hath made thee whole," Jesus said (10:52). Do you see how Jesus put faith into the situation? Grace is the hand that extends salvation to us. Faith is the hand that reaches out to receive it. "For by grace are ye saved through faith" (Ephesians 2:8). "And immediately he received his sight" (10:52). Right on the spot, sight flooded through those darkened eyes. He saw.

That's how instantly anyone can be saved. The moment you ask God to forgive you of your sins and receive Jesus as your savior, instantaneously, that moment, you are saved.

The Bible says he "followed Jesus in the way." He got in the crowd that was heading to Jerusalem with Jesus. "See that man up there? He's the one who made me see."

A medical missionary performed surgery on a poor blind man that restored his sight. Some time after the operation the man disappeared. Then a few days later the medical missionary opened his door and there was the man with a rope. On that rope were ten more blind people.

If Jesus has made you see, it is incumbent on you to find the blind people in your area and bring them to Jesus.

28

The Triumphal Entry

Mark 11:1-11

THE TIME WAS THE PASSOVER, THAT FEAST WHEN THE JEWS BROUGHT their sacrificial lambs to the city of Jerusalem. Thousands were on the move, cramming the streets. Jesus came too, the "Lamb of God" (John 1:29), presenting himself to Israel as messiah and savior. He had been to Jerusalem many times before; this was the last time He would come. Within days of his triumphal entry, He would be nailed to a cross and would die for the sins of the world.

Normally Jesus seemed to avoid publicity. Although He did spectacular things, He often said, "Don't tell anyone." Now, Jesus was making himself the focus of attention. Why? One reason was to fulfill prophecy. The Bible had predicted that He would enter the city of Jerusalem. Prophecy had foretold that the savior would present himself openly to the Jewish people as their messiah. "Behold, thy King cometh unto thee . . . lowly, and riding upon a donkey" (Zechariah 9:9).

Josephus, the Jewish historian, estimated that between two and three million people were packed into Jerusalem on this occasion. When Jesus inserted himself into that situation, it was like throwing a match into a barrel of gunpowder. It had tremendous explosive potential.

I. A DEMONSTRATION (11:1-6)

The village of Bethany was on the eastern slopes of the mount of Olives, slightly more than a mile outside Jerusalem. As the morning began, Jesus was making the preparations necessary to enter the city. Those preparations demonstrate two basic facets of the life of our Lord.

A. His Deity (11:1-3)

First, He sent two disciples on an errand to go into the village and find a colt or little donkey. He told them they would find a colt tied up that had never been ridden. Its owners would be there and would raise questions about why these disciples were taking it.

When Jesus predicted everything that would take place, He was asserting his deity. Some interpreters of this passage say that this was not a miracle. They say that Jesus had already arranged to get this colt. I find that explanation unsatisfactory. When Jesus sent Simon Peter down to the sea of Galilee, He said, "Go down there, catch a fish, open its mouth, and you will find a coin." Did Jesus arrange that with the fish ahead of time? No, in these things Jesus Christ was demonstrating his omniscience.

When we read the life of the Lord, we always have to keep in mind that, yes, He was a man, yet He was more than a man. When He spoke, it was deity speaking.

Jesus Christ was in control of the entire situation. I like that. That brings me comfort today. He's got all the details of my life in his hands. By him all things hold together (see Colossians 1:17). He upholds "all things by the word of his power" (Hebrews 1:3). He's got you and me in his hands.

In this triumphal entry, Jesus Christ also demonstrated his authority.

B. His Authority (11:3)

Jesus was well known in these villages. Only a few hours prior to this He had raised Lazarus from the dead in Bethany, and that was one reason for such a tremendous congregating of people around him when He rode into Jerusalem.

Jesus now said, "Say ye that the Lord hath need of him." He called himself Lord. "Just tell the owner that the Lord needs him." I see a paradox in that statement. How could the Lord ever have need of anything?

The paradox of his earthly life was that although He was rich, He became poor. He possessed nothing, yet was ruler of all things. Jesus Christ created the cattle on a thousand hills, yet He needed a boat from which to preach his gospel. Jesus Christ created the stars and flung them into place, yet He needed somewhere to lay his head at night. He who created the rushing streams of every river cried, "I thirst." He whose chariot was the clouds said, "I need a donkey on which to ride into Jerusalem." That little donkey is called a colt in the King James Bible and is mentioned four times in these verses.

Is there some significance in that donkey? Well, the Lord had need of him, and the Lord has need of you. When a eunuch who had been to Jerusalem to worship came back empty-hearted, the Holy Spirit of God spoke to Philip and said, "Philip, you go down into the desert and tell him about Jesus Christ" (see Acts 8:26-40). God could have spoken directly from heaven to that eunuch if He had chosen to do so. But the Lord had need of Philip. In his sovereignty and grace God has given you and me the privilege of being used to tell other people about the Lord Jesus Christ. It's a wonderful thing to be a link in the chain that has brought someone to Jesus. Maybe all you did was pray. Maybe all you did was invite somebody to a service. If God could use a donkey, he could certainly use you and me.

Then Jesus said, "And straightway he will send him hither." In other words, "As soon as we are through with your donkey we will send him back. As soon as we have fulfilled the task we will return your property to you." That's the way God works. Anything you give to Jesus He will give back to you—only fuller, richer, more precious. You will be amazed what Jesus will do with what you place in his hands. He will take it, cleanse it, sanctify it, and return it to you far more blessed than it was when you gave it to him.

II. A MANIFESTATION (11:7-10)

The donkey was brought to the Lord Jesus and they put their garments on him as a saddle. It was time for the procession to begin. The crowd of pilgrims began to congregate.

Scripture says that Jesus sat on that donkey which nobody had ridden before. Have you ever tried to ride a wild donkey? I have. There is no more vicious animal on earth. When you try to get on him, he will kick, bite, and buck.

I remember getting on a wild goat one time. I was eighteen years old and pastoring, trying to win boys to the Lord. I'd play basketball with them. I'd go swimming with them. One boy who had a wild goat said, "Preacher, you ever rode a wild goat?" I said, "No." "Would you like to try?" I said, "OK." He said, "Get on it then." They got out that goat and I got on it. That thing took off across that pasture going 190 miles an hour with me holding on for dear life. That goat raced to the other side of the pasture and came to a big old briar bush. It got right to those briars and stopped—but I didn't.

It's rough to ride a goat. It's rough to ride even an old donkey, and you just don't get on donkeys that haven't been ridden. Yet the Lord of glory has dominion over the beasts of the field (Psalm 8:6-7). Jesus sat down on that donkey and the people must have shouted when they saw the miracle of what the Lord had done. They started spreading their garments and cutting down branches from trees to make a carpet out of the dusty road.

A. His Lowliness

Jesus Christ was manifesting his lowliness that day. It was not at all the kind of processional you would expect a king to have. A lowly Nazarene, sitting on a donkey with coats for a saddle, and with a motley crew of people waving palm branches instead of swords. When they came marching into Jerusalem, the Roman soldiers must have snickered. When a victorious Roman general would return from war, elephants, tigers, and other animals would accompany him. The general would be in a chariot pulled by handsome horses. The swords of the soldiers behind him would be lifted high. The streets would be filled with the odor of incense. The whole city would be shouting and rejoicing over the victorious king. Can you imagine how Caesar in Rome would have laughed and mocked as he saw this processional? But this was the beginning of a parade that would ultimately topple the Roman empire. Look at that parade. Look at Christ's followers—all those people He had saved, all those people He had healed.

I'm in that parade. It's a long line, that parade of the followers of the Lord. Are you in that parade? If you are saved, you are in it too.

B. His Loftiness

Listen to what the people shouted, fulfilling another prophecy (Psalm 118:25-26). *Hosanna* means "saved now." "Blessed be he that cometh in the name of the Lord." They were lifting up the Lord Jesus Christ with their praises, and He didn't stop them. Luke said that when the Pharisees heard all of this praising going on, all of this shouting, all of this adoration of Jesus, they said to him, "Why don't you rebuke your disciples?" Jesus answered, "If these don't praise me, the very stones would cry out" (see Luke 19:40).

Jesus will be praised on this earth. As long as God is saving people there will be those who praise him. I for one don't want a rock to do my praising for me. I want to praise him. I want to lift him high. I want to live for him. I want to win souls for him.

III. An Examination (11:11)

"Jesus entered into Jerusalem, and into the temple." It is significant that those thoughts are tied together. Jesus' triumphal entry was an examination of the city and the church, of Jerusalem and the temple.

A. The City

Jesus Christ came into that city of Jerusalem (the "city of peace") where it had been predicted that the messiah would come. Amid the praises and shouts and hosannas of his followers, when He beheld the city He wept (Luke 19:41). Glistening tears welled up in his eyes, dripped down his face, and fell on his tunic. In a situation where one might be tempted to pride and pleasure, tears coursed down the Son of God's face as He looked over that wicked city. He saw human beings with needy hearts.

What do you see when you look at your town or city? If we

could see our cities the way Jesus sees them today, I think we would see young people whose lives are being wrecked by alcohol and drugs. I think we would see businessmen whose lives are empty and meaningless. I think we would see struggling mothers whose absent husbands pay no child support.

I think we would also see lonely and sick old people tottering on the precipice of hell. One more step and they will be there forever. Have we Christians forgotten that the Lord Jesus who looked over Jerusalem with tears flowing down his cheeks taught that when people die without him they go to hell?

B. The Church

The Bible says He "looked round about." It was a look of examination.

What does Jesus see when He comes to our churches? He said that "where two or three are gathered together in my name, there am I in the midst of them" (Matthew 18:20). He walks up and down our church aisles. He moves in and out of the pews. He stops and examines every human heart. He knows what we are like inside.

Where do you stand with Jesus? Not, what does the preacher think about you? Not, what do your friends think of you? When Jesus looks into your heart, what does He see?

29

Fig Trees, Temples, and Mountains
Mark 11:12-26

I. EXAMINE US (11:12-19)
  A. Outward Life (11:12-14)
  B. Inward Life (11:15-19)
II. ENCOURAGE US (11:20-26)
  A. Faith (11:22-24)
  B. Forgiveness (11:25-26)

WE ARE IN THE LAST DAYS OF THE LIFE OF OUR LORD. THE countdown to his death is on. During the day He moved about in Jerusalem, teaching in the temple and in various other places. At night He went back to the village of Bethany.

These verses have a combination of unusual components: a fig tree, the temple, and a mountain. What is God trying to say to us by putting those three together? There are two acts of judgment. The Lord cursed the fig tree and cleansed the temple. There is a tremendous lesson on prayer, when Jesus said that it is possible through prayer to move mountains. In those acts of judgment, the Lord examines us. In his lesson on prayer, He encourages us.

I always marvel at how the Holy Spirit takes his word, wher-

ever we are studying, and applies it to our personal situations. I've seen it happen over and over again in my ministry. Wher-

ever I happen to be teaching in God's word, He seems to have a
message for that particular time and hour.

First, let's look at verses that examine us.

I. EXAMINE US (11:12-19)

A. Outward Life (11:12-14)

One examination has to do with our outer life. Is there any fruit
there?

In this passage we read about the experiences of our Lord with
a fig tree. It was morning, and Jesus was hungry. Notice here the
contrast with the previous day, when we had a display of Jesus'
omniscience. He knew all the details about the donkey. There
we saw that Jesus Christ is God.

In this statement we see that Jesus Christ is also human.
Ahead of him He saw a fig tree. I don't know much about fig
trees but I'm told that when you see leaves you can expect fruit
to be there. This particular fig tree had lots of leaves, so He
expected to find fruit. It gave promise of something that could
satisfy hunger. But when the Lord Jesus got there He found only
leaves. Then He did an unusual thing. He spoke to that fig tree.
As Lord over nature, He said, "You'll never bear fruit again." The
next morning that fig tree was dried up all the way down to the
roots (11:20).

That's the last miracle Mark recorded of our Lord Jesus Christ.
It is the only miracle that Jesus performed which might be interpreted as destructive. What was the Lord doing when He cursed
that fig tree? Why do something so severe, so drastic?

Jesus was trying to teach a lesson. He was describing what He
saw in his people, the children of Israel. In the scriptures the fig
tree many times is a figure of speech or symbol for the nation of
Israel. When Jesus came to the nation of Israel He saw all the
leaves of their outward religion. They had a magnificent temple,
and people from all over the world came there to worship God.
They had elaborate ceremonies and all kinds of sacrifices and
offerings. They had every evidence of a vital relationship with
God. Yet when Jesus came, He found no fruit. They had become
so judgmental, so sectarian in their outlook, that they were of no
benefit to the nations around them.

So Jesus, in cursing the fig tree, was examining the nation.

Basically He was pronouncing his judgment on Israel. And in scarcely thirty-five years the Romans would come and conquer the city of Jerusalem. Not one stone would be left on another. It is a picture of the barrenness of religion.

There is a personal examination for our hearts in this passage of scripture. The question is, when the Lord Jesus examines our lives today, does He find the fruit He has a right to expect? In the sermon on the mount, Jesus talked about this kind of fruit (Matthew 7:16-20). He was saying that the test of reality in anyone's relationship to God is not the leaves but the fruit.

Is there any evidence in your life that you are really a born-again child of God? You may have a lot of leaves, but I'm not talking about leaves. I'm talking about a genuine experience with Jesus Christ that is evidenced by fruit.

Of course, at times we don't act the way a Christian ought to act. But if a tree is basically healthy, there will be some good fruit on it. If a person has really met the Lord Jesus Christ there is going to be a change in his or her life. "If any man be in Christ, he is a new creature" (2 Corinthians 5:17). Is there a change in your life? There's got to be some fruit somewhere. When people look at your life, is there any evidence that you are saved?

You say, "I'm a church member." This is nothing but leaves. "I carry my Bible around." Nothing but leaves. "When I get in a jam, I pray." Nothing but leaves. "I've got a sign on my car that says 'Honk if you love Jesus.'" Nothing but leaves.

Leaves are attractive and beautiful and essential, but they are not a substitute for the real thing. In Luke 13, the Lord told another parable about a fig tree. Here was another fig tree with no fruit. For three years they had been trying without success to get fruit from it. The owner came and said, "Cut it down; why cumbereth it the ground?" The gardener pled to give it one more year to bear fruit.

I once preached a sermon on this topic, "One more year to live." What would you do if you knew you had one more year to live? Would there be any changes in your life? What if you had one more day, twenty-four hours, to live? What would you do? Would you come to the Lord in repentance and faith? If I didn't know as sure as I know the sun came up this morning, if I didn't know that my name was written in the Lamb's book of life, I wouldn't make another move until I knew Jesus as my Lord and savior.

B. Inward Life (11:15-19)

There are two words for *temple* in the New Testament. One word means the inner sanctuary of the temple, the temple proper. The other word is the larger term that included the entire temple area, including the court of the gentiles where non-Jews were allowed to come. This latter word is the word used here. It means that Jesus came to the court of the gentiles, the place where the nations of the world could come, where Jews could share the real God with the world's peoples.

What did Jesus find when He got there? He found a flourishing, booming business. Because people came from long distances for the Passover, it would have been impossible for all of them to bring sacrificial animals. When they got to the temple, however, they had to have an offering, so the priests conveniently went into the animal business. You could buy what you needed—for a price. If you brought your own, it had to pass an inspection to make sure it had no blemish. Then too every worshiper had to pay a temple tax of a half-shekel in Jewish currency. It couldn't be in any other currency. So you had to exchange whatever kind of money you had for Jewish coins—of course with a fifteen percent surcharge.

When you got to this temple area you saw a business going on. Can you picture the house of God with cows over here and sheep over there, mooing and bleating? People were pushing and shoving and money was clinking. Here was a place that was meant to be the house of prayer, where people met God. Instead you heard the noise of a marketplace, you smelled the stench of animal excrement, and you realized that dishonesty and corruption were prevalent.

When Jesus got there, can you imagine the fire in his eyes? "He began to cast out them that sold and bought in the temple, and overthrew the tables of the moneychangers" (11:15). He pushed out those who were selling doves. He wouldn't let anybody carry a vessel through the temple. (The temple was a shortcut from one part of town to the other part of town, so they had started passing through that court of the gentiles to get where they wanted to be.)

When they found out what was going on, the scribes and chief priests made up their minds to destroy him. He had disrupted their business. If you want to find out what a person is, touch his money. Hurt his pocketbook and you will find out what kind of person you are dealing with.

Jesus was raising questions about their inward lives. The house of God, intended to be missionary, had become mercenary. Concern for spiritual reality had become subordinate to monetary matters.

Ephesians 2:21 teaches that the church of God is a holy temple unto the Lord. The church today is God's new temple. I raise this question today: Are there things in the house of God that ought not to be there? Has the church of the Lord become more interested in material things than in spiritual things?

Jesus has become big business in our day. You can make money using the name of Jesus. A lot of folks appear more interested in making money in the name of Jesus than they are in winning souls in the name of Jesus. So be careful what you support. I do not minimize other ministries, but I believe in the local church. I want to see firsthand what's going on. I want to know how the money is being used. I want to know if the church is a soulwinning church. If I were not a member of a soulwinning church I'd get out of it and get in one that is. I don't want to waste my time, my treasure, my talent. I don't want to waste anything that's mine in the few years that God has given me on earth by being part of things that don't contribute toward bringing glory to God and getting lost souls to the Lord Jesus Christ.

Our Lord wants to examine us, but also to encourage us.

II. ENCOURAGE US (11:20-26)

A. Faith (11:22-24)

"Have faith in God," Jesus said. "For verily I say unto you, That whosoever shall say unto this mountain, Be thou removed, and be thou cast into the sea; and shall not doubt in his heart, but shall believe that those things which he saith shall come to pass; he shall have whatsoever he saith" (11:22-23). Was Jesus talking about literal mountains? To be perfectly frank, I have lived in places where there were mountains, and I have not seen great value in any of those mountains being cast into the sea.

Jesus was again using a figure of speech. If there is some mountain of difficulty, if there is some obstacle, Jesus here encourages us by talking about mountain-moving prayer. Do you have any problems that look like mountains in your life? Any obstacles that loom like Mount Everest? If so, Jesus says, you have to tap the power of prayer. You have to pray with faith.

His emphasis was on the object of that faith: "Have faith in God." For many of us, when obstacles come, our faith in God wilts.

The first step to success in spiritual matters is faith in God. God can do anything He wants done. God can send revival. God can save that old hardened sinner. Perhaps you have been witnessing to a friend, but it doesn't seem likely that anything can happen. Don't get discouraged, because God can move that mountain.

B. Forgiveness (11:25-26)

Jesus was saying that not only do you have to be right with God when you pray; you have to be right with others. "Forgive, if ye have ought against any" (11:25). Has anybody done you wrong? Snubbed you? Has anybody really hurt you and you are carrying a grudge in your heart? Well, Jesus said, if you have unforgiveness in your heart, God won't forgive you. God won't forgive you if you won't forgive others.

It's a wonderful thing to know that God forgives us when we sin. In 1 John 1:9 we read that if we confess our sins, He will forgive us.

Suppose at the end of this day, you get down on your knees and say, "Lord I know I have failed you today. I've done some things I shouldn't have done. Please forgive me." God says, "No, I won't." So you go to bed, get up the next morning, and those sins of yesterday are still there. You say, "Lord, I sinned against you yesterday; please forgive me." God says, "No, I'm sorry, I won't forgive you." You go all through that day. Now added to the load of yesterday's sin is today's sins. You say, "Oh, Lord, I've got this heavy load of sins; please forgive me." God says, "No, I won't do it." That is what Jesus was teaching here. If you won't forgive those who have sinned against you, your Father in heaven won't forgive you. The channel of God's forgiveness in your life is dependent on whether or not you forgive those who have mistreated you.

You say, "I can't forget. I'll forgive, but I can't forget." Of course, you can't forget. Psychologists tell us that we don't ever forget anything. (If you're still in school, you may wonder about that!) The point is, you don't have to forgive and forget. You really can't forget, but rather you forgive and forsake. You get rid of that old grudge you have been holding against someone.

Jesus encourages us, reminding us that that lost person can be saved. Revival can come. But we have to have faith in God and be sure that there is nothing in our hearts between us and anybody else.

30

Murder in the Vineyard
Mark 12:1-12

IN ORDER TO UNDERSTAND THIS PASSAGE, WE HAVE TO BEGIN WITH Mark 11:27-33, the account of the Jewish leaders coming to Jesus and asking about his credentials. What right did He have to do the things He was doing?

In reply to their question, Jesus asked them a question: "The baptism of John, was it from heaven, or of men?" (11:30). That put them on the horns of a dilemma. If they said that John's baptism was from heaven, then Jesus would say, "Why didn't you believe him?" If they said that it was of men, they would be in trouble with the people. John the Baptist was popular with the people. So they said, "We don't know" (11:33). "In that case," Jesus said, "I won't tell you where I get my authority" (11:33).

There we see the kind of running battle that was going on between Jesus and those Jewish leaders, which would culminate in his arrest, trial, and crucifixion. In that context, Jesus told this parable of the vineyard.

It is often true that those who talk the most about God know the least about him. It was certainly true in the instance of these Jewish leaders. The Lord Jesus Christ had come and had revealed what God was like, and in return they had murder in their hearts. At that very moment they were plotting how they were going to put him to death. They rejected this revelation of God. So, to illustrate that and to reveal what was in their hearts, Jesus told a parable.

The point of this parable is simple: If you receive God's blessings but reject his Son, you must face God's judgment.

In this parable we see a series of pictures of God, revealing what kind of God He is. Most people have a half-god, a god of their own making. They believe in the kind of god they want to believe in, rather than in the God who is revealed in the Bible. They take the characteristics of God that appeal to them, but neglect what God says elsewhere about himself and how He operates.

This parable reveals God's goodness.

I. God's Goodness (12:1)

A man planted a vineyard, built a hedge around it, and put a vessel (vat) down in the ground to receive the juice as the grapes were crushed. He also erected a watchtower so that the whole enterprise could be protected. Here was a man doing everything to make the vineyard what it ought to be. The lesson from this is that God is a good God. Let me explain. The Bible says, "Behold therefore the goodness . . . of God" (Romans 11:22).

A. True of Israel Historically

The primary point of this parable is that God was good historically to the nation of Israel. The man in the parable represents God. The vineyard represents the nation of Israel. The servants who were sent to the vineyard are the prophets of God. The husbandmen or the farmers are the Jewish leaders. The son in the parable is the Lord Jesus. Jesus was recounting the history of God's goodness to Israel.

"Truly God is good to Israel" (Psalm 73:1). God gave them the land. God gave his law to guide them and to care for them. God sent his prophets and preachers to preach the word to them. Many figures of speech are used to describe the nation of Israel in the Bible. Sometimes Israel is compared to an olive tree. Other times Israel is compared to a fig tree. Here Israel is compared to a vineyard. The Lord was saying, "I planted my nation in the land. I cared for them. I cultivated them. I gave them every provision necessary for their lives."

B. True of Us Personally

God has been good to us. He has given us this world, designed for our blessing and benefit. This whole earth has been prepared by God for profitable human habitation. The world is like a giant mall. Everything necessary for our sustenance in life has been deposited there by God. God has placed food in the ground so we can eat. God has placed the ingredients in this world so we can have clothing. God has given us air to breathe.

When we think about how good God is, shouldn't we be thankful? Every day shouldn't we thank God for all the good things He gives us? The scriptures teach that the goodness of God is intended to lead us to repentance. The least we can do as his people, as men and women made in his image (Genesis 1:27), is to turn our lives totally over to him.

II. GOD'S WITNESS (12:2-8)

God has not left himself without a witness (Acts 14:17). In other words, God has revealed himself.

A. He Sent His Servants (12:2-5)

In this parable the owner sent one servant, then another servant. Historically, God sent Israel a series of prophets, a series of preachers, to witness to his goodness and to call them to faith. What happened when God sent those prophets? Jesus said that the husbandmen rejected them. They beat them, sent them away empty, and even killed some of them. A series of rejections took place.

A terrible inconsistency exists in the human heart. We have a penchant for rejecting the goodness and witness of our creator.

God has given us certain freedoms. In this parable these husbandmen were allowed to farm the land as they pleased. They were sharecroppers. Somebody else owned the land. They worked that land and the owner of the land gave them certain liberties.

God gives us freedom to choose a lot of things. We can choose our clothes. We can choose our food. We can choose where to live, where to worship.

The nation of Israel rejected the witness of the servants of God who came to them. The same thing is true today. God reveals himself in this beautiful world of nature. God has given his witness to every person's heart (Romans 1:19). But what do people do? Instead of receiving that divine witness, they worship their intellect. They turn away from the revelation of God and indulge in foolish imaginations (Romans 1:21). They turn to foolishness. Instead of worshiping, loving, and serving God, they start living for material things. Then over and over again God sends his messengers, but people reject them. Still God is patient.

Why does He give people opportunity after opportunity? The scriptures teach that God is longsuffering toward us. He is "not willing that any should perish, but that all should come to repentance" (2 Peter 3:9).

B. He Sent His Son (12:6-8)

Then, Jesus said, "Having yet therefore one son, his well-beloved, he sent him also last unto them" (12:6). God's ultimate revelation of himself was his Son. He had sent prophets, messengers (culminating in John the Baptist), and last of all, He sent his Son. Jesus was God's beloved son (Matthew 3:17).

When the farmers saw this son coming they said, "This is the heir." In Hebrews 1:2, the Bible says, "God . . . hath in these last days spoken unto us by his Son, whom he hath appointed heir of all things." When we accept Jesus Christ we become joint heirs with him, and God's fullness is ours.

What happened in this parable? What did they do? These farmers, these sharecroppers, said, "Let's kill his son the heir, and the vineyard will be ours." When the Lord Jesus came to Israel, God's chosen people, they arrested him, took him outside the city gates as if He were unfit to walk on their streets, drove him with nails to a cross, and smashed him to death. A murder took place in the vineyard.

I love that beautiful spiritual, "Were you there when they crucified my Lord?" The truth is, you were there and I was there. The Bible teaches that we all had a part in the death of God's Son.

I don't think it would be any different today. They say that people are more civilized now than they used to be. I don't think so. I have the feeling that if the Lord Jesus Christ came and walked on earth today, people would do exactly as they did when He came two thousand years ago. When men saw Jesus, they saw their own sins and failures. Instead of receiving Jesus, they stamped him out.

We are living in a world, a vineyard, that is stained with blood. The blood of God's dear Son, Jesus, has been spilt.

Jesus said in John 16:9 that when the Holy Spirit comes, He will convict the world of sin. What is the greatest sin? The sin of rape, cruelly violating the body of another? That's a terrible sin. The sin of child molestation? Child pornography? Murder? That's not what Jesus said. The Holy Spirit would convict the world of sin, "because they believe not on me." This is the greatest sin.

III. GOD'S STERNNESS (12:9-11)

"What shall therefore the lord of the vineyard do?" (12:9). Those farmers had the idea that the owner was way off in a far country. A lot of people have the idea that that's the way God is.

How close is God to you? How real is God to you? Is God a personal God who is involved and interested in his creation, or is He off in outerspace with very little connection to this world?

A time comes when God's patience is exhausted. Did you notice the three dots (the ellipsis) when I quoted Romans 11:22 earlier in this chapter? The entire phrase reads like this: "Behold therefore the goodness *and severity* of God." Too many people want to see only the goodness of God. They do not understand his *sternness* aspect.

There comes a time when only God's judgment remains. We don't like to hear that. But if we are going to be true to the teachings of the scriptures, we have to believe everything Jesus said. When people reject God's Son, there comes a time when they must face God's judgment.

A. Abrupt (12:9)

Do you see how suddenly judgment came? Many years ago my wife and I were in Atlanta watching Georgia Tech play football.

In front of us a man was sitting with his popcorn, Coke, and hot dog, watching the game. We were cheering and having a great time, when all of a sudden that man fell down. We rushed to him. In just a few moments the paramedics came and tried to start his heart—to no avail. One moment he was watching a ball-game. The next moment he was dead and in eternity.

B. Absolute (12:10-11)

In the book of Revelation, Jesus is pictured as both a lamb and a lion. Do you want to meet him as the lamb of God who died for your sins, or as the lion of the tribe of Judah who comes to judge?

Jesus suddenly changed the metaphor in his parable from a vineyard to a building. "The stone which the builders rejected is become the head of the corner" (12:10). God has reversed men's assessment of his Son. God has said, "My son is the only way of salvation." "Neither is there salvation in any other: for there is none other name under heaven given among men, whereby we must be saved." (Acts 4:12).

We either receive or reject Jesus. If we receive him, we experience God's graciousness. If we reject him, we receive God's sternness.

God has done all He can do. It's your move now. Have you said yes to Jesus his Son?

31

Answers for Life's Questions

Mark 12:13-34

A T THIS POINT IN MARK'S GOSPEL THE DIE IS CAST. THE ENEMIES of Jesus had determined that whatever it took, they were going to kill him. Here we see them trying to trick him into saying something self-incriminating. They began with flattery: "We know how impartial and straightforward and spiritually minded you are. So tell us, is it lawful to give tribute to Caesar, or not?" (see 12:14). It was the first of three loaded questions. They needed to trump up some charges, some reason, to put Jesus to death. But the Lord's answers to those questions are important to us also.

Jesus is the great question-answerer. He has ultimate answers to all the questions we face in life.

One of the criticisms some people make of the church is that we are answering questions that nobody is asking. I say that we are answering the questions that people ought to be asking: "What is life all about?" "Is there an eternity?" "What about life and death?" "Heaven and hell?" "Where did I come from?" "Where am I going?" The Bible has the answers to those questions.

The first question the Lord Jesus answered here was about life's political authorities.

I. LIFE'S POLITICAL AUTHORITIES (12:13-17)

Although the Pharisees and Herodians were enemies, in their common hatred of Jesus they joined together in order "to catch him in his words" (12:13). The word *catch* is the word used to describe catching a wild animal by hunters. They covered their traps with flowers of flattery, trying to set Jesus up. "Now, Lord, we know that you don't show favorites. We know that you teach the truth. We know that you are very important." Then they popped the question about Caesar. It was a burning question in their day, a political quandary the people faced frequently. It is reminiscent of the basic church-state relationships we also discuss—what is the role of the state in the life of individuals? Then as now, opinions differed.

The Herodians said that everyone ought to pay tribute, taking the side of the government. The Pharisees said, "Not on your life. It would be unfaithfulness and disloyalty to God. We shouldn't pay taxes at all." This particular tax was a kind of poll tax. Every adult in Israel was required by Roman law to pay this tax once a year, a little silver coin with a value of something less than our quarter. It was a source of irritation to the common people. If Jesus said they should pay the tax, they would be annoyed. If Jesus said they shouldn't pay that tax, He would be in trouble with the Roman government. So they thought they had him between a rock and a hard place.

A. The Authority of Government (12:17)

Notice what Jesus' response was. "Why tempt ye me? bring me a penny [that is, that silver coin], that I may see it. And they brought it" (12:15-16). Jesus took that coin in his strong fingers and asked, "Whose is this image and superscription?" When they looked at the coin they saw the image of Tiberias Caesar on one side. On the other side they saw a superscription that basically assigned qualities of deity to the Roman emperor. Yes, it was clearly Caesar's. Then Jesus replied, "Render to Caesar the things that are Caesar's" (12:17). It was a brilliant reply. By the fact that these men were using Roman coinage, they were admitting that Rome had a legitimate role in their lives.

It *is* the right of government to impose certain requirements on its citizens. The Bible makes clear that Christians are to be good citizens. We are to pay our bills. We are to obey the laws of the land. We are to pay a stipulated portion of taxes. The word of God recognizes that government has certain authorities over life. If we didn't have the state, if we didn't have government, society would be chaotic. Some guidelines are necessary for a society to function the way it ought to function. You and I cannot provide our own water supply, our own road system, our own police protection. We do receive certain privileges, certain benefits, from government. So our Lord said, if you are going to receive the benefits, you must assume certain responsibilities.

B. The Authority of God (12:17)

But also He said, "Render . . . to God the things that are God's" (12:17). Jesus got out of their trap.

Here are two realms of authority in human life: the realm of government and the realm of God. Just as Caesar's image was inscribed on the coin, the Bible says that you and I are made in the image of God. God has created us in his likeness.

Something about you is like God. When God made you, He made you a physical body. That's not what's like God. When God made you, He made you with a soul. That's not what's like God. When God made you, He made you a spirit and that's what's like God. Jesus said, "God is a Spirit: and they that worship him must worship him in spirit and in truth" (John 4:24). Something about you responds to God. Something about you relates to God. Jesus said, "Give to Caesar what is his, and give to God what is his."

We have no right to run our lives. We belong to God. The human spirit has been implanted there by God. We are responsible to respond to God. God is interested not in taking taxes from us, but in redeeming us, changing us, and making our lives what they ought to be.

Have you rendered to God what is his?

II. LIFE'S DOCTRINAL REALITIES (12:18-27)

The Sadducees were a relatively small group in Jewish society, but they were the wealthy aristocratic class. Although most of the high priests came from the Sadducees, the Sadducees didn't believe in the supernatural. They were what we might call the rationalists or the liberals of their day. They didn't believe in angels. They didn't believe in resurrection.

They had concocted a little story to make people who did believe in resurrection look foolish. Coming to Jesus, they said, "Master, Moses wrote unto us, If a man's brother die, and leave his wife behind him, and leave no children, that his brother should take his wife and raise up seed unto his brother" (12:19). They were referring to a practice of levirate marriage, a means devised in Jewish law so that if a man died, his family line could be maintained (Deuteronomy 25:5). It also assured that family property could remain in the same family.

"Now, Lord, this man married this woman, but he died and they didn't have any children. So his brother married her and he died. Then the third and fourth until seven of them died, but with no children. In the resurrection whose wife is she going to be?"

The Sadducees were making light of life-and-death issues. They were talking about the afterlife in a frivolous way.

Every one of us is one day closer to death than we were yesterday. The older we get, the more we think about death. Someone has said that death is a subject that people spend a lifetime trying not to think about. Yet death is the inevitable experience of every one of us, unless the Lord Jesus Christ comes before our individual lifespans are lived out. President Eisenhower once said, "I am interested in eternity. I am going to spend the rest of my life there."

Is there an afterlife? Is there a resurrection? I think that one of the reasons that Easter is such a big day is that deep in the human heart is that desire to know—is there life after death? Job asked, "If a man die, shall he live again?" (Job 14:14).

That dad of yours who died a few years ago, will you ever see him again? That mother of yours, will you ever see her again? The Sadducees said, "No. Never." Were they snickering as they couched their cynical question to Jesus?

A. The Power of God (12:24-25)

Jesus was not smiling when He replied, "Do ye not therefore err, because ye know not the scriptures, neither the power of God?"

(12:24). That's the best definition of a theological liberal I have ever read. A liberal doesn't know either the power of God or the word of God. Clearly, if you take away the power of God and take away the word of God, there is no resurrection.

But then Jesus went on, "For when they shall rise from the dead, they neither marry, nor are given in marriage; but are as the angels which are in heaven" (12:25). He was saying that the power of God is going to transform life in the afterlife to a new and different plane of existence. The marriage relationship, so beautiful and meaningful right now, is going to be insignificant in comparison to what God is going to do by his power in the afterlife. "Eye hath not seen, nor ear heard, neither have entered into the heart of man, the things which God hath prepared for them that love him. But God hath revealed them unto us by his Spirit" (1 Corinthians 2:9-10). God gives us just a little glimpse of a wonderful place called heaven in the next world.

What is it going to be like? I am not sure what it is going to be like. I read what the Bible says. I read the book of Revelation. I read about that next world, with its streets of gold, and all of those things. But I think that when God revealed to John on the isle of Patmos what the next world was going to be like, it was so wonderful that language broke down (Revelation 1:9). John couldn't begin to describe how glorious it's going to be when the child of God steps through the door of death into that next world.

Jesus said you will be like the angels in heaven. He didn't say you are going to be an angel, but you are going to be *as* the angels; that is, you are going to be in a new kind of existence. You are going to be in relationships that so transcend our present earthly human relationships that they will be unimportant. "Will I know my wife in heaven?" Yes, you will know her, but there aren't going to be any wedding bells ringing. You won't be renting tuxedos. Nobody is going to be getting married. It's going to be a higher plane of relationship.

What is the resurrection body going to be like? Jesus had a resurrection body that was able to go through closed doors. One minute He wasn't there, the next minute He was there. I think we will be able to move around with the speed of thought. I think there'll be all kinds of good things to do. In this life we miss out on many meaningful possibilities, but in heaven that won't be so. The best things in this world are only the barest hint of all the wonderful things that are awaiting us there.

B. The Word of God (12:26-27)

Jesus was dealing here with the great question of life after death. "And as touching the dead, that they rise: have ye not read in the book of Moses, how in the bush God spake unto him, saying, I am the God of Abraham, and the God of Isaac, and the God of Jacob? He is not the God of the dead, but the God of the living: ye therefore do greatly err" (12:26-27). The living God is not the God of dead people but the God of living people. Abraham, Isaac, and Jacob were long since dead, yet God referred to them as having conscious existence and in relationship with him.

When death comes, our relationships to this world and to others in this world are changed, but we do not lose our relationship to God. When a person is saved, she or he is "in Christ." The apostle Paul said that he desired to depart and be with Christ (Philippians 1:23). When you are saved, Christ comes to be with you. When you as a believer die, you go to be with Christ. Death and the afterlife for the believer are just more of Christ, more fullness in our relationship with him.

Only one person can speak authoritatively about life after death, and that is the Lord Jesus. He is the only one who ever died, went into the afterlife, and came back to this life.

One of these days they are going to take this body of mine, embalm it, put it in a casket, roll it into a church somewhere—and somebody is going to say, "Poor old Vines, he's dead." I think when they do, I'll be saying, "That's a lie." I will be more alive then than I have ever been in my entire life.

III. LIFE'S SPIRITUAL PRIORITIES (12:28-34)

"And one of the scribes [he seems to have been more sincere than the others] came, and having heard them reasoning together, and perceiving that he had answered them well, asked him, Which is the first commandment of all?" (12:28). That was a big question among the scribes.

The scribes were the experts in the law, the biblical authorities in those days. If you wanted an answer to a Bible question you checked with the scribes. They had so meticulously studied all the commandments in the Old Testament that in the Pentateuch alone they had isolated 613 commandments of God. Then they

had divided those commandments into heavy commandments
and light commandments. Some were more significant than others. The big question was, What is the greatest commandment
of all? Jesus answered:

> The first of all the commandments is, Hear, O Israel; the
> Lord our God is one Lord. And thou shalt love the Lord
> thy God with all thy heart, and with all thy soul, and with
> all thy mind, and with all thy strength: this is the first
> commandment. And the second is like, namely this,
> Thou shalt love thy neighbor as thyself. There is none
> other commandment greater than these (12:29-31).

A. Vertical: Love for God (12:29-30)

Jesus brought all the commandments down to two. The number-
one priority is to love the Lord thy God. Love him with your
whole being—heart, soul, mind, and strength. Love him with
everything you've got.

B. Horizontal: Love for Others (12:31)

Then a second priority comes right alongside the first. Love your
neighbor as yourself. People talk a lot about loving their neighbors as themselves. That's good and we should. But we can't
obey the second commandment until we obey the first commandment. We can't love others the way we ought to love them
until we love the Lord the way we ought to love him.

To say we love the Lord is one thing, but we show that we love
the Lord by our actions, by the things we do, by the life we live.

The Lord wants us to love him. The Lord longs for us to love
him. He is the God of love. "God commendeth his love toward
us, in that, while we were yet sinners, Christ died for us"
(Romans 5:8). When we understand and respond to his love in
faith, and receive Jesus, the love of God is spread abroad in our
hearts through the Holy Spirit.

The scribe saw how well Jesus had answered and responded,
"Master, thou hast said the truth: for there is one God; and there
is none other but he" (12:32). And when Jesus saw that the man
answered discreetly (or wisely) He looked at him and said, "Thou

art not far from the kingdom of God" (12:34). Jesus was saying, "You are right on the verge of the kingdom of God. You understand that God loves you and that you must love him in return. You are just one step from salvation. That step is to receive me as your personal savior."

32

The Widow's Mite
Mark 12:38-44

I. WHERE JESUS SAT (12:41)
   A. In the Temple (12:41)
   B. At the Treasury (12:41)
II. WHOM JESUS SAW (12:41-42)
   A. Money
   B. Motives
III. WHAT JESUS SAID (12:43-44)
   A. Her Liberality
   B. Her Sacrificiality
   C. The Totality of Her Gift

THIS SHORT PARAGRAPH AT THE END OF MARK 12 IS A WELCOMED relief. It's like a lovely flower in a cucumber patch. The Lord Jesus had been doing battle with the scribes, the Pharisees, and the Sadducees. They were a great burden, a source of misery to his heart. But in contrast this woman was a source of great encouragement to him. As far as we know, Jesus didn't speak to her and she didn't speak to him. Perhaps she never knew that Jesus even noticed her. Yet what she did was so beautiful that it has been memorialized forever on the pages of scripture.

She was unnamed, yet she has a place in the Bible Hall of Fame. She has become one of the best-known characters in our Lord's life. She has become the heroine of all those unnamed and unnoticed saints of God who keep our churches going. She represents those who, just because they love Jesus, do the work of the Lord unselfishly.

First, we must notice the contrast between this widow and the scribes in the preceding verses (12:38-40). They were interested in wearing long, flowing robes of honor. She was garbed in widow's clothing. They were concerned to receive honorific salutations in the marketplaces. Probably few people spoke to this poor widow as she passed by. When they went to the synagogues, to social gatherings, and to parties, they were given the chief places. She was probably anonymous in most situations and certainly was not invited to the upper crust's soirees. They were interested in all they could get out of life. She was interested in what she could give in life. They received the condemnation of the Lord Jesus. She received his commendation.

I. WHERE JESUS SAT (12:41)

A. In the Temple (12:41)

Jesus was sitting in the temple. He had been teaching there, dealing with the scribes and Pharisees.

B. At the Treasury (12:41)

Specifically we are told that Jesus was sitting "against the treasury," the place where the people brought their freewill offerings. It was known as the women's court. Alongside the inside walls of the women's court were thirteen collection boxes, each labeled to designate what the offering in it was for. Because it was Passover time, Jerusalem was filled with worshipers. People were giving tremendous amounts of money (12:41).

II. WHOM JESUS SAW (12:41-42)

Jesus was interested in people. The word *beheld* indicates that He was more than just an indifferent spectator. It doesn't mean just a passing glance, but rather "to look with interest and perception."

A. Money

Jesus is interested in what people do with their money. The Bible nowhere says that money is evil; rather, it says that the *love of money* is the root of all evil (1 Timothy 6:10). If you tell me how a person relates to his or her money, I suspect I can tell you something about how that person relates to God.

So, as Jesus watched, He saw the wealthy cast in much. If God has blessed you with a large salary or a large inheritance, then you ought to give large gifts. But you must never get to the point that you feel you have been blessed financially because of *you*. It's not your ingenuity or genius that has enabled you to make money if you have made money. Do you think your brains have produced what you are able to do? Well, just one submicroscopic alteration in the chemical combination of your genes and you would become a blubbering idiot.

Everything you have comes from God. Everything you get is because God has given it to you (Deuteronomy 8:18). Everything you have—that job, that salary—comes as a blessing from the Lord.

What would Christian schools be today without people who have money giving it to build buildings and see things grow? Where would churches be if it weren't for the generosity of God's faithful saints giving their money to build buildings, send missionaries, and do the work of the Lord? If God has blessed you with large amounts of money, I exhort you to use that money now for Jesus. Don't leave it for your children to fuss over. Pray that God will help you be faithful in what you do with it.

Money can do more *to* you than it can do *for* you. Money is a good servant but a poor master. When you learn to give, you learn to control your money and not let it control you.

Jesus was also watching as that widow gave her two mites, two little pings in the temple treasury.

Jesus sees the little things that most people never see. The hand that formed the sun and moon and stars is the hand that formed the wing of the fly and the tongue of the gnat. Little deeds done unselfishly in his name and for his glory are important to him. Don't ever think that what you have is too little for him to notice.

B. Motives

Jesus also saw people's motives in giving. He beheld how the people gave (12:41). See that little word *how*. He was not so interested in what they gave as in how they gave. He was seeing some things that nobody else could see. He was looking at the motives of their hearts. He was concerned about why this widow did what she did. Jesus is concerned about why you do what you do.

In Matthew 6, Jesus made clear that what mattered was not giving, fasting, or praying, but why a person did those things.

Why do you give? The IRS doesn't care what your motive is in giving. All it is interested in is the figures on the tax form. But God cares what your motive is. God is interested in why you give. Are you giving just to get a tax write-off, or is your motive that you love the Lord Jesus and want to get his work done on this earth?

III. What Jesus Said (12:43-44)

A. Her Liberality

Jesus called his disciples to him and pointed that widow out. He wanted them to perceive the liberality of her gift. "This poor widow hath cast more in, than all they which have cast into the treasury" (12:41). On human scales that was not true, but God weighs things on another set of scales. Furthermore, millions of dollars have been given because of this woman's example. Jesus noted the liberality of her gift.

B. Her Sacrificiality

"They did cast in of their abundance; but she of her want did cast in." They gave out of their plenty; she gave out of her poverty. For her it was a sacrifice to give. When she gave those two mites, she gave everything she had. She didn't have anything left. She gave sacrificially.

What is important in the matter of giving is not how much you give but how much you have left.

C. The Totality of Her Gift

Jesus said, She has given "even all her living" (12:44). She had not one thin penny to buy bread for the next day. Those other people had plenty to fall back on. They had plenty for a rainy day. She didn't have one thing. She cast herself totally on the mercy and faithfulness of God.

This Jesus, who complimented the widow for giving her all literally, gave his all on Calvary's cross for us. The question is, What will we give in response?

33

Blueprint for the End

Mark 13:1-37

GOD HAS PLACED WITHIN US AN INTEREST IN THE FUTURE, AN awareness that life as we know it is not going to continue indefinitely. There is going to be a time of the end.

The devil has used in detrimental ways our innate desire to know the future. The devil has those who claim to foretell what the future is going to bring. So people turn to psychics and they make their predictions. Astrologers syndicate daily horoscopes in newspapers. In the midst of all those satanic imitations, some Christians raise the question, "Is it possible for God's people to know what's going to take place in the future?"

Of course, we know certain aspects of the answer to that question. The scriptures give us some awareness of what we can expect.

Here in Mark 13 we have a kind of blueprint of the end times. But we need to understand the context. The Lord Jesus had been in the temple, dealing with those who had determined to put him to death. The temple represents the ultimate failure of the Jews to know God in a personal way. Although dedicated to his worship, the temple had now become a den of robbers and a place of merchandise. When the Lord Jesus walked away from the temple that day, He stunned his disciples by saying, "Your house is left unto you desolate" (Matthew 23:38). That was more than the disciples could understand. The most substantial thing they knew in their national life was this magnificent temple. It was an imposing building, built out of beautiful marble. When you looked at Jerusalem from a distance and the sun was shining, that temple was like a magnificent colossus standing there above the city. Jews knew nothing more solid, nothing more permanent-appearing, than the temple of God.

The disciples in a tone of incredulity replied, "Lord, look at this temple. Look at these massive stones." Some of those stones weighed a hundred tons. They were forty feet long, eighteen feet wide. Hearing them say that, Jesus said, "Do you see these stones? Do you see this building? Not one stone will be left upon another. It will all come down" (13:2). Can you imagine how they reacted?

We know that that is exactly what took place. In A.D. 70 the Romans came and invaded Jerusalem. Although the general had commanded that the temple should be spared, a soldier tossed a torch, the fire began, and before it was over the temple was destroyed. All there is today of that temple is what the Jews call the Wailing Wall.

When Jesus made that prediction, the disciples wanted to know when those things were going to take place (13:4). So, moving from their question about the destruction of the temple, Jesus leapt out into the future and discussed the time of the end. The destruction of the temple was a pre-picture of that period when the Lord would deal with the earth in judgment and there would be, as our Lord called it, "great tribulation on this earth." In this chapter the Lord noted basically three aspects.

I. PRETRIBULATION MARKS (13:5-8)

A. Spiritual Deception (13:5-6)

Describing the closing days of the age, Jesus cautioned, "Take heed lest any man deceive you" (13:5). One mark of the pretribulation days will be spiritual deception. Jesus said, "Be very careful. Take heed in those days. There will be those who will profess to be Christ and will deceive people spiritually" (13:6-9; 22-23).

In every age there have been those who have claimed to be Christ. In our day there is the false Jesus of the cults, or the false Jesus of the gurus of eastern religions, or the false Jesus of liberal theologians. God's people need to be careful that the Jesus we follow is the Jesus we see in the pages of the New Testament. As we approach the time of the end, it is important for us to be observant and discerning of all the false religions that will come. They will do signs and wonders, supernatural miracles. But on the basis of this scripture and many other scriptures it is clear that the devil can give power to false teachers and false prophets to perform signs and wonders. The thing we have to look for is the character of the teacher and the content of his message. Is it consistent with the word of God?

B. International Disruption (13:7-8)

Another mark of the pretribulation days will be international disruption. Jesus said there will be wars and rumors of wars. In almost every part of the globe today there is war. There is war in the Middle East, fighting in Lebanon, conflict in Central America.

C. Physical Destruction (13:8)

The pretribulation days will be marked by physical destruction, earthquakes, famines. Jesus specifically said, however, that those things in and of themselves are not an indication that the end is near. He said,

—"Be not troubled [don't let these kinds of things bother you]."
—"The end shall not be yet."
—"These are the beginnings of sorrows."

To some extent deception, disruption, and destruction have characterized every age since Jesus spoke those words. There has never been a time that was not characterized by false religions, international turmoil, and physical disasters. Such things are the beginning of sorrows (literally, the beginning of pains). The word Jesus used means the pains of death, death throes, as well as the pains of a mother giving birth to a child. These will be the death throes of an old age that is passing out, but also the birth pains of a new age that is about to be born. They will grow in intensity and when they get closer and closer together, these are the indications to us that the consummation of the age is approaching.

Then Jesus moved on to describing a period of time known as the tribulation.

II. TRIBULATION MISERIES (13:9-23)

A. Personal Miseries (13:9-13)

Jesus said that believers would be delivered up to synagogue councils; they would be beaten; all kinds of persecutions and sufferings would take place. All of that happened to the first disciples, the men that Jesus was talking to right then.

The early Christians went through severe persecution. Some of them were martyred for their faith. Since that time, believers in all ages have experienced all kinds of persecution and hostility.

But there will come a time on this earth which the Lord calls the great tribulation, a time of unprecedented anguish. Notice what will take place. On the one hand there will be hatred against believers such as they have never known before. On the other hand there will be great effectiveness in preaching the gospel as never before. God made a promise to believers that when they are in a time where they have no opportunity to prepare what they are going to say, in those situations when they are called on to answer for their faith in the Lord Christ, the Holy Spirit will give them the words to say.

In those days, Jewish believers who have received Christ as their savior will spread out over the world and will preach the gospel to all nations. Revelation 7 says that a multitude of gentiles that cannot be numbered will be brought to faith in Jesus in those days.

B. National Miseries (13:14-23)

In the book of Daniel there is a prediction of the abomination of desolation. A world ruler will come on the scene during these tribulation days, who will solve the problem of the Middle East. That's one problem the leaders of the world haven't been able to deal with.

This world ruler will be a scintillating statesman. He will

make a treaty with the Jews for a period of seven years and will allow them to rebuild their temple. The Jews will reinstitute their sacrifices and systems of offerings. It will appear that there is peace on the earth. But in the middle of that tribulation time, according to scripture, after three and one-half years, this world ruler will do a dangerous and damnable thing. He will have an image of himself constructed. He will order that that image be placed in the temple and that he be worshiped as God by the whole world. That image will stand in a place, Jesus said, where it ought not. It will be an abomination of desolation. The Jews will refuse to go there anymore and, Jesus said, when that happens, if you are in Judea you had better flee to the mountains (13:14). If you are out in the field, don't go back to get your clothes. If you are up on the rooftop, don't go down inside to rescue anything. A time of unprecedented trouble and horror and misery on this earth is ahead. There is no time to lose. The world has never known and will never know again such an atmosphere of terror. The antichrist (that's who he is), this world ruler, will impose his domination on the world and exact its worship. All those who will not bow down to his image will be slain. That's what Jesus predicted will take place.

At that point in time it will appear that the antichrist and the devil are in control of the world. It will look as if God has lost his sovereignty over the whole universe. But if you are born again, you won't be here then.

III. POST-TRIBULATION MANIFESTATIONS (13:24-27)

A. God Will Shake His Creation (13:24-25)

"But in those days, after that tribulation, the sun shall be darkened, and the moon shall not give her light. And the stars of heaven shall fall, and the powers that are in heaven shall be shaken" (13:24-25). Just when it looks as if the devil has control of this universe, God is going to shake his creation. God does that from time to time. Sometimes puny man gets the idea he is running this thing. Sometimes man thinks he is in control of things down here. Then God shakes the universe and lets him know. God touches the universe and the lightning crackles. God touches his universe and the thunder booms. An earthquake rocks and rolls. A volcano spews up its innards.

One of these days there will be disturbances in the heavens. The sun will turn black as midnight. The moon will be like a burned-out lightbulb. Stars will fall. "The powers that are in heaven shall be shaken" (13:25). God will put an earthquake up there in the heavens. The great God of this universe will do something about a world that has turned its back on Jesus.

B. God Will Send His Christ (13:26-27)

"And then shall they see the Son of man coming in the clouds with great power and glory" (13:26). Jesus is going to come back and take charge. He will send for his elect wherever they may be at that time.

The second coming of Jesus to this earth will be very different from his first coming. The first time, He came in humility. This time He will come in power and glory. The first time, He came to suffer and die. This time He will come to reign as king of kings and lord of lords on this earth.

Did you know you are going to be with him? You are. In Revelation 19:11-16 it talks about the heavens opening and the Lord Jesus Christ coming out on a white horse. Then, the Bible says, the armies of heaven will follow on white horses. You had better learn to ride a horse, because you are going to have one. You are going to come riding out of heaven with Jesus back down to this earth. You don't have to worry about training to fight. You won't have to do any fighting. The Lord Jesus is going to win this battle. He will conquer the devil and subdue a rebellious remnant by the word out of his mouth. He will bring everything into submission. This world will become the kingdom of our God and of his Christ forever and forever.

Jesus then wrapped it up with two great words of encouragement for believers. We are to learn from the parable of the fig tree. When you see the leaves coming out, you know it's about time for summer. Just about any day now it's going to be summer.

The first word that Jesus laid out before us is *be watching.* We ought to live "looking for that blessed hope, and the glorious appearing of the great God and our Saviour Jesus Christ" (Titus 2:13).

The second word is *be working.*

> For the Son of man is as a man taking a far journey, who left his house, and gave authority to his servants, and to

every man his work, and commanded the porter to watch.
Watch ye therefore: for ye know not when the master of
the house cometh, at even, or at midnight, or at the cock-
crowing, or in the morning: Lest coming suddenly he find
you sleeping. And what I say unto you I say unto all,
Watch (13:34-37).

This is no time to be asleep.

34

Do What You Can
Mark 14:1-9

I.   THE WOMAN'S DEVOTION (14:3)
   A. Its Costliness (14:3)
   B. Its Recklessness (14:3)
II. THE DISCIPLES' REACTION (14:4-5)
   A. The Mentality It Revealed (14:4-5)
   B. The Carnality It Revealed (14:4-5)
III. THE LORD'S EMOTION (14:6-9)
   A. The Loving Nature of Her Deed (14:7-8)
   B. The Lasting Nature of Her Deed (14:9)

IN MARK 14 WE SEE HUMAN NATURE AT ITS WORST AND AT ITS BEST. Here a woman expressed her love for the Lord Jesus in such a meaningful way that He instructed gospel preachers throughout the ages to tell her story.

In just a few hours He would die on the cross, yet in the closing hours of his life the Lord Jesus went to a supper in his honor. The supper was held in the house of a man named Simon, the leper. This man had evidently been healed by Jesus and he was so appreciative that he got together a group of his friends and had a supper in honor of Jesus. There in that lovely scene did they share their testimonies of what Jesus had done in their lives? Did they pray together? Surely they fellowshiped together, they loved Jesus together.

In that atmosphere we are told about a lovely deed done to Jesus by a grateful disciple.

I. The Woman's Devotion (14:3)

In the midst of all this a woman came in with a box of very expensive ointment. She opened it and poured its entire contents on Jesus' head. John says that it was poured on Jesus' feet as well. Then, according to John, she wiped Jesus' feet with her hair. It was a beautiful act of devotion on the part of that woman.

A. Its Costliness (14:3)

This particular perfumed ointment was worth about a year's wages of a common laboring man. Only the very wealthy could afford it. This may mean that this woman—her name was Mary, the sister of Martha—was quite well-to-do. Mary loved the Lord Jesus and that is what caused her devotion to be so very costly. I have come to believe that if love is real love, if you love someone the way you ought to love him, it's always going to be a costly thing in your life. In the Old Testament, David said, "Neither will I offer burnt offerings unto the Lord my God of that which doth cost me nothing" (2 Samuel 24:24).

Has your love for Jesus cost you anything lately? Have you given what you could? Have you done what you could?

B. Its Recklessness (14:3)

In those days when a guest came into your home it was customary to take a few drops of perfume and put it on that person's head. But this act was an absolutely lavish gesture. Mary poured it all on the Lord Jesus Christ.

Love is kind of reckless. If you are a man, do you remember when you first fell in love? You just fell head over heels in love. Nothing was too much for her. Love is also extravagant; it doesn't necessarily know where to draw the line.

I pray that God will help every one of us to get carried away with the Lord Jesus Christ, get sold out completely to him, and do whatever we have to do to get his job done. In Romans 16, speaking of Priscilla and Aquila, Paul said in effect, "For my life, they have risked their lives." The word there was a gambling term that meant to toss the dice. Paul was saying that they had gambled their lives for his life. In doing so, they were reckless in their devotion to the Lord Jesus Christ. This is the kind of devotion we have pictured here as Mary came and poured the fragrant ointment on Jesus.

II. The Disciples' Reaction (14:4-5)

Sadly, I have to paint another picture for you. Some of the disciples were indignant and said, "Why was this waste of the ointment made?"

Who in the world would say something like that? It sounds just like the scribes and Pharisees, doesn't it? But Matthew's account says specifically that the ones who were critical were the disciples of Jesus Christ. Those who professed to love him were the first to criticize. In other words, here were Christians who had become narrow-minded and fault-finding.

A. The Mentality It Revealed (14:4-5)

It is a sad thing when people who say they love the Lord Jesus Christ act like the lost world. It is a pitiful thing when God's people become judgmental and unkind. The disciples saw this act of devotion and asked, "Why this waste?" That's the way the world looks at it too. This world looks at something done for the Lord Jesus and describes it as "waste."

Here is a man who gives himself to drink. Every party he goes to he gets intoxicated. People believe he's the life of the party.

I was coming back on the plane yesterday from Atlanta. There was a couple in their sixties and another man sitting across the aisle from me. The three of them got on the plane drunk and they were about as loud and obnoxious and profane as any people I've ever heard in my life. I stood it a long time. Finally I said to myself, if they are going to pour their profanity and their liquor on me, I'm going to pour my Jesus on them. I reached in my bag and got out a BIG Bible. I opened up my Bible and started singing, "Amazing grace, how sweet the sound that saved a wretch like me." It was amazing how subdued they got. In fact, the whole plane got quiet. Then I saw folks whispering and pointing at me.

Apparently there was nothing wrong with being drunk and blaspheming the name of God and making yourself obnoxious to a whole plane. That's fine. But if somebody is sold out to Jesus, that's a waste.

Apparently there is nothing wrong with a man giving his life to money. He's just a successful civic leader. Nothing wrong with becoming a great athlete; he becomes a hero. Nothing wrong with being a politician; he becomes a noble servant. But let somebody get sold out to Jesus and they say, "My, what a waste of talent."

I was a freshman at Mercer University in Macon, Georgia. They had a scholastic organization there, and if you made straight A's you got initiated into it. I got initiated into it at the honors' supper and I was sitting across from the dean of the school. He looked over at me and said, "Vines, what are you going to do?" I said, "I'm going to be a preacher. God's called me to preach." He frowned. "Oh, my," he said, "I thought you would amount to more than that."

I have come to the conclusion that *waste* is whatever you do that you do not do for Jesus. The only thing that will really last in this world is what we do for Jesus.

The world will build a stadium that costs several million dollars. That's great, good for the community. It will have a fireworks display, and spend several thousand dollars. Good for public morale. But let a church build a building to reach people for the Lord, you'll hear them say, "They're wasting all that money on buildings." The disciples at times had that mentality too.

B. The Carnality It Revealed (14:4-5)

They said, "Why this waste? You could have sold that for three hundred pence and given it to the poor." That's true. With a year's wages you could buy a lot of food and feed a lot of hungry people. But that was not the problem here. Behind the criticism of those disciples, John told us what the problem really was.

"Then saith one of his disciples, Judas Iscariot . . . This he said, not that he cared for the poor; but because he was a thief and had the bag [he was the treasurer], and bare what was put therein" (John 12:4, 6).

Behind the criticism of the disciples of that woman's deed was the carnality of Judas Iscariot. The basic problem in the life of Judas Iscariot was money.

If anyone looks at life only from a dollar-and-cents perspective, that person will miss what life is really all about. Judas Iscariot is a reminder to us that every time there is a criticism of Christian generosity, somewhere behind that criticism there may be a Judas abroad.

III. THE LORD'S EMOTION (14:6-9)

I think this was a deeply emotional scene for Jesus. First, there was a sense of grief in his heart at the disciples' carnality. He said, "Let her alone; why trouble ye her?" (14:6).

A. The Loving Nature of Her Deed (14:7-8)

I think there was also an emotion of gratitude in the heart of Jesus, which absolutely overwhelmed him when He saw what this dear woman had done. He said, "She hath wrought a good work on me." The word *good* means noble, beautiful. The disciples' opinion was *Wasteful.* The Lord's opinion was *Beautiful.* The Lord Jesus Christ lifted her action into the realm of the spiritual.

The Bible has a lot to say about good works. God has created us in Christ Jesus unto good works. We ought to be zealous of good works. Do you know how to take the common deeds of life and lift them into the spiritual realm of good works? Jesus said, "Ye have the poor with you always, and whensoever ye will, ye may do them good: but me you have not always" (14:7). The common deeds of life become good works when they are done for him.

Then He said, "She hath done what she could" (14:8). She couldn't do everything, but she could do something. Among all the followers of Jesus, Mary came close to his heart. She understood that He was going to die and be buried. Jesus commended the loving nature of her deed.

B. The Lasting Nature of Her Deed (14:9)

Jesus said that wherever the gospel was preached, what she had done would be spoken of as a memorial for her. Jesus took her generosity and memorialized it for eternity.

Everything we do for Jesus is never forgotten. It has eternal value. Nothing we do for him escapes his notice.

You can't do everything, but you can do something. You can't win all of the lost people in the world, but you can win some of them. You can't comfort all the lonely people in the world, but you can encourage some of them. So do what you can for Jesus today.

35

The Betrayal

Mark 14:10-21, 43-50

MANY NAMES GO DOWN IN INFAMY: HITLER, STALIN, MUSSOLINI, Jim Jones, to name just a few. But no name is so despised or despicable as the name of Judas Iscariot, who betrayed the Lord Jesus Christ. Judas is a wonderful name, really, meaning praise. Judas had a noble name and did something terrible to it. We never name our children Judas. Dante's picture of hell takes us down to the lowest pit of hell, where the worst sinners are, and depicts Satan right in the center with Judas in his mouth being torn to pieces. In his description, Dante was trying to say that of all the sins ever committed, what Judas did when he betrayed the Lord was the worst of them all.

These verses in Mark say three times that Judas was one of the twelve (14:10, 20, 43). He traveled with Jesus. He heard him say wonderful things and preach as no man had ever preached before. He saw the miracles Jesus performed. Yet none of it seemed to have an effect on him. He never really came to the Lord in a personal salvation experience. The story of Judas is a warning to all of us who profess the name of Jesus, a reminder that we can be close to the things of the Lord, we can be conversant with spiritual concerns, we can walk with the Lord's people, yet in our hearts never really love Jesus and serve him the way we ought to serve him.

I. THE BETRAYAL PLANNED (14:10-11)

Judas Iscariot evidently carefully planned the betrayal of Jesus. I think we see the beginning of this plan of betrayal in Mark 14:1-9. We know that Judas Iscariot was the one who led the criticism of the disciples against what Mary had done (John 12:4-6).

We know that Judas Iscariot was the treasurer. When we read what he said, we discover that he betrayed Jesus for money. Something meant more to Judas than anything else. When he saw a year's wages of perfume poured out on Jesus, it was more than he could take. A Judas will always be critical of anything that is done in a lavish manner to praise and honor the Lord Jesus Christ. That's the Judas mentality. When he saw the generosity of Mary, he said, "Why this waste?"

The Lord had warned his followers to beware of covetousness. "What shall it profit a man, if he shall gain the whole world, and lose his own soul?" (8:36).

A. The Die Is Cast (14:10)

I think that Jesus' rebuke stung Judas. He saw that things weren't going the way he wanted them to go. He was not going to get all that much materially in the kingdom of the Lord Jesus.

Has it ever entered your mind to sell the Lord out, do something that would bring reproach on his name, because the Christian life is not going the way you want it to go?

B. The Deal Is Made (14:11)

Shortly after that, Judas Iscariot went to the enemies of Jesus and offered to betray him. Not surprisingly, they were delighted. They had been looking for some way to get the job done. In Luke's gospel it says that he communed with them about a price; the word really means that they bargained over it. Finally, they agreed that he would receive thirty pieces of silver to betray this troublemaker from the north country.

Some people today betray Jesus for a lot less. Some folks will betray him for a can of beer, questionable amusement, a moment of stolen pleasure. Jesus is put on the bargain counter of life and is sold very cheaply in this world today.

II. The Betrayal Predicted (14:12-21)

Next we see the disciples preparing and eating the Passover meal together. How stunned they were when Jesus said, "One of you which eateth with me shall betray me" (14:18).

A. The Scriptures (14:21)

"The Son of man indeed goeth, as it is written of him" (14:21). The scriptures had predicted the betrayal of Jesus.

> For it was not an enemy that reproached me; then I could have borne it: neither was it he that hated me that did magnify himself against me: then I would have hid myself from him: But it was thou, a man mine equal, my guide, and mine acquaintance. . . . The words of his mouth were smoother than butter, but war was in his heart: his words were softer than oil, yet were they drawn swords (Psalm 55:12-13, 21).

> Yea, mine own familiar friend, in whom I trusted, which did eat of my bread, hath lifted up his heel against me (Psalm 4:9).

Those verses specifically predict that one of the inner circle of Jesus, one of his own, one of his friends, would betray him. We don't know whether Judas was literate or not, but if he was, he could have read about himself in the Old Testament scriptures.

We see ourselves in the Bible. When we read the Bible, it shows us not only what God is like but also what we are like. Sometimes that's not a very pleasant picture.

The one who wrote the Bible made us. He knows what is in our hearts. He knows the capabilities and potentialities of our lives.

B. The Savior (14:21)

After Jesus spoke those awesome words the disciples all started saying, "Is it I?"

Why do you think they asked that question? I think it was because when they searched their hearts every one of them saw that capability there. The possibility of betraying the Lord is in the heart of every one of us. At some point in time, every one of us has betrayed or will betray him. If I were to say that five years from now you would be an adulterer, you wouldn't want to believe it. If I were to say that five years from now you would be involved in embezzlement, you wouldn't think it possible. The Bible says, "Let him that thinketh he standeth take heed lest he fall" (1 Corinthians 10:12). But for the grace of God we are capable of doing anything anybody else in this world does. Only God's power can keep us true to Jesus.

Another passage says that Judas Iscariot himself asked, "Lord, is it I?" Nobody suspected him. He was trusted. They had enough confidence in him to make him treasurer of their group. There may be Judases today whom nobody would ever suspect. They have their baptismal certificates, they have their places of work in their local church, they are there every time the door is open, but down in their heart of hearts they are planning right now a betrayal of the Lord Jesus. They may not look at it as a betrayal, but that's what it is. A young woman may be thinking about yielding to the insistent sexual proposals of her boyfriend. An older man may be considering getting involved in a questionable business deal. Someone else may be thinking about taking part in some kind of activity contrary to the proper lifestyle of a born-again child of God.

I believe that Jesus did everything possible to awaken Judas and bring him to a point of repentance. In fact, scripture indicates that Judas was seated at the place of honor alongside the Lord Jesus that night.

A sop is a little morsel of food. In those days if you gave somebody a sop, it was a token of special honor. Jesus dipped into the dish and as a token of affection, He gave a tidbit to Judas Iscariot. Can you imagine how Judas must have felt? The Bible says he soon went out. His guilt drove him out.

III. The Betrayal Perpetrated (14:43-46)

John's gospel tells us that Satan put it into the heart of Judas to betray Jesus (John 13:2). Satan is always looking for a heart somewhere as a beachhead from which to do that. After Judas received the tidbit of food, Satan entered into him (John 13:27). It's a very short step from satanic suggestion to satanic possession. "He . . . went . . . out: and it was night" (John 13:30).

A. Where He Stood

A little later in the garden of Gethsemane, Judas Iscariot came with the soldiers of the chief priest. John says that when they got there, Judas stood with them.

Where do you stand? When the name of Jesus Christ is up for grabs, where do you stand? When the battle for morality and decency and the things of Jesus is on, are you outspokenly on his side? If you don't stand for him, in essence you will betray him.

B. What He Said (14:45)

Judas went to Jesus, and then his kiss, a token of tender affection, became a token of betrayal. "Master, Master," he said. The venom of hell was in that kiss.

We read no more about Judas in Mark, but that was not the end of the story. God has given man a conscience. Scripture says that Judas repented. That doesn't mean a godly repentance, a godly sorrow that leads to salvation. It means he was sorry for the mess he had gotten himself in. He went back to the chief priest, that money burning holes in his hand, and said to them, "I have betrayed innocent blood."

I can see Judas as he threw those thirty pieces of silver on the floor and rushed out. He took a rope, wrapped it around his neck, and swung out into eternity. The Bible says he went to his own place. He went to hell, heaven's graveyard. It was too late for Judas.

But it is not too late for you and me.

36

The Denial

Mark 14:27-72

I. STAGES OF SPIRITUAL DECLENSION (14:27-71)
   A. Pride (14:27-31)
   B. Presumption (14:37-38, 47, 54)
   C. Pressure (14:66-71)
II. STEPS TO SPIRITUAL CONVERSION (14:72)
   A. Repentance (14:72)
   B. Restoration

IT IS GENERALLY BELIEVED THAT MARK WAS A YOUNG PROTEGE OF Simon Peter, and that many of Simon Peter's sermons became the substance of the gospel of Mark. From time to time in Mark we have important glimpses into the life of Simon Peter.

Simon Peter was a man filled with enthusiasm. He was the kind of boisterous man who did whatever he did in a big way. The Lord Jesus knew that Simon Peter was destined to become a leader of the disciples. But there had to be a crisis in his life that would bring Simon Peter to see his weaknesses as well as his strengths. The flaws in his personality that kept him from being what God wanted him to be had to be confronted and corrected. That crisis was what we commonly call "the denial."

Every Christian ought to study the denial of Simon Peter. We may never betray the Lord Jesus as Judas Iscariot did, but there is always the danger that through life or lip we may deny him in some twentieth-century equivalent.

I. STAGES OF SPIRITUAL DECLENSION (14:27-71)

How did it come about that a man who so obviously loved Jesus
would deny three times he ever knew him? You remember that
when Simon first came to know Jesus as his savior, Jesus looked
at him and said, "Your name is Simon, but I'm going to give you
a new name. Your name will be Peter or Cephas or Rock."

There was one thing Simon Peter was not and that was a rock.
He was as unstable as the shifting sand on the seashore. When
Jesus said to Simon Peter, "I'm going to make a rock out of you,"
it must have absolutely captured his heart. There was inside
Simon Peter the potential for him to be a great man of God. But
the Lord Jesus Christ had to work on his life to reveal those characteristics. So when Jesus said to Simon, "I'm going to make
something out of you; I'm going to make a rock-like personality
out of you," I think that Simon that day fell head over heels in
love with Jesus.

Being saved is not merely giving assent to a set of doctrinal
propositions. Being saved is a love relationship to Jesus. Everyone who can say in his or her heart, "I'm a child of God," can
also say, "I love Jesus."

How then could Simon Peter deny Jesus as he did? It didn't
take place all at once. A series of stages leads to spiritual declension.

A. Pride (14:27-31)

After the Lord's supper, Jesus said to these disciples, "Before this
night is over you will all forsake me and flee." Anger must have
welled up in the heart of Simon Peter. "Lord," he said, "I
wouldn't be surprised at the rest of these men, but I'd never do
that. Regardless of what they do, Lord, you can count on me."
Pride was building up in Simon Peter's heart. When we read
about him and follow the gospel accounts of his life we discover
that several times he bragged about a dedication which he really
did experience on occasion.

The Bible has a great deal to say about pride in the life of a
believer. "Pride goeth before destruction, and an haughty spirit
before a fall" (Proverbs 16:18). One of the most subtle temptations in our lives is the temptation to pride. It is a subtle trap in
the devil's arsenal. The Bible warns us that we are not to take

a novice, a new Christian, and put him in a place of leadership, "lest being lifted up with pride he fall into the condemnation of the devil" (1 Timothy 3:6).

It's easy for Christians to get filled with pride. God begins to bless us and if we are not careful we start taking credit for those blessings instead of praising God for them. Maybe you are blessed materially. Maybe you have been given a place of responsibility in the church. The devil whispers in your ear, "You are somebody. Look at you. Folks have recognized your abilities. They have given you this job." Then, if you aren't careful, when people start praising you, pride will rise up in your heart. Someone has said that pride is being stuffed full of yourself.

That was the problem with Simon Peter, although his pride was unfounded. His career to that point, his discipleship, had been bumpy to say the least. There was a time when he said, "Thou art the Christ, the Son of God." He soared to the heights spiritually. In the next breath he said, "Lord don't let that [death on the cross] happen to you." Jesus said to him, "Get thee behind me, Satan." One moment Peter was out there walking on top of the waves. The next moment he plunged into the depths of the sea and was crying out, "Lord, save me." There was no basis for the pride in his life.

As children of God, what do we have that we did not receive (1 Corinthians 4:7)? Whatever we are as children of God, God has made us that. Whatever blessing we may be in the lives of others, it is because of what God is doing.

B. Presumption (14:37-38, 47, 54)

Simon Peter presumed several things incorrectly that led to his denial of Jesus. In the garden of Gethsemane, Jesus wept and prayed a prayer such as was never heard by human ears before. In the midst of that prayer vigil, Jesus found his disciples sleeping (14:37). He said, not to all of them, but to Simon Peter, "Sleepest thou? couldest not thou watch one hour? Watch ye and pray, lest ye enter into temptation. The spirit truly is ready, but the flesh is weak" (14:37-38). Had Simon presumed he was so mature spiritually, so capable in the things of God, that he could neglect prayer?

That's a subtle thing that takes place in the lives of Christians.

When Christians allow pride to get in their hearts, it's easy for them to feel that they don't need prayer anymore. The daily quiet time is neglected. Forgotten is the daily "morning watch" with God—when you open up the Bible and let God speak to you and correct your life by his word, when you bow in prayer quiet and alone before the Lord and ask for his strength—that gets lost in the hustle and bustle of life. I don't care who you are; I don't care how long you have been serving Jesus; I don't care how spiritual and how strong you are as a child of God—after only one or two days of neglecting your prayer life, you are one or two days away from denying Jesus Christ.

None of us is so strong that we can do without meeting God every morning. Miss your breakfast, but don't miss your Bible. You need that time with God in his word. You need that time when you draw on the power of God. But here, Simon Peter was asleep when he ought not to have been asleep.

In just a moment we are told that the soldiers came with Judas Iscariot and were getting ready to arrest Jesus. "And one of them that stood by drew a sword, and smote a servant of the high priest, and cut off his ear" (14:47). Who do you think that disciple was? Which one do you think did that? Yes, John tells us it was Simon Peter. Simon was sleeping when he should have been praying. Now when a crisis came, he reached for his sword, the steel glistened in the light of the torches, and he swung. Let me tell you something: he wasn't swinging for an ear. He was going to split that man right down the middle of his head. But the servant moved quickly, so he just lost an ear.

Simon Peter did damage to another human being, which is characteristic of people who are not in the word of God and in prayer. When you start down the downward slide that leads to denying the Lord Jesus Christ, and are so presumptuous as to think you can live apart from daily contact with God, you will discover that you are hateful and hurtful in your relationships with others. You become ugly in your dealings with them.

So Peter cut off the ear of one of the servants of the high priest. Further, Peter presumed something else. Look at 14:54. Jesus was now arrested and they were getting ready to take him to trial. "And Peter followed him afar off." He was still following Jesus, but from afar. He still loved Jesus, but from a distance.

Many of God's people get to that point. They still love him, they are still serving him, they are still coming to church—but they begin to follow him from afar. An example of this would be that they drop out of Tuesday night visitation. "I'll be a witness wherever I go. To do that one night a week is just organized legalism. I'm not going to get into that." Wednesday night services? "Look, I need a little family time. I work hard. Going up there Wednesday night is just asking too much." The next thing you know he or she drops the Sunday night church service. "I need my rest. I've got to go to work in the morning." Probably we all have seen that happen with people we know. They start following Jesus afar off. They start rationalizing and excusing themselves for their lack of devotion to him. What they don't realize is that they are on a path that leads to denying the Lord Jesus Christ.

C. Pressure (14:66-71)

Peter came into the palace of the high priest, sat with the servants, and warmed himself at the fire. When you follow Jesus from afar and do not warm your heart in constant contact with him, the devil will provide you with a fire to warm yourself by. Many a child of God who used to be warmed and blessed by the things of God, who used to be stirred and thrilled by daily fellowship with Jesus Christ, is now seeking warmth at the fire of some enemy. It may be some amusement or some questionable social contact—but that's where he or she gets warmed now.

Peter was susceptible to the pressures of others. We all are, especially when we are young. When we are young we are very interested in what our peers say. We are very responsive to their opinions. The facts are, however, that things you think are important, pressures from that crowd at school that are so significant today, aren't really going to matter a few years from now. There are a lot of things you may think you have to do to be acceptable, a lot of places you may think you have to go in order to be popular, but you really don't have to. When you are grown up, you will look back surprised at how insignificant those things are. But we are all susceptible to people-pressure.

What really got Simon Peter was that the temptation came from an unexpected source. If those soldiers had charged Simon Peter, he would have fought to the last drop of blood in his body. But when he got himself in a spiritually weakened condition, the devil could come at him from the blind side and he never knew what hit him until much later. He was warming himself by that fire and here came one of the palace maids. "Oh, aren't you one of those disciples of Jesus?" "I don't know what you're talking about," Simon Peter said.

A little later that scenario repeated itself, again piercing his false front. "You are one of his, aren't you?" Peter began to panic. "Listen," he said, "I don't know what you're talking about." Then the people around the fire picked it up. "Hey, I can tell that accent. You're one of those country fellows from northern Galilee." Peter's voice became louder and more insistent. He started cursing and blaspheming. "I don't know this Jesus." He had vowed he would never deny his Lord; but what he said he would never do, he did three times.

Are you a person who threw a stick on the fire at camp and said you would serve him till you die? Or did you walk down a church aisle, kneel down, cry, and say you would love Jesus supremely? And then one day you denied him? Did some kids at school start criticizing your church? Did they say, "You go to church over there, don't you?" And you said, "No, I don't go much." You denied Christ. Or was it some business deal, and you knew what they were planning to do wasn't right, and you didn't say a word? You denied Christ. Was it some questionable social activity you knew was wrong and somebody should have taken a stand, but you didn't do it? You denied Christ.

About that time the cock crowed. Jesus in his omnipotence had predicted exactly when the rooster would crow. That rooster crow was the poor man's alarm clock. It meant it was time to get up. But to the soul of Simon Peter it was the alarm clock of God. That crowing brought Simon Peter to the realization that he had denied Jesus three times.

II. Steps to Spiritual Conversion (14:72)

In Luke 22:31-32 Jesus said, "Simon, Simon, behold, Satan hath desired to have you, that he may sift you as wheat." That chaff of pride in Simon Peter's life had to be sifted out before God could use him effectively. "But I have prayed for thee, that thy faith fail not: and when thou art converted, strengthen thy brethren."

The conversion referred to here is not soul salvation, that conversion which takes place once. But since our souls' conversion most of us have had several other conversions along the way.

Most of us had to have a habit conversion; some of our old habits had to be converted.

On this occasion Simon Peter saw himself as he really was. His pride was dealt a deathblow. His arrogance was slain. It was not his faith that failed, because Jesus had specifically prayed that his faith would not fail. His problem was that his love failed. His point of strength became his point of danger. The point where you are strongest is apt to be the point where the devil will hit you and tempt you to deny Jesus.

Two steps brought Simon Peter back to the Lord.

A. Repentance (14:72)

When Simon Peter heard that rooster crowing, he became aware of what he had done. Luke says that at that moment the Lord turned and looked at Simon Peter. I think it was a look of love and forgiveness. Peter saw the face of one who loved him so much that in spite of his denial He would go on to the cross. His heart was broken.

If you are truly born again, when you sin against the Lord Jesus Christ, it will have an effect on you. A child of God cannot go on and on in sin and not be brokenhearted. The look of the Lord would have done Simon Peter no good if he himself hadn't been looking at the Lord when the Lord was looking at him. He was looking at Jesus, turning his eyes back to Jesus. Now, when he remembered the words of the Lord, he went out and wept bitterly. Did he go to that upper room? Did he go out to Gethsemane and prostrate himself where Jesus did? We don't know, but we do know that Simon Peter repented. Judas did not repent. Yes, he was remorseful; he was very sorry he had sinned. But repentance is much deeper than remorse. Peter was not only sorry for his sin, but he was sorry that his sin hurt his Lord.

B. Restoration

Those were sad days for Simon Peter. He witnessed the crucifixion of Jesus. I can imagine him looking at that cross from a distance, aware that the Lord was dying for his denials, his sin, and the sins of the world.

Then came the message that the tomb was empty, and Simon Peter and John ran to that tomb. They saw the empty grave clothes. Whatever did that mean? What should they do next? What *could* they do?

Peter and the disciples went fishing. They fished all night and didn't catch a thing. The next morning on the shore there was a fire, fish cooking, and someone said, "Children, have you caught anything?"

"It's the Lord!"

Simon jumped into the water and swam to Jesus.

Jesus asked three times, "Simon, do you love me?"

What was He doing? I think He was restoring his love. Jesus restored this man who had three times denied him.

Regardless of what we have done, if we will look toward Jesus, return to fellowship with him, and ask his forgiveness, He will restore us and again use us.

37

Gethsemane
Mark 14:32-42

I. The Mystery of Gethsemane (14:32)
   A. The Place (14:32)
   B. The Prayer (14:32)
II. The Agony of Gethsemane (14:33-36)
   A. Physical Agony
   B. Mental Agony
   C. Spiritual Agony
III. The Victory of Gethsemane (14:37-42)
   A. Renunciation of One's Will
   B. Resignation to God's Will

Gethsemane was just outside Jerusalem, across from a little brook named Kidron. At this time of the year Kidron was a full stream. The name *Gethsemane* means "oil press." It must have been an enclosed garden with olive trees, and in its center was an olive press. We are now on holy ground.

> It is midnight and on Olive's brow,
> The star is dim that lately shone.
> 'Tis midnight in the garden now,
> The suffering Savior prays alone.

We can learn many lessons from this garden of Gethsemane experience. We learn lessons on suffering. We learn what life is all about for a believer.

I. THE MYSTERY OF GETHSEMANE (14:32)

There is a mystery about this Gethsemane experience. When we begin to come to grips with what took place in this garden, it defies our ability to understand it. Our human minds are staggered, our language is bankrupt, when we try to describe what Jesus went through in this place.

A. The Place (14:32)

We are told elsewhere in the gospels that Jesus often went to Gethsemane. That is why Judas knew where to find him that night. It may have been a place owned by a friend. It seems to have been a place where Jesus went alone to pray.

The place of prayer was now also the place of pain. Jesus went into a garden and prayed, "Not my will, but thine be done."

The first Adam was in a garden and exerted his will to the ruin of the human race. The last Adam was in a garden and deserted his will for the redemption of the human race. In the garden of Eden the first Adam faced a tree and yielded to the will of Satan. The last Adam prayed, facing a tree on Calvary, and yielded to the will of God.

B. The Prayer (14:32)

The disciples many times had heard Jesus pray. There was such confidence, calm assurance, and jubilation in the prayers of Jesus. Many times He would just lift his heart up in prayer and say, "O Father, I thank thee." Sometimes He would pray and there would be a spirit of victory in his prayer.

But this prayer was different. It was not the kind of prayer that Jesus normally prayed. When we listen we can almost see tears fill his eyes. We can almost feel the pain in his voice. This prayer filled the heavens with its grief. It's an amazing mysterious prayer.

Many times Jesus knelt when He prayed, but here He fell on his knees and ultimately prostrated himself in agony: "If it be possible, let this cup pass from me." Until we get to heaven we will never fully understand what Jesus went through in the garden that night when He prayed the Gethsemane prayer.

II. The Agony of Gethsemane (14:33-36)

The phrase Mark used here, "sore amazed" (14:33), means that
Jesus began to be terrified or horrified at an approaching object.
The Bible also says in this verse that He was "very heavy" (literally, "not at home"). Jesus Christ experienced a sense of
estrangement, isolation, loneliness, at this time. "My soul is
exceeding sorrowful" (14:34). The word *sorrowful* means "to be
circled by sorrow." It's as if a whirlwind of sorrow were envelop-
ing him. The agony Jesus was experiencing was connected with
what He referred to as his "cup." "Abba, Father, all things are possible unto thee; take away this cup from me" (14:36).

Jesus had already talked about that cup to his disciples. "Can
ye drink of the cup that I drink of?" (10:38). They foolishly said,
"We are able." They didn't know what they were saying. Later
on, Jesus said, "The cup which my Father hath given me, shall
I not drink it?" The agony that Jesus Christ was going through
was somehow related to this cup. In the Bible, drinking from a
cup is a symbolic way of saying you are going to experience
something to the fullest.

A. Physical Agony

What did Jesus see when He looked in that cup? What kind of
agony did this cup represent in the life of our Lord? I think it
means that his humanity recoiled from the suffering He was
going to experience at Calvary.

Something about all human nature makes us recoil from suffering. None of us invites suffering. We do everything we can to
spare ourselves physical pain. We live in a wonderful day when
God has made possible the discovery of medicines that can alle-
viate suffering, dulling pain and easing human agony.

Jesus Christ was going through physical agony here. His perspiration was like "great drops of blood falling down to the
ground" (Luke 22:44). An angel from heaven came to strengthen
him. When Jesus said He was sorrowful unto death, it could
mean that if He had not received heavenly strength He might
have died right there in the garden.

I don't think this means that Jesus was afraid to die. Countless

Christian martyrs have faced death bravely. God has given supernatural strength, dying grace, to many of his children in the hour
of death and they have not been afraid. Mark was saying that Jesus
Christ had a human nature. He knew what was ahead. He knew
what his physical nature would have to endure. He knew that in
just a few moments the thorns around his brow would puncture his
skin. He knew that He would be going through physical scourging.
He knew that nails would be driven into his hands, the spike would
be driven into his feet, the sword would be thrust into his side.

B. Mental Agony

Jesus also saw his imminent emotional agony in that cup. Jesus loved
people, and his personality shrank from the approaching separation.
     The Lord Jesus Christ was taking the steps now that would
lead him into a place of isolation where no one else will ever go.
In just a few hours on the cross, He would cry, "My God, my
God, why hast thou forsaken me?" When our savior died, He was
by himself. He understands what it is to be alone.

C. Spiritual Agony

Deity recoils from sin. Jesus Christ was the sinless, holy one. In order
to get to the depths of what Gethsemane was all about, we must interpret it by Paul's words, "God hath made him who knew no sin to be
sin for us." Jesus Christ was facing the sins of the world in that cup.
     We don't know the true nature of sin. We don't know how sin
can ruin a life. Literally millions of people in this world have fall-
en for the lies of the devil that sin is fun. Sin is the popular thing.
We don't understand sin the way Jesus understood it in the garden of Gethsemane or we would hate sin the way He hates sin.

III. THE VICTORY OF GETHSEMANE (14:37-42)

In what Jesus experienced at Gethsemane you and I can learn the
twofold secret of victory in life.

A. Renunciation of One's Will

In Gethsemane, Jesus Christ made the sacrifice of his will. The
essence of sin is assertion of our own will. Satan fell from heaven

because he said, "I will. I will." Simon Peter denied the Lord
Jesus Christ because he didn't understand the depravity of his
own will. He said to Jesus, "I never will. Others may deny you.
I will not."

When you and I come to the point that we are willing to deny
our will, we are on the path that leads to victory. Can you pray,
"Father, not my will be done"? Are you willing to take all your
selfish desires, hopes, life aspirations, and say no to them? Then
you are on the way that leads to victory.

B. Resignation to God's Will

"Not my will," Jesus said, "but thy will be done." He was saying
that God the Father had a plan for his Son's life and He wanted
that plan fulfilled to the letter.

God has a plan for every life. God has a purpose for your life.
The grandest decision anyone ever makes in life is to come to the
Lord and say, "Lord, I take hands off my life. I'll do what you
want me to do for you. Your will be done in my life." If you make
up your mind to do that, you will have the most meaningful life
any person could have. When I was sixteen years old, I prayed
a prayer like that and put my life in the hands of God. I could
never have imagined what God had in store for me.

When Jesus was praying that prayer, almost simultaneously
we hear the clanking of swords. We see the reflection of torches.
The Lord Jesus said, "Arise, let us be going." Was He going to flee
from his accusers? No, He was going to meet them. He was going
to the cross because that was the will of God for him. Today you
should say, "God, I don't know what's best in my life, but you do.
Please give me that."

38

Guilty of Love in the First Degree

Mark 14:53-65; 15:1-20

I. BEFORE THE HEBREWS (14:53-65)
    A. The Lord Accused (14:55-59)
    B. The Lord Arraigned (14:60-64)
    C. The Lord Abused (14:65)
II. BEFORE THE HEATHEN (15:1-20)
    A. His Silence (15:3-5)
    B. His Substitution (15:6-14)
    C. His Scars (15:15-20)

THE TRIAL OF JESUS CHRIST WAS THE MOST FAMOUS, FAR-REACHING trial in human history. Not only was He tried before the world, but the world was tried before him. When the four gospels are put together, we discover that actually there were two trials of Jesus: a religious trial as He was brought before the Jewish leaders and a civil trial as He was brought before the political authorities.

There were six phases to the trial of Jesus. First He went to a man named Annas, who was the father-in-law of Caiaphas, the high priest. Annas, a wicked old man of about seventy, was in charge of the lucrative business of the temple shops. Second, from there they took Jesus to Caiaphas himself, who was supposed to be the spiritual leader of the Jewish people. Once a year Caiaphas would go into the holy of holies to represent the peo-

ple in the presence of God. Third, early in the morning of the
day He was crucified, Jesus was brought before an official gathering of the Sanhedrin, a group of seventy-one men. These men
had the ability to try cases but not the power to carry out their
sentences.

Then there were three phases to the civil trial of Jesus. First,
Jesus was brought before Pontius Pilate, then Herod, and again
Pontius Pilate. Lawyers who have studied these proceedings pro-
nounce the trial of our Lord a travesty of justice, a mockery of
legality. Although there are many different illegal aspects to the
trial of Jesus, I will discuss only a few of them here.

The place where Jesus was tried was illegal. The Sanhedrin
was required to hold its hearings in the hall of stones in the temple. Jesus was tried in the homes, the private residences, of
Annas and Caiaphas.

The periods of time involved were illegal. A case could not be
tried at night, yet Jesus was tried at night. You were not to try on
one of the feast days, yet Jesus was tried during Passover.

The proceedings themselves were illegal. The judge was the
prosecutor, the one who actually pressed the case against Jesus.

The witnesses had to agree, but these witnesses did not
agree.

If a man had been condemned to die, they were supposed to wait
a day in order to give the members of the Sanhedrin time to look
for some possible way to extend mercy to the accused. Jesus was
condemned, yet He was rushed right on through to crucifixion.

Jesus was convicted before He was tried. He was condemned
before his case was ever really heard.

The condemned had to have someone testify on his behalf. No
one was allowed to come forth and speak on behalf of the Lord
Jesus Christ.

Mark 15:10 states that the reason they brought Jesus to trial in
the first place was the Jewish leaders were envious of him.

We too must reach a verdict about the Lord Jesus. We must
decide if Jesus Christ was who He said He was or if He was an
imposter.

Having studied all of the facts about the Lord, having looked
at all the proceedings of the trial of Jesus, I have come to the conclusion that Jesus was guilty. He was guilty of love in the first
degree.

I. Before the Hebrews (14:53-65)

Mark did not tell us about Annas, but rather that the Lord Jesus
was brought before Caiaphas.

A. The Lord Accused (14:55-59)

The chief priest and the council did everything in their power
to get witnesses who would say something devastating to the
case of Jesus. Yet they were not able to get their witnesses to agree
(14:56). Later on, some men came in and said, "We heard him
say, I will destroy this temple that is made with hands, and within three days I will build another made without hands" (14:58).
This was a misquotation of what took place. Jesus had said,
"Destroy this temple [talking about his body], and in three days
I will raise it up." He was making a prediction about his resurrection. He was not talking about a temple made of stone or tim-
ber, but about the temple of his own body (John 2:21). But this
was the charge they brought against him.

These were the only witnesses that were brought in. That
night, as Jesus stood before those Jewish leaders, many others
could have been brought before them to testify for him. There
were ex-lepers, those who no longer were blind, former demo-
niacs. All kinds of people could have testified about who this
Jesus was and what this Jesus could do.

I wonder if anyone reading this book would say that Jesus
didn't do what He said He would do? Would any reader say that
Jesus has been unfaithful to you, a disappointment to you? If that
is so in your life, I hope you will find some mature Christian in
your town and talk to him or her about it.

Let's go to the other side too. If you have found Jesus to be
faithful, everything the Bible says He is, would you testify on his
behalf today? What would you say to a non-Christian friend or
relative about him?

So, the Lord Jesus was brought to trial, yet the witnesses who
needed to testify on his behalf were never allowed to do so.

B. The Lord Arraigned (14:60-64)

By this point, the high priest was desperate. He knew he was losing his case. "I adjure thee by the living God," he said to Jesus,

"that thou tell us whether thou be the Christ, the Son of God" (Matthew 26:63). He was putting Jesus on oath. He was requiring Jesus by Jewish law to give a direct answer to his question. Under those circumstances, our Lord said, "I am: and ye shall see the Son of man sitting on the right hand of power, and coming in the clouds of heaven" (14:62). As Jesus stands before this religious group, we see him arraigned and condemned on the charge of being Christ (14:64). Either Jesus is the Christ or He is the greatest imposter who ever lived.

C. The Lord Abused (14:65)

Once his sentence was pronounced, some began to spit on him. Can you imagine that? Their foul-smelling spit running down the face of Jesus. Spitting in the face of God. Then they began to buffet him, to strike him with the palms of their hands. Scripture says, "I hid not my face from shame and spitting" (Isaiah 50:6). Jesus came into this world to be the savior, and what did men do? They spit at him and slapped him.

Charles Wesley wrote:

Amazing love, how can it be
That thou my God shouldst die for me?

II. BEFORE THE HEATHEN (15:1-20)

The Jewish leaders next hastily called the Sanhedrin, the whole council, together. To make their charges stick before Pontius Pilate, they would have to change them somewhat. They had condemned Jesus for blasphemy, a religious charge, but they knew it would have to be reworked if it were going to have any bearing on Pontius Pilate.

Scripture elsewhere tells us that their charge became threefold. Number one, they charged him with perverting the nation. Number two, they charged him with saying they ought not to pay tribute to Caesar. Number three, they charged him with claiming to be a king in competition with Julius Caesar. As we read through these opening verses in chapter 15, we discover that over and over again this phrase, the "King of the Jews," comes up. Pilate asked him, "Art thou the King of the Jews?"(15:2) He was trying to discover if Jesus was guilty as charged.

A. His Silence (15:3-5)

The Bible had predicted that Jesus would be silent before his accusers. "As a sheep before her shearers is dumb, so he openeth not his mouth" (Isaiah 53:7). At times Jesus spoke—when being silent would have helped his cause. At times Jesus was silent—when speaking would have helped his cause. The Jews so bumbled the case that Jesus could have gotten out by just a word or two in appropriate places, yet He refused to say those words. Jesus was in total control of this situation.

B. His Substitution (15:6-14)

Then Pontius Pilate hit on a brilliant idea which he thought would get him out of this no-win situation. He knew that Jesus was innocent, but he was in the hot seat between the Jewish leaders and what he knew to be the prisoner's innocence. Every year at that time it was customary to release some prisoner. Why not this one? Another prisoner at that time was named Barabbas, an insurrectionist and murderer (15:7). The name *Barabbas* means "son of a rabbi." Evidently he had joined a revolutionary group in Israel at that time, hoping to overthrow Roman power. So Barabbas was an insurrectionist, a murderer, but also a kind of hero with the people.

The heroes of a society tell you a great deal about that society. Who are the heroes in America today? Whose pictures are on the walls of our young people's rooms? Whose names are given to our babies? There was a time in America when we named our children after Bible characters. But no longer.

"Will ye that I release unto you the King of the Jews?" Pilate asked the people. "But the chief priests moved the people, that he should rather release Barabbas unto them" (15:11). The word *move* there is akin to our word *earthquake*. They stirred the mob into a frenzy, inciting them to demand the release of Barabbas. "What should I do with Jesus?" Pilate asked.

Crucify him. Crucify him (15:13-14). A tragic choice.

One of the most beautiful doctrines of scripture is the doctrine of substitution. Jesus took our places on the cross. Can you imagine how those last few hours were for Barabbas? He had already been condemned to die. He had already been found guilty of murder. Can you imagine his dread as he counted down the

hours and minutes to the time he would be executed? I can imagine the night before as Barabbas tried to sleep. It was a fitful, rest-
less sleep. Early in the morning he heard them driving the nails
in a cross getting it ready. Was that the cross being prepared for
him? Every time he heard movement in the jail he wondered if
they were coming to get him. Then the hour arrived for his exe-
cution. He heard the tramp of the soldiers. He heard the key as
it was placed in the lock of the door. It turned. The door opened.
He was going to his death. He stood there, his heart leaping in
his throat. "Barabbas," they said, "there is a man named Jesus.
They have put him in your place. He is going to die. You're free.
You can go home."

C. His Scars (15:15-20)

"And so Pilate, willing to content the people, released Barabbas
unto them, and delivered Jesus, when he had scourged him, to
be crucified" (15:15).

   Scripture says, "I gave my back to the smiters" (Isaiah 50:6).
   The Bible says, "With his stripes we are healed" (Isaiah 53:5;
1 Peter 2:24).

39

The Meaning of Calvary

Mark 15:20-32

I. PATHWAY TO THE CROSS (15:20)
   A. Started in Eternity
   B. Continued in History
II. PEOPLE AT THE CROSS (15:21-28)
   A. Simon (15:21)
   B. The Soldiers (15:21-27)
   C. The Thieves (15:27)
III. PURPOSE OF THE CROSS (15:29-32)
   A. To Save Others
   B. To Sacrifice Himself

CALVARY IS AT THE CROSSROADS OF HISTORY AND ETERNITY. MARK called Calvary *Golgotha*, a Hebrew word that means "the place of the skul" (15:22). It seems to have been a familiar place, one that all the people of Jerusalem would have known. It was located outside the city gates, approximately a mile from where Jesus was condemned to die.

None of the gospel writers really described the crucifixion. Few details were given of what actually took place. It's as if the gospel writers just drew a curtain over the scene. Rather, we are allowed to look at the men and the groups of people represented there.

When I think of Calvary, several things come to my mind.

I. Pathway to the Cross (15:20)

The road leading to Calvary was called the Via Dolorosa, the way of sorrow.

A. Started in Eternity

Actually the pathway to the cross began in eternity. The book of Revelation says that Jesus was the lamb who was slain before the foundation of the world. The heart of God had determined from all eternity that there would be a cross. When God put Adam and Eve in the garden He knew that they were going to sin and that the whole human race would be plunged into disaster. So, in eternity, God determined that his Son, the Lord Jesus, would pay the price for the forgiveness of our sins.

The cross was no ambulance sent to an accident. The cross was not an afterthought with God. The cross was on the drawing board of the heavenly Father from the beginning eons of the ages.

B. Continued in History

All through human history the cross was predicted; it was destined that Jesus Christ one day would die there. A red river of redemption flows all through the pages of the word of God. There was no other way for us to be saved. The cross is the only pathway that makes it possible for us to get to God.

> I must needs go home by the way of the cross:
> There is no other way but this.
> I will never catch sight of the gates of light
> If the way of the cross I miss.

There is only one way to get to heaven. We can meet God only at the cross. It is the divinely designed meeting place between helpless sinners and a loving God. Psalm 85:10 says, "Mercy and truth are met together; righteousness and peace have kissed one another." It was at the cross that God's mercy and humanity's need for a savior met and were reconciled.

II. People at the Cross (15:21-28)

Various groups of people gathered there the day Jesus was crucified, some probably out of morbid curiosity. Something in human nature is very curious about these kinds of things. In the early part of this century public hangings were common. I remember hearing my grandfather talk about hangings. They would hang men in the center of the town and the whole town would come to witness it.

I heard about a great preacher who was preparing a sermon on the meaning of the cross. When he went to bed that night he dreamed about the cross. He saw the nails driven into Jesus' hands. He saw the crown of thorns as it punctured his brow, the sword thrust into his side. It was more than he could bear. He ran to one of those soldiers, pulled him around, and when he looked into that soldier's face he saw his own face. In his dream he was experiencing the truth that all of us were represented in one way or other at the cross that day when Jesus died.

A. Simon (15:21)

A man named Simon was there. They compelled Simon, a Cyrenian who passed by, to bear Jesus' cross. As a Cyrenian, he was from north Africa. Possibly he was a black man. Simon was there because of compulsion. He was pressed into service.

Some people go to church out of compulsion. They really don't want to go. Maybe their parents make them go. They would rather be watching TV or reading the sports page. Maybe some husbands go to church because their wives nagged them into going. They come just to shut her up. If that is so, they ought to be grateful that somebody cared enough about them to want them to come. David once said, "No man cared for my soul" (Psalm 142:4). The children or husbands I'm talking about can't say that. They may live to thank God for the day that someone nagged them to come to the house of God. They may live to praise the name of Jesus that somebody made them get up out of bed and go to church. Many a person who has come to know Christ did not attend a certain service because he or she wanted to. They came resentfully but they left repentant.

B. The Soldiers (15:21-27)

Of course the soldiers were there. It was their job to be there. One soldier would take a board and write on it the crime of the person who was accused. That's what they did with Jesus. Mark gave an abbreviated version of the superscription (15:26). Probably the full version was: "This is Jesus of Nazareth, the King of the Jews." That was the only crime they could find to hang on Jesus. But the truth is, He's king of the world, king of this universe, king of kings and lord of lords. One of these days, every knee will bow and every tongue will confess that Jesus Christ is Lord (Philippians 2:10).

Those soldiers were sin-hardened. They could sit around a cross and gamble for the clothing of the dying person. They sat there throwing dice at the feet of the Son of God.

> The Roman soldiers shook the dice
> As for the stake they vied,
> Quite unaware that on the cross
> The world's Redeemer died.
>
> But in the circus of our day
> We thoughtless act the clown
> While God is speeding up his work
> To ring time's curtain down.
>
> The Roman soldiers shook the dice
> As for the stake they vied.
> Are we as unconcerned as they
> That Christ for us has died?

We are violence-hardened, aren't we? We've seen so much on television, we hear it on the radio. Five hundred died over here. Thousands got slaughtered over there. If Jesus died today, would a television crew be sticking a camera in his face to hear what He was going to say?

C. The Thieves (15:27)

"And with him they crucify two thieves; the one on his right hand and the other on his left" (15:27). Three crosses were there that day, and one of those thieves got saved. Mark didn't record it, but Luke did. One man died *in* sin; one man died *to* sin; one man died *for* sin. Thank God for that middle cross.

> Was it for crimes that I have done
> He groaned upon the tree?

Amazing pity, grace unknown,
And love beyond degree.

Yes, it was for crimes that we have done. "And he was numbered with the transgressors" (15:28, quoting Isaiah 53:12). When Jesus hung on that middle cross He identified himself with the crimes of those thieves. He was paying the price for whatever wrongs they had done. He was paying the price for your crimes and my crimes. Most of us don't want to think about our crimes, our sins. It's a lot easier to think about everybody else's.

I was talking to somebody recently who said, "I'd like to become a Christian, but I'm afraid I might sin after I accept Jesus." That's one of the common objections to accepting Christ: I'd like to be saved, but I'm afraid I might sin again, down the road.

Here's what I said. "How long has it been since Jesus died on the cross?"

"I don't know, a long time."

I said, "It's probably been about two thousand years. When Jesus died on the cross, did He die for sins?"

"Yes, I believe He died for sins."

I said, "All right, when Jesus died two thousand years ago on the cross for sins, were all of your sins, at that point in time, future?"

"Yes."

I said, "Does that mean all the sins you have committed?"

"Yes."

"Does it mean all the sins you may commit today? Does it mean all the sins you may commit tomorrow? If Jesus died two thousand years ago for all of your sins and He's already paid for all of those sins that are out there in the future, it means that whatever sin you may ever commit, Jesus has already shed his blood on the cross for it."

"Well, does that mean I can just go on out there and sin because He paid for it?"

"No. Every time I sin now I know that that's just one more sin that was added to the load that made him suffer on Calvary's cross. It makes me want not to sin anymore."

Yes, we were there at Calvary.

III. PURPOSE OF THE CROSS (15:29-32)

The scribes, chief priests, and religious leaders were there, along with the crowd. "They that passed by railed on him, wagging their

heads" (15:29). Wouldn't you think that a dying person ought to
be entitled to die in some serenity? This is like yelling at a man on
his way to the electric chair. Wouldn't you think they could at least
stop at that point? They had him going to the cross; that's what
they wanted. They wanted him killed. Was there to be no let-up?
No. The venom that filled their hearts spewed out on him as He
died, suffering and bleeding as no human being ever suffered.

They taunted and ridiculed him. They shouted, "Come on
down from the cross. If you are who you say you are, if you are
a king, come on down from the cross" (15:29-30). Each time I
read that, something inside me wells up and I want to say, "Lord,
show them you can do it; come on down." He could have. Jesus
said He could have called for legions of angels. He could have
called ten thousand angels to destroy the world and set him free.

If you listen carefully you will hear another voice in that statement: the voice of the devil. All through the ministry of Jesus,
the devil sought to get him to avoid the cross. The chief priests
and scribes took up the same mocking. "He saved others; himself
he cannot save" (15:31).

A. To Save Others

In formulating that ironic dichotomy, the priests were speaking
the essence of the gospel but they didn't know it. Jesus came to
save others. That was the purpose of the cross. Here is an admission on their part that He did save others: the man with the palsy,
Legion, the little dead girl, the poor woman with her diseased
body. Jesus saved others all over Israel. People who had been
crippled were walking. People who had been blind were seeing.
People who had been deaf were hearing. He saved others.

What did He save them from? He saved them from their physical ailments, yes, but more than that, He saved them from their
sins. "Thou shalt call his name Jesus: for he shall save his people
from their sins" (Matthew 1:21).

What's the big problem we face as a people? International
problems? National problems? Home problems? Individual problems? It's a problem summarized in one word—*sin*. That's my
problem. That's your problem.

Recently, I was listening to a hymn and wondered who had
been tampering with the words. This is the way we used to sing
a favorite of mine:

Alas! and did my Savior bleed?
And did my sovereign die?
Would He devote that sacred head . . .
For such a worm as I?

Now here is the way it reads:

Would He devote that sacred head
For sinners such as I?

We've changed it. We've gone modern. We've watered it down. It isn't just for "sinners such as I" that He died on the cross; it's for "a worm such as I." When you know yourself, the way you really are, when you see yourself in the light of God's perfect holiness, you see how sinful you are.

Jesus died to save others. He died to save me. He died to save you.

For God so loved the world, that he gave his only begotten Son, that whosoever believeth in him should not perish, but have everlasting life (John 3:16).

B. To Sacrifice Himself

It is because Jesus did not come down from the cross that we believe in him. It is not that He could not come down. It is that He would not come down.

Was it the tenacity of the nails that held him there? Was it fear of the soldiers that kept him on the cross? No. It was the cords of love that kept him there. He did not spare himself in order to spare you and me. That was the purpose of Calvary. That is the meaning of it all.

40

Sin's D-Day
Mark 15:33-41

I. THE LONELINESS OF SIN (15:33-34)
  A. Darkness (15:33)
  B. Desolation (15:34)
II. THE BITTERNESS OF SIN (15:35-36)
  A. The Tantalizing Drink
  B. The Bitter Cup
III. THE OBSTRUCTIVENESS OF SIN (15:37-39)

OF THE GOSPEL WRITERS, MARK IS THE ONE WHO TELLS US THE TIME when Jesus died. It was the third hour, about nine in the morning (15:34). At the sixth hour, darkness had covered the whole land (15:33). That was twelve noon. At the ninth hour, three o'clock in the afternoon, Jesus cried, "My God, my God why hast thou forsaken me?" Jesus was on the cross approximately six hours.

On June 6, 1944, the allied forces landed on the beaches of Normandy and went on to overcome Hitler's army. That day was actually the beginning of the end for the forces of evil led by Hitler. At the cost of tremendous sacrifice, at the giving of the lives of many thousands of men, D-Day was a victory day.

Two thousand years ago there was a spiritual D-Day. It was sin's D-Day because Jesus stormed the beaches of hell's portals. On that day Jesus won the battle that ultimately put away sin forever. The gospel is "Christ died for our sins according to the scriptures" (1 Corinthians 15:3). What Jesus did those six hours when He was on the cross has made it possible for you and me to be forgiven of our sins, to be saved from the penalty of sin—and day by day, as we grow, to be saved from the practice of sin. One day ultimately when we get to glory we will be saved from the presence of sin.

I. THE LONELINESS OF SIN (15:33-34)

Sin has brought loneliness into the lives of human beings. Jesus conquered that loneliness.

A. Darkness (15:33)

When darkness covered the whole land, it was not an eclipse of the sun. It was the Passover at this particular time, which means that it was the time of the full moon. So it was physically impossible for there to be an eclipse of the sun. The darkness that came over the cross for three hours as Jesus hung there was supernatural in origin. God brought that darkness over the earth. "And it shall come to pass in that day, saith the Lord God, that I will cause the sun to go down at noon, and I will darken the earth in the clear day" (Amos 8:9).

At noon, when the sun was at its brightest, God turned down that sun. God used his heavenly dimmer so that there was darkness over the whole land. When the darkness came, an Egyptian philosopher living at that time (Diogenes) said, "Either the deity himself suffers at this moment, or He sympathizes with one that does."

When Jesus died at Calvary's cross it was as if God were putting a funeral drape over his creation. When Jesus was dying for the sins of the world that day it was as if the universe went into mourning. It was as if the sun refused to shine. It was as if what was taking place there were so dark that God's creation itself could no longer stand the event.

> Well might the sun in darkness hide,
> And shut his glories in,
> When Christ, the great Redeemer, died
> For man, the creature's sin.

In that time of darkness the Bible teaches that Jesus was being made sin for us. "For he [God] hath made him to be sin for us, who knew no sin; that we might be made the righteousness of

God in him" (2 Corinthians 5:21). Jesus tasted death for every man. Jesus bore the sin debt for every one of us. In that darkness he cried, "My God, my God, why hast thou forsaken me?" He experienced the loneliness of sin.

Before this Jesus had known what it was to have communion with the heavenly Father. All through his ministry Jesus talked about his relationship to the Father. It was Jesus who taught us to pray, "Our Father, who art in heaven." Many times Jesus would lift his heart toward heaven and say, "Father, I thank thee."

B. Desolation (15:34)

In the gospel of John, Jesus said these words to his disciples: "Behold, the hour cometh, yea, is now come, that ye shall be scattered, every man to his own, and shall leave me alone: and yet I am not alone, because the Father is with me" (John 16:32). Yet, in Mark's gospel, we are told that Jesus was forsaken by his Father and cried that terrible cry.

The Bible says that our God is a holy God. His eyes are so pure that He cannot look on sin. So, in that moment, when Jesus bore all the sins of humankind, when Jesus literally was made sin, the holy God could no longer look on that sin. God turned away from his Son, and Jesus experienced the ultimate loneliness—what it means to be abandoned by God. Literally his words mean, "Why have you left me down in?" Acts 2:27 says about Jesus: "Because thou wilt not leave my soul in hell, neither wilt thou suffer thine Holy One to see corruption." Hell came to Calvary that day. Jesus descended into hell that day. Jesus experienced what it means to be abandoned by God.

Loneliness is a problem common to every human being in this world. Sometimes we talk about the loneliness of the elderly. That's true. Many elderly people experience terrible loneliness. We talk about the loneliness of singles. It's possible for a person to be walking in the midst of a city of a million people and be lonely in her or his heart.

Loneliness is a state of heart. Loneliness is some of the baggage that came with original sin when it entered this world. There is no lonelier place in the entire world than the human heart without love. That is what sin has brought into this world, and Jesus experienced the ultimate loneliness of sin.

When Jesus talked about hell He used many terms, but one of the terms was "outer darkness." I've heard people laugh about going to hell. I've heard lost people make fun of it and say, "If I go to hell that will be all right; I'll have plenty of company down there. We'll have a big party together."

But the Bible describes hell as a place of darkness. You are not going to see anyone in hell. You are not going to be having a big party in hell. You are going to experience what it means to be lonely, as no human being has ever been lonely in this life. Think about it. For eternity, never to see anyone else. For eternity, to cry to God for mercy and never hear an answer.

God has promised, "I will never leave thee, nor forsake thee" (Hebrews 13:5). When your father and mother forsake you, the Lord won't forsake you. When your friends turn their backs on you, God won't forsake you. A child of God can be on a bed of affliction, can have pain wracking throughout his body, yet in the midst of it he can experience the joy and peace that only Jesus can give. It's wonderful to know that when we go through the dark valleys of this life we don't have to fear any evil because the Lord is right there with us (Psalm 23:4).

Jesus also conquered sin's bitterness.

II. THE BITTERNESS OF SIN (15:35-36)

The devil doesn't want you to know that bitterness is attached to sin. Jesus experienced that bitterness. "And some of them that stood by, when they heard it, said, Behold, he calleth Elias. And one ran and filled a spunge full of vinegar, and put it on a reed, and gave him to drink, saying, Let alone; let us see whether Elias will come to take him down" (15:35-36).

A. The Tantalizing Drink

Earlier they had offered Jesus a mixture of wine and myrrh, a painkiller, which He refused (15:23). Jesus would not take the painkiller. He chose to taste death to its bitterest degree. He would speak with a rational mind.

John gave a little fuller account of Mark 15:36. "After this, Jesus knowing that all things were now accomplished, that the scripture might be fulfilled, saith, I thirst" (John 19:28). Do you remember the rich man in hell who lifted up his eyes and said,

"Father Abraham, have mercy on me and send Lazarus, that he may dip the tip of his finger in water, and cool my tongue; for I am tormented in this flame" (Luke 16:24)? Jesus experienced hell's flames for us.

"Now there was set a vessel full of vinegar: and they filled a spunge with vinegar, and put it upon hyssop, and put it to his mouth. When Jesus therefore had received the vinegar . . ." (John 19:29-30).

Jesus' body was experiencing normal thirst. Jesus was fully God, yet fully man. He knew what it was to be thirsty. When it is unsatisfied, thirst is a terrible craving of the human body but it is one of our normal appetites. Now, instead of giving Jesus something to quench his thirst, they gave him stinging acid. "In my thirst they gave me vinegar to drink" (Psalm 69:21). That is a picture of what sin will do to you. It will give you bitterness as you try to satisfy what are normal thirsts.

God has given you certain normal desires. Sin is the attempt to satisfy normal desires in abnormal ways. Sin doesn't start off bitter. "Stolen waters are sweet, and bread eaten in secret is pleasant" (Proverbs 9:17).

Sin starts off being attractive. It shows you its sweetness. I'm not saying that folks in sin aren't having a good time. They sometimes are. I would be lying if I said they weren't. You know they are having a good time. I know they are having a good time. The Bible alludes to "the pleasures of sin for a season" (Hebrews 11:25). But remember, it is only for a season.

Sin gives the best first, and then it gets worse and worse. Sin gives you that secret thrill of premarital or extramarital sex. Everybody's doing it. Go to the movies. Turn on the TV. It's exciting, alluring. So you bite the devil's bait and it's sweet.

But there's another aspect: more sin brings less satisfaction. The second cup is not nearly so sweet as that first cup was. The next cup is worse, the cup of guilt. You didn't know you would have to drink that cup of guilt.

One of the main reason for teenage deaths today is suicide. We are living in a generation that has decided that there is no such thing as right and wrong. Sin is fun. Sin is all right. A generation of young people have been told, "If it feels good, do it." But they haven't been told that "at the last it biteth like a serpent, and stingeth like an adder" (Proverbs 23:32).

Early one morning years ago my telephone rang. It was a boy

in our church. He said he needed to see me; it was an emergency. "Can you come over here to the school? I've got to see you this morning." I went and there stood this teenager shaking like a leaf. He said, "Preacher, I need help; I'm desperate. My girlfriend told me this morning that she's pregnant." The devil didn't tell that boy when he partook of that sweet secret sin that there was going to be a bitter cup of an unwanted pregnancy down the road.

B. The Bitter Cup

When Jesus took that bitter vinegar, He was taking into himself all the bitterness of sin, all our shame, all our guilt. Jesus drank the bitter cup. Now He wants to give us a sweet cup to drink, that sweet cup of forgiveness.

Jesus also conquered sin's obstructiveness.

III. THE OBSTRUCTIVENESS OF SIN (15:37-39)

Sin obstructs us. Sin is a barrier that keeps us out. "Jesus cried with a loud voice, and gave up the ghost" (15:37). We know that was when He said, "It is finished." He expired. No one took his life from him; Jesus gave up his life at Calvary. Then the veil of the temple was torn in two from top to bottom (15:38).

The temple was a series of obstructions, a series of walls. If you were a gentile you could go to the court of the gentiles, but then there was a wall, and you couldn't go any farther unless you were a Jew. After that there was the court of the women. If you were a Jewish woman you could come there, but then there was a wall and only Jewish men could go beyond that wall. After that there was another wall and only the priest could go into the holy place with its huge veil—sixty feet high, thirty feet wide, thick as the palm of a hand. It was made out of fine linen with threads of blue and purple and scarlet. That veil separated the priest from the holy of holies, where the mercy seat was, and only one man, the high priest, only once a year, on the day of atonement, could go in there, take the blood of the lamb, and apply it on the holy of holies. The temple was a reminder of the fact that sin keeps human beings from God.

When Jesus died on the cross, the unseen hand of God took that veil and tore it in two. It took place at three in the afternoon, the time when the priests were in the holy place tending to the sacrifices. At that very moment, they saw into that holy of holies. The ultimate barrier to God's presence was rent asunder. That's why in Acts 6:7 it says that a great company of the priests were obedient to the faith. That's why there is no more sacrifice, no altar where lambs are slain in our churches. We worship a living savior who gave himself as a sacrifice at Calvary's cross.

God has opened up the door. I don't have to go to any priest to pray to God for me. The Bible says that we can come boldly to the throne of God (Hebrews 4:16). The writer of Hebrews said that we have entrance through the veil, that is, the body of the Lord (Hebrews 10:20). Through Jesus Christ we can come into the presence of God.

Every day of my life I have the blessed, glorious opportunity as a child of God, on the basis of the blood of Jesus, through the rending of the body of the Lord Jesus Christ, of walking right into the presence of the creator of the universe, the God of my salvation. I have the privilege of saying to him, "My Father." Jesus conquered the obstructiveness of sin. He removed the barriers.

After the centurion watched Jesus die and heard what He said, he exclaimed, "Truly this man was the Son of God" (15:39). Is that your conclusion too?

41

He Is Risen
Mark 15:42–16:8

I. His Death Was Perceived (15:42-45)
   A. By a Friend (15:43)
   B. By a Foe (15:44)
II. His Burial Was Prepared (15:46)
III. His Resurrection Was Proclaimed (16:1-8)
   A. The Women's Arrival (16:1-4)
   B. The Angel's Announcement (16:5-8)

MARK BEGAN HIS ACCOUNT BY ASSOCIATING JESUS CHRIST, THE Son of God, with "good news," which is what the word *gospel* means. The Bible says, "As cold water to a thirsty soul, so is good news from a far country" (Proverbs 25:25). The gospel of the Lord Jesus Christ is the good news from a far country. It is the good news from heaven that God has done something about humanity's desperate need. God has taken steps to deal with our sin problem to make it possible for us to be forgiven.

If somebody should ask you what the gospel is all about, what would you say? The best words I've ever read to describe what the gospel really means are those of the apostle Paul. "I declare unto you the gospel . . . Christ died for our sins according to the scriptures; and that he was buried, and that he rose again the third day according to the scriptures" (1 Corinthians 15:1, 3-4).

There are three essential ingredients of the good news, which Mark set before us in these verses: the death, burial, and resurrection of Jesus Christ.

I. His Death Was Perceived (15:42-45)

Jesus died, and his death was perceived.

A. By a Friend (15:43)

First of all, Joseph of Arimathaea came to care for him at his death. This Joseph is described as an honorable counselor, which means that he was an influential member of the Jewish Sanhedrin. Luke wrote that Joseph, a good and just man, was one member of the Sanhedrin who had not consented "to the counsel and deed of them" (Luke 23:50-51). Joseph of Arimathaea was a wealthy man. Now he was going to use his riches to express his devotion to the Lord Jesus Christ. He was waiting for the kingdom of God (15:43) as one of that Jewish remnant who really believed what God had to say. He was looking anxiously for the coming of the messiah. This man had come to believe that Jesus was indeed the messiah, the Christ, that He was everything He claimed to be.

John's gospel tells us that Joseph was a disciple, "but secretly for fear of the Jews" (John 19:38). That is why we've not seen him on the pages of our Bible before. Joseph was one of those people who had faith in the Lord Jesus, but his faith was not vocal. It was not the kind of thing he talked about.

Isn't it amazing how reticent some people are to proclaim their faith in the Lord Jesus? I look around in our world and I see people who are not ashamed about their allegiance to many things. I see all kinds of decals on their cars, bumper stickers proclaiming membership in all kinds of organizations. People wear uniforms or silly hats. They are proud of their schools, their teams, their political parties. Everywhere you turn, people are proud to promote what they stand for, yet there seems to be a hesitancy on the part of some to admit their love for the Lord Jesus Christ.

But something happened in the life of Joseph of Arimathaea. The death of Jesus on the cross did something in his heart. He now came forth boldly, with courage, and asked Pilate if he could have the body.

In the light of Calvary's cross I do not believe that any secret discipleship today is justified. I do not believe that anyone can intelligently discern the fact that Jesus died on the cross for our sins and never go public with her or his faith. Jesus said, "Whoever therefore shall confess me before men, him will I confess also before my Father which is in heaven. But whosoever shall deny me before men, him will I also deny before my Father which is in heaven" (Matthew 10:32-33).

The boldness of Joseph encouraged someone else. John in his gospel said that Nicodemus also came and brought spices to anoint the body of Jesus (John 19:39). Fear is contagious. Discouragement is contagious. Pessimism is contagious. But courage is contagious as well. Witnessing for Jesus is contagious.

This is a time when God's people need to take their stand. We need to say, "I'm on the Lord's side, and I don't care who knows it. I don't care who tries to intimidate me." We are living in a world that is heading down a slide to hell and if God's people don't preach the gospel unashamedly we are going to see multitudes die in their sins.

B. By a Foe (15:44)

When Joseph came, Pilate marveled that Jesus was already dead. It was normal for a person on a cross to remain there for several days. Crucifixion was a slow, excruciating form of death. The Jews were afraid of this, so they had asked Pilate that his legs be broken (John 19:31). Yet Jesus' legs were not crushed. No bone of his was broken—as the scriptures had predicted (John 19:36; Psalm 34:20).

This gospel of Mark sets before us Jesus' death. You and I are living in a world of death. We have to die. If Jesus Christ doesn't return to earth, the Bible teaches that every one of us will have to die. We are not living in the land of the living. "It is appointed unto man once to die" (Hebrews 9:27). Jesus identified himself with us in tasting death for everyone (Hebrews 2:9).

II. His Burial Was Prepared (15:46)

Normally the Romans left a body to die and rot on the cross. They would just leave it there for the scavenger dogs or vulture birds to eat. The Jews had scruples about leaving a body on the cross: A dead body was not to be allowed to remain overnight (Deuteronomy 21:23). Dead bodies had to be buried. Because of the religious rules of the Jews it was necessary that the body of Jesus be taken from the cross. Isn't that interesting? Here these men were; they had condemned him, yet they were worried about keeping their law.

The Bible had predicted that the Lord's servant would make "his grave with the wicked, and with the rich in his death" (Isaiah 53:9). And God had already prepared Joseph and Nicodemus. They came and requested the body of Jesus for burial.

Notice the preparation that was made for the burial of the body. Joseph "bought fine linen, and took him down, and wrapped him in the linen, and laid him in a sepulchre which was hewn out of a rock, and rolled a stone unto the door of the sepulchre" (15:46). In the Bible, linen has symbolic significance as a picture of righteousness. It is a reminder that God requires righteousness for us to get into heaven. It is also a reminder that the Bible says we have no righteousness. That leaves all of us in bad shape. You and I in our sinfulness have no hope whatsoever of getting to heaven. But Jesus Christ was God's righteousness epitomized. Because Jesus never sinned, He has bought a perfect righteousness for us.

> When He shall come with trumpet sound,
> Oh, may I then in Him be found;
> Dressed in His righteousness alone,
> Faultless to stand before the throne.

When I go to heaven, although I will not go there because of my own goodness, I will not have to stand there in my sinfulness. I will go there in the imputed righteousness of the Lord Jesus Christ.

Jesus was buried in a borrowed tomb, Joseph's own tomb, and they rolled the stone shut.

Joseph knew a truth that is engraved in every human heart: Somewhere out there is a grave for every man and woman. The burial of Jesus Christ means that our sins have been forgiven. God has put our sins away in the person of Jesus Christ.

> Living He loved me, dying He saved me,
> Buried He carried my sins far away.

God has removed our sins as far as the east is from the west (Psalm 103:12). He has put our sins behind his back, to remember them no more (Isaiah 38:17). He has wiped them out as a thick cloud (Isaiah 44:22). He has cast our sins in the depths of the sea (Micah 7:19). And no fishing is allowed.

III. HIS RESURRECTION WAS PROCLAIMED (16:1-8)

A. The Women's Arrival (16:1-4)

Mark tells of three women who came to the tomb of Jesus early in the morning bringing spices to anoint his body. They were wondering who would move the stone from the door of the sepulcher. They had no inkling what had occurred.

Our Christian faith rests solidly on the fact that Jesus Christ did not stay in that tomb. When those women got there they found that the stone had been rolled away. Stepping inside they saw a young man in a long white garment, a messenger from another world. An angelic being was sitting there.

B. The Angel's Announcement (16:5-8)

"And he saith unto them, Be not affrighted: Ye seek Jesus of Nazareth, which was crucified: he is risen; he is not here: behold the place where they laid him" (16:6).

Jesus was gone. Jesus Christ rose from the dead. That's the gospel. That's the good news. Every day is Easter Sunday. Every Christian service is a resurrection service.

> He lives, He lives, Christ Jesus lives today!
> He walks with me and talks with me
> Along life's narrow way.
> He lives, He lives, salvation to impart!

Jesus Christ is alive today. He is not in that tomb. Unlike the devotees of the world's other religions, we Christian believers go to a tomb that is empty. "He is not here. He is risen."

Then the young man said to the women, "But go your way, tell his disciples and Peter that he goeth before you into Galilee; there ye shall see him, as he said unto you" (16:7). We have a living savior who goes before us today. Wherever you are going, when you get there, Jesus will be right there. Jesus has kept his word.

One of these days, the Bible says, "The Lord himself shall descend from heaven with a shout, with the voice of the archangel, and with the trump of God: and the dead in Christ shall rise first" (1 Thessalonians 4:16).

He went before them into Galilee; He goes before us into glory.

My savior is in heaven today. Because He's there, one of these days I'm going to be gone. I'll go home to be with the Lord. And you can too. That's the good news.

42

How the Gospel Ends

Mark 16:9-20

NEWER TRANSLATIONS OF THE BIBLE OFTEN HAVE A NOTE IN THE margin saying that these concluding verses of Mark's gospel are not found in the oldest manuscripts. The New Testament documents were first written on papyrus. From those original manuscripts, copies were made, and then translations.

The area of study known as textual criticism goes into these matters of the original manuscripts in order to discover as nearly as possible what the New Testament writers actually wrote. It is indeed a formidable task, since there are over five thousand extant manuscripts of ancient copies of our New Testament. The role of the textual critic is to take these manuscripts, compare them with one another, and determine which is the most accurate text.

Textual critics have done as much as any other discipline to give us confidence in the integrity of our New Testament text. We can be confident that our Bible is an accurate representation of what was originally written. Although we do not have the original documents, we can rest assured that we have the text as God the Holy Spirit gave it to Spirit-inspired writers.

When we come to the gospel of Mark and get to these last nine verses, in the oldest manuscript we have, these particular verses are not found. On the basis of that, some scholars believe that they were added by later writers or by some editor to what Mark had to say. When we look at the eighth verse, however, it is obvious that this was not the conclusion to Mark's gospel. It stops with a spirit of fear, saying that the three women were afraid. Surely scripture must go on to complete this gospel and make sense. Those same scholars also point out that several words appear here which Mark does not use in any other place in his gospel.

On the other hand, other scholars argue that these concluding words are indeed authentic. They point out that in the earliest translations we have—Latin, Syrian, Coptic—a writer does not have to use a word more than one time in order for it to be authentic. Personally I am not qualified to go into matters of textual criticism and manuscript evidence, but I can say unequivocally that everything we find in these verses can be found in the other three gospels. There seems to be no question that what we have here is the result of divine revelation. No major doctrine is changed by these verses. No major doctrine is diminished by these verses. When properly interpreted, these verses are in harmony with the rest of New Testament teaching. I myself feel a lot like the faithful Christian who walked into a bookstore one day and said, "I want a copy of the Bible—the King James Version—just like Paul wrote it."

Mark's gospel ends the way it began. It began with the gospel of Jesus Christ, the Son of God. It ends with the gospel of Jesus Christ, the risen Lord. These verses call Jesus the Lord. In Acts 2:36, Simon Peter said, "God hath made that same Jesus, whom ye have crucified, both Lord and Christ."

I. THE LORD'S APPEARANCES (16:9-14)

Three times we are told that Jesus appeared: first to Mary Magdalene (16:9), then to two of them (16:12), and finally to the eleven (16:14).

There are actually ten or eleven appearances of Jesus after his resurrection. For a period of forty days Jesus walked on the earth, revealed himself to his disciples, and gave them unquestionable proof that He is alive. Acts 1:3 says that Jesus showed himself "alive . . . by many infallible proofs." These people, who were not expecting the resurrection of Jesus, came to be absolutely convinced that He had walked out of the tomb and is alive forevermore.

A. To Reward Love (16:9-11)

In Jesus' first appearance, to Mary Magdalene, I think He rekindled love. Mary Magdalene had a great reason to love Jesus; Mark said that Jesus had cast seven demons out of her (16:9).

There is no evidence in scripture that Mary Magdalene was a sexually immoral woman. A few years ago there was a blasphemous rock musical entitled *Jesus Christ, Superstar.* In it Mary Magdalene was pictured as a prostitute making attempts to seduce Jesus. That rock musical also made Judas the hero and Jesus the buffoon of the whole thing—a gross perversion of New Testament teaching. Mary Magdalene's love for Jesus arose from her appreciation of what He had done for her, freeing her from satanic oppression and giving her new life in him.

If you have an awareness of how much Jesus has done for you, it will create in your heart also an unbounded love for him. One of the most profound truths that can grip the human heart is the truth that "Jesus loves me; this I know, for the Bible tells me so."

My heart is overwhelmed today when I think of the love of Jesus. My love responds to his love. If you love someone you want them to love you. Do you remember when you were a child you used to get a fuzzy dandelion and would pluck the petals off the dandelion? She loves me, she loves me not. I always rigged it so it would come out "she loves me." Sometimes I would have to pull off three petals at a time, but when it was all over she always loved me. We always want to be loved, don't we? As believers in the Lord Jesus we know and serve a savior who is alive and who loves us with an everlasting love.

"And she went and told them that had been with him, as they mourned and wept. And they, when they had heard that he was alive, and had been seen of her, believed not" (16:10-11).

B. To Restore Hope (16:12-13)

The second appearance of the Lord was to two on the road to Emmaus. This is recorded more fully in Luke 24. They had lost their hope. In fact, before they realized who He was, they said to Jesus, "We had trusted [we had hoped] that it had been he which should have redeemed Israel" (Luke 24:21). They had lost their hope so they were going back to their homes, to their previous pursuits.

When Jesus Christ revealed himself to them as the living savior, in their renewed hope they turned and went back the eleven miles to let it be known that He was alive, but "neither believed they them" (16:13).

This message of the resurrection of Jesus is the message of hope that our world so desperately needs. The literature of the times portrays an age of hopelessness. The music of our day underscores the reality that most people feel hopeless. Everywhere we turn, people seem to have lost hope. Those who do not know Christ, who do not know the promise of eternal life that Jesus has given, are making all kinds of efforts to deal with impending death. Look at the fitness craze right now. Of course there is a great deal of good to be said for it: running, jogging, walking, lifting weights, aerobics, jazzercise. But some people do these things in an effort to prolong life and to evade the reality of death. But however skinny we are, or however muscular and in shape, one day we are going to have to die.

The Bible says that if you die without Jesus Christ you will die in your sins and have no hope in eternity. Our only hope for life after death is in the fact that Jesus Christ rose again from the dead and will make himself real to us in a new-birth experience.

The risen Lord places hope in our hearts. Ten thousand years from now the children of God will be more alive in their glorified bodies than they are in these mortal bodies right now. We are going to live forever because Jesus died and rose again and came forth the victorious living Lord.

C. To Renew Faith (16:14)

Jesus appeared to the eleven (16:14). We have noticed that all through these verses it says they didn't believe the earliest witnesses to the resurrection. Again, it is important to remember that these disciples were not preprogramed to believe that Jesus was alive. In fact, their unbelief was rather stubborn. They were persistent in their unbelief. The only thing that renewed their faith was the appearance of their resurrected Lord.

In order to be valid, faith has to be grounded on facts. In one sense of the word, everybody has faith. Everybody believes something. But the question is this: Is your faith grounded on some fact that is substantial?

Suppose you are in a tall building and the building is on fire. There is no way to get down. The elevators are out of commission. The stairways are filled with smoke. There you stand at the window way up in the building. Your only possible hope is to jump out of that building. I say to you, "Go ahead and jump. It'll rescue you, save you from the fire." You say, "Is there anything down there to catch me?" I say, "It doesn't really matter whether there is anything down there to catch you or not, just as long as you believe there is. Just as long as you have faith that something is there." This is crazy, but there is no other way out, so you jump. You go down twelve floors, but when you get to the bottom—I don't care how much you believe, I don't care how strong your faith is—unless there really is a safety net to catch you when you hit the ground, you will die. It's all over for you. Our faith is only as substantial as the object of our faith.

The Bible says, "If thou shalt confess with thy mouth the Lord Jesus, and shalt believe in thine heart that God hath raised him from the dead, thou shalt be saved" (Romans 10:9).

II. THE LORD'S ASSIGNMENT (16:15-18)

Jesus gave an assignment to those eleven disciples. One of them had denied the Lord with curses. Now they had all been sitting behind closed doors, their knees knocking. The Lord looked at that pitiful group and said, "Go ye into all the world, and preach the gospel to every creature" (16:15). I can imagine their saying, "Who's He talking to?"

What an audacious assignment, to assign to eleven unimportant people like that the job of shaking the world with good news. But they did it. Before the first century was over, church historians estimate that out of a population of 200,000 in Jerusalem over 100,000 were won to faith in the Lord Jesus Christ.

We need to stretch our minds in order to comprehend the tremendous potential in the preaching of the gospel of Jesus. Did you know that a church in Korea has over 200,000 members? When I started preaching back in Georgia, if a church had a thousand in Sunday school, that was a phenomenon. Now it's fairly common all over the country.

A. Proclamation (16:15)

You and I are feeling the effects of that first-century witness. The word *preach* in Greek means "to announce as a herald." It was a word used for an ambassador who had an announcement to make from the king. You and I have an announcement to make from the king of kings and lord of lords. It's the good news about Jesus Christ. Every human being in this world has a right to hear it. Missionary statesman Oswald Smith said many years ago, "Why should anybody in the world hear the gospel twice until everybody has heard it once?"

Jesus broke down the assignment into reasonable segments. We're to go, beginning at Jerusalem, and Judea, and Samaria, and then to "the uttermost part of the earth" (Acts 1:8).

Obviously I cannot go everywhere and preach the gospel to every creature. So I will give money to send missionaries who can go. But I will get personally involved in my Jerusalem, right where I am, telling the gospel to every person. God has given us each an assignment to preach the gospel.

B. Reception (16:16)

"He that believeth and is baptized shall be saved; he that believeth not shall be damned" (16:16). The main thought in that verse is not baptism. Jesus was not teaching that you have to be baptized to be saved. The crucial word is *believe*. Baptism does not confer salvation; it confirms it. Baptism is an outward act that demonstrates an inward experience. Jesus did not say, "He that believeth not and is not baptized shall be condemned." It is he that believeth not who is condemned; that is, he shall be under judgment.

The Bible says that God has given "to every man the measure of faith" (Romans 12:3). God has placed within every person the ability to believe. To believe is not merely an intellectual matter.

It is that, but more is involved.

To believe as the New Testament talks about belief in Jesus Christ is a three-in-one decision. It is an intellectual matter, it is an emotional matter, and it is a matter of your will.

If you have never received Jesus Christ as your personal savior, at what stage of the process are you? Do you believe that Jesus lived? Do you believe that Jesus died on the cross for your sin? Do you believe that if you ask him to forgive you of your sin and come into your life, He will do it? If your answer to the last three questions is yes, you are one-third there.

In your heart is there a desire to know Jesus? Is there a desire to go to heaven when you die? Do you have that *want to*? You say, "I don't know when it will be, but sometime on some occasion, I do want to know Christ as my savior." You are two-thirds there.

The third step is this. "I know I need Christ; I want Christ; I will receive Christ as my savior. Right now." If you turn from your sins and invite Jesus personally into your heart and life, salvation will occur.

C. Confirmation (16:17-18)

"And these signs shall follow . . ." There was no New Testament. So the Lord said signs would authenticate their message. In the absence of the New Testament revelation, these signs would confirm their message. His followers would cast out demons; they did that. They would speak in new tongues; they did that. They would take up serpents; Paul did that. They would drink any deadly thing; we have no record of that. They would lay hands on the sick and they would recover; the apostles did that. "And they went forth, and preached everywhere, the Lord working with them, and confirming the word with signs following" (16:20).

Hebrews 2:3-4 and 2 Corinthians 12:12 make clear that God gave the apostles definite signs that validated their ministries. Today we have the New Testament revelation. We need only the authority of "thus saith the word of God" to validate what we say. These verses are a promise that when we go and seek to win souls to Jesus Christ, He will give us the necessary power and will provide the protection to do everything we need to do.

I don't have victory over dogs, as I have already told you. I'm afraid of dogs. If you are lost and you have a dog, you better tie it up or I'm not coming to see you. Every time I see a dog that starts looking a little bit irritable toward me, I pray for my personal protection. When I go out visiting and soulwinning and there is a dog around I claim the promise of God's protection.

Jesus was saying, "You preach the gospel and I'll take care of you." He was saying that the child of God is immortal until he or she has done what God wants done by him or her.

III. THE LORD'S ASCENSION (16:19-20)

A. His Heavenly Reception (16:19)

Finally we have the beautiful passage of Jesus Christ being received up into heaven, welcomed by the angels of glory, welcomed by the Father, and sitting down at his right hand. The battle was over; the victory was won; the sacrifice He made was complete and concluded.

B. Our Earthly Mission (16:20)

Now Jesus works in his spiritual body, in us believers, as He seeks to win the lost. That's how the gospel ends. It begins with Jesus. It ends with Jesus.

Mark wrote the beginning of this gospel. Each of us writes the ending of this gospel when we conclude its purpose by opening our lives to Jesus.